Drama Was a Weapon

Drama Was a Weapon

THE LEFT-WING THEATRE IN NEW YORK
1929–1941

by

MORGAN Y. HIMELSTEIN

With a Foreword by JOHN GASSNER

GREENWOOD PRESS, PUBLISHERS
WESTPORT, CONNECTICUT

Library of Congress Cataloging in Publication Data

Himelstein, Morgan Yale.
  Drama was a weapon.

  Reprint of the 1963 ed. published by Rutgers Univer-
sity Press, New Brunswick, N. J.
  Bibliography: p.
  Includes index.
  1. Theater--New York (City)--History. 2. Theater--
Political aspects. 3. Communism--United States--
1917-   I. Title.
[PN2277.N5H5 1976]   792'.09747'1   76-14934
ISBN 0-8371-8939-X

Copyright © 1963 by Rutgers, The State University

Originally published in 1963 by Rutgers University Press,
New Brunswick, New Jersey

Reprinted with the permission of Rutgers University Press

Reprinted in 1976 by Greenwood Press,
a division of Williamhouse-Regency Inc.

Library of Congress Catalog Card Number 76-14934

ISBN 0-8371-8939-X

Printed in the United States of America

FOR LIBBY

Politics and Theatre
By John Gassner

Since *Drama Was a Weapon* is a thoroughly scholarly work, it is sufficient unto itself. It presents the self-contained thesis that the communist movement of the nineteen-thirties endeavored, but failed, to win control of the American theatre. The author of this work, Morgan Himelstein, argues cogently and documents his contentions so well that he does not need the support of any on-the-spot observer like myself. But it is one of the merits of this study that it propels the reader into areas of interest adjacent to the author's central argument, and the more one enters these the more one arrives at a just picture of an exciting period in the theatre. Mr. Himelstein is himself quite aware of the total reality of what was the theatre of the thirties, for he supplies much detailed data on the subject. The larger the base of his investigation, however, the more provocatively he invites considerations into which he himself cannot deviate without overloading his argument.

It is important to realize that the leftism of the theatre of the period was many things at the same time, if it was not indeed many different things to many different people. Depending upon the way one looked at it, it was Marxist and non-Marxist, foreign to American culture and native, large in

vii

compass and small, influential and uninfluential, productive and sterile. It started with the Depression or it started long before. It ended with the end of the Depression and the start of World War II or it never died. Something can be said for each of these contentions, and the continuity of creative work by graduates of the social theatre (Odets, Hellman, Kingsley, MacLeish, Blitzstein, Kazan, Clurman, Bobbie Lewis, Cheryl Crawford, Strasberg, and others) and the influence on Williams, Miller, and others in the next two decades should certainly make one hesitate to write *finis* to a chapter on the thirties without some qualifications. One may, finally, consider the esthetic problems highlighted, although hardly resolved, by the leftist theatre movement. Where, for example, does propaganda start or stop in a dramatic work? And how is it to be served best? By fiat or example, directly or indirectly, with dramatic realism or with nonrealistic stylization? Debate raged over these and related questions, and over the question of whether politics was swallowing up esthetics or esthetics undercutting politics. Patently there is sufficient material here for a supplementary book on the period's socially oriented theatre. But while a Foreword is not a substitute for such a book, it can perhaps suggest the further ranges of the subject brought to our attention by Mr. Himelstein's study.

For one thing, it is to be observed that the social orientation of our theatre goes back a long while. The American stage was consciously political and social virtually from the beginnings of the Republic, when the Tories and the Revolutionists exchanged insults in their amateur stage productions. Then ensued the considerable vogue of comedies like *The Contrast* and *Fashion,* favorable to our frontier virtues and democratic ideals. In the middle of the nineteenth century, abolitionism found popular expression in an immensely successful stage version of *Uncle Tom's Cabin;* and when the late nineteenth and early twentieth century period of social reform set in, there was no lack of dramatic writing about the issues of the day in workmanlike exercises such as Steele MacKaye's labor play, *Paul Kauvar, or Anarchy,* Charles Klein's antitrust drama, *The Lion and the Mouse,* and Edward Sheldon's *Salvation Nell, The Nigger,* and *The Boss.* In the theatre of the prosperous nineteen-twenties, the light-minded comedies of Kaufman and his collaborators riddled our mass culture with laughter, while a heavier assault was launched by O'Neill, George Kelly, Elmer Rice, Paul Green, and a New Playwrights company that included Mike Gold, John Howard Lawson, and John Dos Passos. The socially slanted theatre of the thirties had a long background of journalistic topicality and democratic sentiment, although both friends and foes tended to overlook this fact, the friends acclaiming leftist social drama as a noble Marxist invention while the foes called it an alien abomination. Only a special species of plays and productions could be designated as "leftist" in any precise sense. But they were influential for a time and could be distinguished from other plays because their authors implemented their social sympathies with revolutionary Marxist visions of the overthrow of the capitalistic system in the course of an apocalyptic "final" conflict between capital and labor.

That this point of view made only a small dent in our theatre is well established by Mr. Himelstein. Yet the label of "leftism" got attached to the entire serious-minded stage in America. And the label of "leftism" was not used pejoratively, as it came to be used in the 1950's, but in a vaguely complimentary sense by proponents of liberalism. "Leftism," for them, was the banner under which one fought *against* fascism and Nazism and *for* human decency and social reforms soon to be incorporated in the law of the land without commitment to the overthrow of capitalism and the establishment of a "dictatorship of the proletariat." Men of good will and, I venture to say, sound (if politically limited) intelligence ranged themselves around this banner, and what they had in common may be lumped together as a sentiment, or a collection of sentiments, important politically because sentiments affect politics, and important *theatrically* since feelings and attitudes are of the essence in the theatre.

A moderate optimism, consisting of a belief that social evil could be destroyed, injustices eliminated, inequities eradicated, humanity saved, and the "good society" erected, was shared by all contributors to leftist theatre. There can be no doubt, of course, that Communist leaders endorsed this view and fostered it to expected, perhaps even calculated, advantage of their cause.

But if this optimism was derived in the case of Marxist bellwethers from the gospel of dialectical materialism, it came, in the main, from distinctly different sources to the majority of the theatre's liberals and radicals. It came from the sanguine American temperament, from native movements of reform, the spacious tradition of the frontier, and, ultimately no doubt, from the eighteenth-century Enlightenment that had pervaded American life from the very beginnings of the Republic. The history of the country was viewed as a sustained struggle between materialism and idealism, specifically between vested property interests defended by Hamiltonian conservatives and the democratic spirit championed by Jeffersonian liberals, Jacksonian frontier egalitarians, and Emersonian moralists or mystics. The native roots of this liberalism and radicalism were everywhere apparent. I, personally, never encountered so many people in the theatre with Populist, frontier, hobo, or rustic backgrounds before or after the thirties. (Both the leader of the militant New Theatre League in the mid-thirties and the editor of *New Theatre* magazine were recent arrivals from Davenport, Iowa; and some of the most politically articulate and active performers were corn-fed confederates.)

Finally, I should not like to underestimate the very simple factor that optimism was also the other side of despair and the alternative to a passiveness disgraced by the appeasement policies of the governments. A great fear of social acedia, of evading or having evaded one's social responsibility, pervaded the world of the artist and the intellectual as the Depression grew deeper and the fortunes of fascism in Italy, Spain, and Germany rose higher. The one thing the artist and the intellectual feared most from an embattled leftist critic was the charge of "escapism" frequently thundered at them from the doctrinaire left. Engagement to a cause became a guilt-enforced virtue that was to lead to some kind of activism such as signing a petition or a protest, marching in a parade, and writing a story, poem, or play of so-called social consciousness. Thus *enthusiasm,* an important factor in the practice of the arts, became a ferment in the depressed nineteen-thirties just as *depression* concerning humanity's condition and prospects became de rigeur for the intelligentsia of the prosperous nineteen-fifties. Some of the most effective plays and stage productions of the thirties were inspired by confidence and enthusiasm just as some of the most impressive works after 1950 were sparked by disillusion. A veritable longing for heroism or the heroic gesture was apparent in circles that in the blasé nineteen-twenties would have brazened out a modish scepticism and diffidence. The intellectuals of the thirties were determined to avoid the opprobrium of having it said of them as Eliot said of the previous slothful generation that

> . . . Here were decent godless people,
> Their only monument the asphalt road
> And a thousand lost golf-balls.

This is not to say, of course, that communism did not exist in the thirties and make converts among the neophytes of the stage, or that Marxism did not exert an influence on the leftist theatre of the thirties. But the uninitiated majority of playwrights, actors, producers, and directors manifested larger and less definable promptings. Even when they adopted the political catchwords of the period, the heart and mind of the artist belonged not to a "party," but to the human race. If Marxism was an element in the more or less uncommitted thinking of the sympathizers of the left, it was frequently parroted rather than understood by them; had its implications been grasped, Marxism would have frightened them away almost as much as fascism did. Marxist theory was just one more piece of driftwood afloat in the current of fashionable intellectualism, along with amateur Freudianism and hazy antibourgeois romanticism.

It was, in fact, this inchoate radicalism that infuriated Communist spokesmen and led them to charge the play-wrights with the cardinal sin of "confusion." What troubled them most was the "political unreliability" of the men of good will and democratic sentiment who contributed most of the dramatic substance of the theatre of the thirties. These writers and artists rarely offered any effective intellectual defense against such accusations, but they had a built-in defense, so to speak, in their "innocence." They could create only as their talents, temperament, and conditioning dictated. They couldn't have followed blueprints from the Union Square headquarters successfully, even if they had thought they should do so in a time of social crisis. S. N. Behrman was self-consciously moved to offer an apologia in *No Time for Comedy* when he showed a successful writer of comedies allowing himself to be talked into writing weighty dramas such as the age presumably demanded but returning to the craft of comedy after badly fumbling as a would-be writer of "serious" plays.

I must not, for that matter, be too exclusive in my qualifications of leftism lest we overestimate the orthodoxy of the talented young who actually tried to adhere to Marxist

doctrine or to some segment of the "Party line." Their deepest desire was to relate their work to the tensions and aspirations of their times; and however public these may have been
on the surface, their protests and hopes were personally
rooted. Not the least of their motivations, besides, was a
search for stability in a period of uncertainty veering toward
chaos; for a means of overcoming their sense of frustration
and isolation in a society in which the need for artistic ful-
fillment seemed inconsequential beside simple economic
necessity; and for giving meaning and a sense of direction
to their lives. If they lashed out at existing society with some
ferocity, they did not—and by temperament probably *could
not*—launch a planned assault. "Society" was often an ab-
straction in their work, and it was the very last thing they
actually saw and knew; they were apt to confuse it, indeed,
with their close relatives and neighbors, whom they knew a
great deal better than they knew the so-called System. Nothing, I believe, is more ridiculous than to envision them as
the well-trained, cool and consistent cadres of "the revolution." Their worst vice (and perhaps also greatest virtue),
from a detached point of view, was an excess of zeal, just as
the chief vice of the cold-war generation has been an excess
of caution.

Except for the ending artificially grafted on *Awake and
Sing!*, Odets' first and best full-length play was a strongly
localized family drama replete with lower middle-class manners and sensibilities. If vaguely stirring in the final version
of that work was the notion that the family is the breeding-
ground of rebels against the capitalist world, it was the pleni-
tude of pathetic and humorous and slightly bizarre characters
and life situations rather than Marxist ideology that made
Awake and Sing! an appealing drama and drew attention to
the author's talent. If the ideological content of the same
young author's *Waiting for Lefty* was based on the Marxist
prescript that labor strikes should be viewed as "dress rehearsals" for the revolution, it was certainly no such idea but

the over-all dramatic rhythm and imaginative dramaturgy of the play and the vibrancy of life in its individual episodes that distinguished this one-acter from the routine propaganda pieces of the political left. It was not the author's fleeting membership in a Communist cell tucked away in the Group Theatre but personal associations, attachments, and rejections that gave life to the work. It is doubtful that a single play for which one could claim some modicum of life was significantly a demonstration of ideology, or was exempt from criticism by the Communist press. Only the nondramatists who invaded the theatre with propagandist designs upon it hewed to a straight line, and the greater the propaganda the less the effect except on a small politically-minded and pre-convinced coterie.

If the drama was expected to be a "weapon," its edge was soon blunted when realistic plays with dimensioned characters displaced the original leftist plays. Short hortatory pieces, called agitprops ("agit" for agitation, "prop" for propaganda), these plays lost their vogue early in the thirties because of their transparent crudity. The blunting must have come, in part, from what I shall call the blessed confusedness of writers, which prevented them from following a Party line in any work dealing with human beings rather than mere puppets. Once characterization and individual motivation became important, as they were bound to become in realistic playwriting, discrepancies between apparent intention and actual execution began to appear—often to the advantage, rather than the disadvantage, of the individual play. Propagandist clarity became supplanted or obfuscated by humanity. Thus, working-class characters were no longer simon-pure heroes nobly ranged against capitalist villains; *Waiting for Lefty* even had a couple of proletarian villains, a corrupt labor leader and his stooge. Conversely, middle-class characters could be presented as sympathetic and diversified human beings, as in the case of an entire family in *Paradise Lost* and the dentist-hero in *Rocket to the Moon*. From these plays and the earlier *Awake and Sing!* it was abundantly evident that their author, Clifford Odets, the white hope of the thirties and of the left-wing theatre, was a middle-class, rather than "proletarian," writer. He was perhaps the most authentic American author of *drame-bourgeois,* a form of literature advocated nearly two centuries before by the eighteenth-century philosopher Diderot.

Leftist orthodoxy required "conversion-endings" for plays; that is, the principal characters were expected to acquire awareness of the class struggle and to actively participate in it. Action carrying the characters of a play from a state of ignorance to recognition or knowledge (Aristotle's dramatic element of *anagnorisis*) has been considered an honorable and effective mode of progression ever since the age of Sophocles; it is described in Aristotle's *Poetics* as a highly desirable plot element. But the brisk conversions of agitprop drama became discredited. The conversion element either vanished in leftist drama altogether—there is no conversion, for example, in *Golden Boy*—or was fumbled when appended to plays of private life written with predominantly realistic observation: Thus, the boy-hero of Odets' first full-length play, called *I've Got the Blues* before it acquired a "positive" conversion ending under the title of *Awake and Sing!,* decides to ask for "steam heat" in the factory, and his sister, the heroine of this drama, is converted to love without benefit of clergy when she runs away from her husband and child with the family's star boarder! It is a wonder that orthodox leftist critics did not rise up in arms and accuse the author of having perpetrated a travesty. So far as I know, they did not, although I would judge from their press notices that they felt somewhat embarrassed.

One tendency that did not greatly abate during the period was that of attributing individual failure to society ("the System") rather than to character, probably because social determinism had had a vogue in literature ever since Taine and Zola. But the most flagrant tendencies to refer every private distress to social causation were modified. The character had to bear at least part of the responsibility for failure because the decisions were his own, as when the violin-playing prizefighter Joe Bonaparte in *Golden Boy* abandoned the fiddle for the fist. In one way or another, even the doctrinairism of the rebellious young writers, the hard core of the leftist theatre, underwent considerable softening. So far as absolutist Marxist drama is concerned, it remained pretty much a formula in an unwritten handbook once creativity rather than creed asserted itself on the professional stage.

The decade proved far more fruitful than one could have expected from the deepening of the economic depression, the spread of fascism, the imminence of a second world war, and the profusion of poor dramatic criticism—flabbily impressionistic on the "right" and dogmatic, almost formulaic, on the "left." To the theatre of the thirties, notably augmented by nonleftist producers (such as The Theatre Guild, Guthrie McClintic, and Gilbert Miller) and playwrights (O'Neill, Wilder, Barry, Behrman, Anderson, Sherwood, Saroyan, and Sidney Howard), social fervor and compassion gave an indisputable vitality found nowhere else in the world during the decade—a vitality plainly not yet recovered in some twenty New York seasons. This was, moreover, the case with noteworthy variety, with considerable use of both realism and imaginative stylization, and with advances in several genres. Since the period, moreover, placed no interdict on plays of such general interest as *Mourning Becomes Electra, Our Town, The Man Who Came to Dinner,* and *Life with Father,* it cannot be argued that the social drama overran the theater and stifled all other growth. A proper understanding of its complex character can win considerable respect for the theatre of the nineteen-thirties. To that understanding Mr. Himelstein's book brings objectively accumulated data and a historical account that students of both social history and theatre will find enlightening.

Acknowledgments

I WISH to acknowledge aid from many sources that do not appear in the Bibliography. Among the scholars and critics who helped, I am particularly indebted to Eric Bentley for encouraging me to write this book and for guiding me through the research and the early stages of the writing. I wish also to thank Lewis Leary for his carefully detailed criticism of an earlier draft, and Robert Gorham Davis for allowing me to draw on his special knowledge of the nineteen-thirties. There are many others to whom I am grateful. My chief thanks go to the staff of the Theatre Collection at the New York Public Library for permitting me access to typescripts of unpublished plays, to scrapbooks, to photographs, and to playbills. I wish to thank Harold Rome and the copyright owner, Mills Music, Inc., from whom permission was secured to quote the lyrics from *Pins and Needles*. I wish also to thank the Educational Department of the ILGWU for allowing me to use the manuscripts of that production. Adelphi College aided with a grant for July and August of 1962 so that I could get the manuscript ready for the printer. For assistance and encouragement I am also indebted to Grace Volick, to Constantine Leondopoulos, and to my mother, Dorothy Himelstein. Most of all, I wish to acknowledge the help of my wife.

M. H.

Garden City, New York
1963

Contents

Drama Was a Weapon

"Drama Is a Weapon"

ARMED with the slogan, "Drama is a weapon," the Communist Party attempted to infiltrate and control the American stage during the Great Depression of the nineteen-thirties. The Communists believed that the theatre could help foment their revolution against American capitalism and all of its Depression evils. They believed further that the drama would be useful as a propaganda agency in the period of reconstruction when the Party would lead the country forward first to the proletarian state and then to the classless society.

The theatre, as well as the country, was nearing an economic crisis in 1929. By the early thirties, because of the competition from Hollywood, the "road" had been reduced to a few key cities, and the number of Broadway theatres and productions was starting to shrink. By the middle of the decade the famous playhouses of Forty-second Street were grinding out movies and burlesque. The legitimate stage was thus changing, and the Communists sought to change it even further into a new theatre to propagandize their planned revolt.

But they were not alone in seeking to create a new theatre movement for the thirties. They were aided by the intellectual Marxists, the fellow travelers who followed the Party

3

line but did not want to do the dirty work of the revolution.

The Communists were also accompanied by liberals and non-Marxian leftists who attempted to use the theatre as a weapon—not to promote a revolution but rather to fight for some radical reforms in the society that produced unemployment, bread lines, Hoovervilles, farm foreclosures, and bank failures. The Communists capitalized on this liberal desire for reform.

The new theatre movement thus encompassed plays written from many political points of view. There were the liberal dramas, as left-wing as the New Deal. There were the Marxist plays that explained the Depression problems by the philosophy of economic determinism. There were liberal plays with Marxian overtones. And, finally, there were Communist dramas that not only followed the Marxian analysis of American society but also called for the violent "transition" to a Soviet America. Because there were virtually no plays advocating a right-wing revolution, the new theatre movement acquired the alternate name—theatre of the left.[1]

It was, indeed, a new movement on the American stage. Unlike the nineteen-twenties, when New York had but two minor companies devoted to the social drama—the Workers' Drama League and the New Playwrights' Theatre [2]—the thirties saw the creation of many more social theatres. These new theatres were designed to indoctrinate a new audience, that is, the poor workers who could not afford to see Broadway shows and the wealthier theatre patrons who sympathized with the plight of their oppressed brothers. Proponents of the new movement also encouraged Broadway producers to sponsor plays of social protest.

Although social plays had been written in Athens as early as the fifth century B.C., the special problems of the nineteen-thirties gave the American social drama a sense of novelty. The nineteen-twenties had seen a few plays of social significance, like *The Adding Machine* by Elmer Rice, but the thirties saw many more. There was also an increase in the intensity and explicitness with which the Depression playwrights dramatized their political beliefs.

The advocates of the new movement also urged writers to create new forms of drama and new techniques of the theatre to propagandize the radical ideas of the thirties. Although most of the social plays were really conventional melodramas, two new forms—the agitprop and the living newspaper—gave the decade an illusion of theatrical experimentation and dramatic importance.

This illusion was sharpened by the large amount of publicity given to the new theatre movement, especially by the Marxian press. In 1935, for example, several writers of the left claimed that the movement had "vitality, drive and a fresh slant on life" and, furthermore, that "the theatre would become what in its great days it always was—a school, a forum, a communal institution, a weapon in the hands of the masses for fashioning a sound society." [8] In the same year Ben Blake, one of the self-proclaimed founders of the movement, recorded its five-year history in a pamphlet called *The Awakening of the American Theatre,* to which John Howard Lawson, a prominent playwright and Marxist critic, prefaced these remarks:

Behind these pages is a story best appreciated, perhaps, by those like myself who have labored long at the task of establishing this theatre movement. . . . A long road still lies ahead. But history has already been made.

Not only the Marxist press but even such "bourgeois" organs as *The New York Times* regarded the new theatre as a flourishing movement:

What the future of the workers' theatres will be is still pretty much in the cards, but there can be no equivocation about one point. They've gotten off to a flying start. [4]

The impression of the thirties as a theatrical decade devoted predominantly to the social drama has persisted to the present time, but the accuracy of this image has not, until now, been checked. The present study of the theatrical history of the nineteen-thirties demonstrates that the social drama did not, in fact, dominate the American stage. Although many plays of social significance were produced in the Depression decade, their importance has been overstated by the friends of the new movement.

Also persisting to the present time has been the impression that this period was the Red decade in the American theatre. This image was created by the Communists themselves, who indeed attempted to infiltrate, organize, and control the American stage, in the belief that the drama was a Party weapon. They continued to convey this idea of a Red decade even after it had ended because they liked to believe that their theatrical efforts—as well as their political ones—were of tremendous importance. Looking back over the decade in 1940, Michael Gold, the chief literary spokesman for the Party, claimed conscious Communist control over the entire body of left-wing literature:

... it was only because a Marxist body of thought already existed, and because there were Communist literary men to teach the orphans of the storm, to organize them that the decade took on its character.[5]

Although Gold admitted that many of the orphans found other shelter as the decade wore on, he still gave major credit to the Party.

His view of the Party's importance in the theatre was reinforced by the House Committee on Un-American Activities in its search, during the forties and fifties, for Communist actors and playwrights.

But the Communists and their pursuers both overstated their case. A careful study of the Depression theatre, of its social plays, and of the Party's reactions to them reveals the exaggeration in the term "Red decade." This book sets forth the story of the Party's attempts to organize new theatre troupes and to dominate old ones, to formulate a theory of drama in the articles and reviews that appeared chiefly in the *Daily Worker* and *New Masses,* and to force playwrights to conform to the Communist line in their plays. This book also records the Party's failure to achieve these goals.

Because the new theatre movement was centered in New York City, the study has been limited to the plays produced there. Although there were a few left-wing theatres in such cities as Boston, Philadelphia, Chicago, and Los Angeles, they were largely reflections of the New York stage.

This book thus treats theatre of the left and the Party's attempt to direct this American theatrical movement. The following pages are not intended as an exposé of Communists; information regarding the political affiliations of persons connected with the new theatre is already part of the public, written record. There have been no secret sources of information. There has been little attempt to penetrate the pseudonyms apparently used by some of those who were active in theatre of the left. One man, for example, may have written criticism under two different names. In this book the criticism is more important than the critic.

Originally this study was to have been supplemented by personal interviews with participants in the new theatre movement. But the plan was abandoned when clear patterns began to emerge from these interviews. Some of those questioned had simply forgotten the facts of thirty years ago. Others were elaborately defensive—nostalgic, apologetic, or hostile—about their roles. For instance, one individual interviewed could hardly answer a question without digressing to mention the names of the famous people he had known during that glorious chapter of American history. Another revealed very little information because he spent so much time defending his Marxist criticism as a natural impulse of youth and then protesting that it was not really Marxist after all.

Since these interviews were more interesting than valuable, it was decided to study what those involved in the left-wing theatre wrote and did during the Depression, not what they would like to recollect now. We can thus steer a more objective and dispassionate course between an unduly glowing view of the times and an unduly hostile one.

In the following pages, it is well to remember that playwrights, actors, directors, and producers who followed the Party line were not necessarily Party members. By the same token, the critics who wrote for the official and unofficial publications of the Communist Party were not necessarily members either. But, since this criticism did appear in the Communist press, we can assume that it had the sanction of the Communist editors and thus reflected the Party line. The innocent critic may not have intended to work for the Communists, but they did use him and, indeed, anybody left-of-center. It is perhaps true that the Party editors did not dictate directly to the innocent critic, but it is equally true that, had he written a right-of-center review, they would never have published it.

With these reservations in mind, we can turn to the history of the left-wing theatre: first to the Party's own troupes —both amateur and professional—and then to the Party's assault on the non-Communist stage.

Chapter 1

The Communist Party's Earliest Amateur Troupes

SEEKING to create its own amateur theatres, the Communist Party labored prodigiously to bring forth theatrical dragons to devour capitalism but managed to bear only a few theatrical mice—the German-speaking *Proletbuehne,* the Workers' Laboratory Theatre (WLT, later called the Theatre of Action), and the Theatre Collective. None of them succeeded in changing the theatre or the world.

But one of them, the *Proletbuehne,* did introduce the agitprop [1]—a new dramatic genre—to the American stage in 1930. This event marked the beginning of the new theatre movement and, the Communists hoped, an augury for a Soviet America. The agitprop, a very short play written for the purpose of political *agitation* and *propaganda,* was supposed to lure non-Communists to Party headquarters and send Communists to the barricades. To illustrate the Marxist doctrine, the agitprop was presented in stylized productions; it was loosely constructed of episodes; it offered satiric cartoons instead of characters; it had the actors speak directly to the audience; and it called on the audience to participate in the show. Agitprops could be performed either indoors or out.

Although these stylized devices were theatrically ancient,

9

their combination with Marxist propaganda was new. In 1920, in Soviet Russia, a group of students, wearing the blue blouses of workers, performed the first agitprop. They presented their show not to foment another revolution but rather to instruct the backward Russian people in the new Socialist way of life.[2] The Communists soon organized similar agitprop troupes throughout Russia, and more revolutionary ones throughout the rest of Europe, because the Party theorists liked this genre better than the conventional, realistic drama as a vehicle for Marxist doctrine. Because of its mobility an agitprop troupe could go straight to the people, and because of the direct agitation and propaganda the actors could lead the audience forward to the proletarian state.[3]

Although these agitprop companies were performing widely in the Soviet Union, in Germany, and in Czechoslovakia by 1930,[4] the same year saw but two troupes—the *Proletbuehne* and the WLT—in New York. The Communist Party introduced the agitprop to the United States as a weapon in the election campaigns of the early thirties, undoubtedly on orders from Moscow. Although the American medicine shows had tried to sell their nostrums long before 1930, the agitprop did not attempt to sell its panacea until the Depression had created a large mass of prospective customers.

Agitprops were not expensive to put on. The actors needed the script, some homemade props, a soapbox for a stage, and a busy street corner for a theatre. *Vote Communist,* an agitprop written for a political campaign of the early thirties, begins with an actor playing the Capitalist ascending the little platform. Wearing a top hat on his head and a large dollar sign over his heart, in addition to his street clothing, he gathers his audience by shouting Herbert Hoover's slogan, "Prosperity! Prosperity is just around the corner!" Mingling with the people who stop to see the show are other actors who pretend to be workers. Using megaphones, they heckle the Capitalist with such lines as "We are starving!" The Capitalist tries to get votes for himself by masquerading first as a Republican—he places a placard inscribed "Republican" over his heart. But the actor playing the Communist reaches out from the audience and pulls off the card, thus revealing the dollar sign. The Capitalist next pretends to be a Democrat, then a Socialist, but each time the Communist exposes him in the same way. The Communist then replaces the Capitalist on the soapbox and recites highlights from the Communist Party Platform. He then shouts, "Vote for the Communist Candidates!" The workers, spread out in the crowd, shout "Vote Communist!" repeatedly through their megaphones and encourage the spectators around them to join in.[5]

Although this dramatic form was imported for political reasons, it achieved some artistic respectability because of the interest shown by non-Communist artists of the American theatre. In 1931, for example, Hallie Flanagan, the director of the Vassar College Experimental Theatre, and later head of the Federal Theatre, presented three agitational plays on the college stage.[6] The first two, *Miners Are Striking* and *We Demand*, were agitprops that had already been presented by Communist units on the streets of New York. The third, *Can You Hear Their Voices?* was a longer play Mrs. Flanagan and Margaret Ellen Clifford had adapted from Whittaker Chambers' short story about the plight of some Midwestern tenant farmers. Mrs. Flanagan did not produce the agitprops to spread communism to the girls at Vassar. She was interested in this genre because it seemed novel and because it was highly theatrical, much in the manner of the "advanced" expressionistic productions of Europe during the nineteen-twenties.

Most American agitprops, however, were produced by the Party's few theatrical troupes. The Communists officially blessed the agitprop during the early part of the thirties, but they liked it for its clear revolutionary slogans, not for its theatricalism. The Marxian theorists frowned on dramatic art for its own sake because art was, after all, a political weapon.

The *Proletbuehne*, the first of the Party's amateur troupes on the American scene, produced many agitprops under the direction of John Bonn, who was known also as Hans Bohn. On April 17, 1932, this group won the first prize in the First National Workers' Theatre Spartakiade in New York with Bonn's *15 Minute Red Revue*, a typical product of this company.

This short "revue" has six parts. In Part One, ten actors portraying workers line up on the stage as they recite such couplets as

> Comrades, workers, listen, stop—
> Prolet-Buehne agit-prop.
>
> Agitprop—against hunger and destitution—
> Agitprop—theatre of revolution—
>
> Agitprop—and the bosses quake with fear—
> Agitprop—for the workers' day is near.

Part Two is a similar recitation, during which the workers change their position from a straight line at the front of the stage into an inverted V toward the backdrop, a large map of Russia.

In Part Three one of the workers praises the Soviet Union but wonders if the Capitalist will surrender. At this point the Capitalist enters and declares that he would rather fight Russia than renounce his profits. In Part Four he directs his servants—Censor, Justice, Church, Press, Police, Radio, Art, and Science—to tell the proletariat "lies" about the Soviet

Union. They obey, but a new character, the Soviet Union, corrects the "slander."

The fifth episode compares the "truthful" Red press, symbolized by a worker carrying a sign inscribed "Daily Worker," with the "untruthful" publications of the Socialist Party and the AFL. Next Soviet and American workers exhibit slogans that contrast the "slavery" of American workingmen with the "freedom" of their Soviet brothers. In the final section the actors on stage repeatedly shout their allegiance to the Soviet Union and ask the audience for a show of solidarity. "With clenched fists" raised, the spectators, led by other actors planted in the audience, reply that they will fight "FOR THE SOVIET UNION." [7]

This skit is hardly dramatic. Although the allegorical characters are either good proletarians or evil capitalists, there is no visible conflict between them. Class war is assumed rather than dramatized. Little more than a pamphlet of Communist slogans written in dialogue, this agitprop is composed of rhetorical questions and Marxist answers.

It is not likely that the *15 Minute Red Revue* recruited any nonpartisan workers for the Communists, nor did it succeed in forcing the faithful to reaffirm their belief in communism and its chosen people—the Soviet Russians. A good show might have been valuable as political ritual, but the *15 Minute Red Revue* was heavyhanded and dull. Besides, it was performed in German.

Unhindered by the *Proletbuehne's* language barrier, the WLT had a chance for greater success because more New Yorkers spoke English than German. This group was controlled by the Workers' International Relief, a Communist front,[8] and was affiliated with the International Workers' Dramatic Union of Moscow.[9]

In 1930 this proletarian theatre was run by Alfred Saxe, a recent graduate of the University of Wisconsin with a major in dramatics; Harry Elion, a "worker" who had just graduated from the City College of New York; Will Lee, a dental mechanic; Jack and Hiam Shapiro, both of whom had been active in dramatics at a settlement house in New York; and Ben Blake, who billed himself as a playwright.[10]

From 1930 through 1934 the WLT was primarily an amateur group that produced agitprops dealing with the Depression, the New Deal, the New York City political scene, and foreign affairs. The company performed all over New York for the benefit of many revolutionary causes. For instance, the actors appeared at a "Colonial Night" to aid the Anti-Imperialist League, at the Labor Temple to benefit the striking dressmakers and the Kentucky miners, at the Manhattan Lyceum to help the Chinese unemployed, and at the Rockland Palace to help the Party make its "Monster Dance and Election Rally" a success. The WLT claimed a repertory of 83 skits, including such titles as *Who's Got the Baloney?*, *La Guardia's Got the Baloney,* and *Fat Fiorello—* all aimed at destroying the political career of Fiorello La Guardia.[11]

Not until the spring of 1933 did the WLT form a regular unit of about a dozen full-time actors to present agitprops at factory gates, on street corners, and on the docks. This "Shock Troupe" or "'Shock Brigade" had been planned at least two years earlier, but the WLT had to wait because it lacked the needed money.[12] The shock troupers, living on a "small subsidy" from the WLT and on "voluntary contributions," seemed proud of their collective activities and even more proud of their poverty—the outward sign that they were properly proletarian in a capitalist country. Not only were they ready to bring their revolutionary agitprops to the public at a moment's notice, but they also taught evening classes in dramatics and directed rehearsals for about one hundred amateur actors.[13]

Members of the Shock Troupe had to prepare themselves

for their own performances by the study of such subjects as dialectical materialism and the art of acting. The actors rehearsed in their own theatre, a large room with rows of benches and a small stage, over which hung a red banner inscribed "The Theatre Is a Weapon." When Al Saxe, the director, started a rehearsal, his "comrades" maintained perfect discipline. At one session, when the agitprop in preparation was *Scottsboro,* there was a guest of honor—Ruby Bates, the woman who had recently testified for the defense of the Scottsboro boys.[14] Since the Communists were also working for their defense, her presence added a note of political importance to the impending production.

In November 1933 the WLT produced its best agitprop—*Newsboy,* which Gregory Novikov adapted from a poem by V. J. Jerome, the Party's boss in charge of culture. The curtain rises on a darkened stage. The first light reveals only the feet of a crowd milling around. A newsboy cries out his wares—murder, rape, scandal, sports, and war—as a spotlight illuminates his face. Then amber light reveals the whole crowd, which has taken up his cries, especially the call for war to cure the Depression. A black man, the *raisonneur,* explains that the press is preparing the nation for another war. After the stage has been darkened again, a spotlight picks out William Randolph Hearst ordering war headlines, Huey Long proclaiming the glory of war, and Father Coughlin reciting "Our country, right or wrong." As the masses, with their newspapers rolled up as rifles, start to march up and down, the black man tries to call his "comrades" out into the light, but he fails. When an unemployed worker begs a nickel from three rich persons, they tell him to join the CCC (the Civilian Conservation Corps) or the army; he replies that he will starve in the one and be killed in the other.

Then as the left side of the stage becomes brightly illuminated, a second newsboy enters shouting "Fight against war

and fascism." To expose the profits of the munitions makers
and the "war preparations" of the CCC, he distributes his
copies of *Fight,* the newspaper of the American League
Against War and Fascism—a united front organization of
Communists, liberals, and leftists that was created and controlled by the Party. The crowd is quickly converted to his
beliefs when they read of the millions killed in the last war.
These readers are so'situated that their papers form a bar-
ricade, and the second newsboy waves his copy of *Fight*
above it. The first newsboy retreats as the black man con-
cludes the agitprop with the summons to action:

Black Men, white men, field men, shop men.—It's time to fight
war. It's time to fight fascism. . . . Get yourself a trumpet,
buddy, a big red trumpet . . . and blare it out . . . time to
fight war . . . time to fight fascism.[15]

Newsboy, like the *15 Minute Red Revue,* probably made
few, if any, converts to this Communist front, but the ritual
of this little drama was on a higher artistic plane because
the dramatic and theatrical devices were much subtler.
Since it was produced indoors, lighting was used extensively
to intensify the feelings conveyed; for example, the bright
light represented the ideological illumination brought to the
crowd by the Communist newsboy, appropriately from the
left entrance. Because the players moved about in various
patterns almost like ballet dancers and because the "masses"
repeated the unrhymed phrases in several different rhythms,
the monotony that plagued the *15 Minute Red Revue* was
overcome. The characterization, also, gained in subtlety, for
the abstract worker was replaced by the black man and the
second newsboy, and the cartoon capitalist was turned into
the historical figures—Long, Hearst, and Coughlin.

Furthermore, the content, while unmistakably Marxist,
was less rigidly doctrinaire. The concluding call to action
no longer required the audience to shout allegiance to the

Soviet Union or to the local Party. The spectator was asked merely to fight two social evils by aiding the League Against War and Fascism. A "red trumpet" referred to the Communist leadership of this front.

For all this subtlety, however, the ideology of the playlet was still simple-minded. The tableau of the masses joining the front merely because they have read a single issue of *Fight* represented the playwright's and the Party's wishful thinking, for the American masses—as the Communists and Fascists were learning—were not converted that easily. For those who did join the front, the obvious dangers of war and fascism were cause enough, without the theatrical inducements of Novikov's agitprop.

Newsboy, although a much subtler playlet than its predecessors, was still primitive drama. The agitprop was to undergo further development in the next few years.

The year 1934 saw the end of the WLT as an agitprop troupe when this group, rechristened the Theatre of Action, was "reorganized on a full professional basis" for the indoor presentation of realistic plays.[16] Unlike the stylized agitprop, the new technique required the playwright to weave the Marxist ideas into a realistic plot.

A newly created Advisory Council included a united front of writers, a coalition representing many varieties of liberal and left-wing opinion. From Broadway's commercial theatre came Moss Hart; from the Group Theatre came Lee Strasberg; from the Party's professional company, Theatre Union, there were Paul Peters, George Sklar, and Charles Walker. Edward Dahlberg and John Henry Hammond, Jr., completed the list. The Theatre of Action's new Executive Board included John Howard Lawson, who had become an extremely zealous Communist; Herbert Kline, an officer of the Party's New Theatre League and an editor of the Party's unofficial publication, *New Theatre;* and Alfred Saxe, who had been with the WLT since 1930.[17]

The Communists apparently had some doubts about this change in the WLT's purpose, for Leon Alexander, the *Daily Worker's* drama critic, claimed that the Theatre of Action would go on producing the crude agitprops, contrary to the wishes of "some of our professionally minded comrades." But he also admitted that the company was searching for realistic one-act plays, not agitprops.[18]

This group began its realistic period in November 1934 with the presentation of Peter Martin's one-act dramatization of "Daughter," a story by Erskine Caldwell about an impoverished father who shoots his daughter because she is starving. Critics on the left, including Leon Alexander, agreed that this new, realistic style of drama and theatre added power to the play,[19] and, although *Daughter* achieved only a few performances, the Theatre of Action felt itself ready for a move to Broadway.

The company offered its next realistic drama at the Park Theatre in May 1935—*The Young Go First* by Peter Martin, George Scudder, and Charles Friedman. This three-act play was hailed by the Communist press more for the realism of the production than for the political correctness of the script. *New Theatre* sent Herbert Kline, a member of the Theatre of Action's Executive Board, to review the show, and he was, of course, impressed with the miraculous transformation of the agitprop troupe into a professional company. He praised the directors, Al Saxe and Elia Kazan, the latter a rising young actor in the Group Theatre. Kline also praised the playwrights for their exposé of the CCC, but he criticized them for having failed to include even one Communist in their camp; there were militant neighbors but no militant campers. All the reviewers for the Marxist press felt that this self-deprecatory gesture of good will toward the non-Communist left was entirely unrealistic. The play was brought into line politically during the third week of the run,[20] but this change and a publicity campaign in the *Daily Worker* were not enough to keep the drama running more than one month.

The company, having failed to capture Broadway, waited another year, until March 1, 1936, before unveiling its next production—Michael Blankfort's *The Crime*. This short play, again directed by Elia Kazan and Al Saxe, was presented at the Civic Repertory Theatre under the auspices of the New Theatre League. The Communist press was not happy with this drama about a meatpackers' strike, especially with its slight reversion to the agitprop.[21] An actor planted in the audience pretends to be the real leader of the union about which the drama was written. In the prologue a master of ceremonies asks him to say a few words. After the nine realistic scenes have been performed, the actor playing the real leader leaps to the stage to announce that the strike will continue. This theatrical flourish, like those of the agitprop, discloses the deception.

The play was repeated on a few successive Sunday nights. With the end of these performances, the Theatre of Action was dead.

The trend toward realism on the Party's stage actually predated the Theatre of Action. In 1932 the Theatre Collective was organized as a subdivision of the WLT in order to stage full-length realistic plays in the conventional manner of Broadway.[22] Unlike the dramas of the commercial theatre, however, the Collective's plays were supposed to illustrate the Communist Party line.

From 1932 to 1934 the Theatre Collective devoted itself largely to two major productions, both off Broadway. The first of these, *1931–* by Paul and Claire Sifton, opened on May 20, 1933. This drama about unemployment had originally been produced on Broadway by the Group Theatre in 1931 for a run of 12 performances. The Collective's revised version pleased the critic for *New Masses*, Etienne Karnot, who reported that the thesis had been "clarified" to show that "the only way out of the crisis is revolution," even though this conclusion was proved emotionally rather than logically. Despite such minor reservations, this reviewer was thrilled by the *idea* of the Theatre Collective, for he felt that he had witnessed a historic performance involving a theatre, a play, a production, and an audience that were all proletarian. When the curtain fell on the night of May 21, 1933, the audience rose and sang the "Internationale." [23] The play had obviously succeeded in reconvincing the comrades who attended, but so few attended that the production closed after four performances.

The second offering did not open until May 31, 1934, one year later, when the company presented *Marion Models, Inc.*, a "collective play" written by Olga Shapiro, John Bonn (who ran the *Proletbuehne*), and Jack Shapiro "on the struggle of a New York needle trade shop." [24] The critic for *New Theatre*, Nathaniel Buchwald, complained that the play was an unhappy marriage of realism and the agitprop. While the bosses and the model were human, he said, the slogan-spouting union organizers were not.[25] *Marion Models, Inc.* played out its scheduled three performances. Perhaps the lack of dramaturgic skill was to blame; perhaps the leftist spectator was simply getting tired of the old slogans in any theatrical disguise.

Members of the Theatre Collective, in a post-mortem, written by Jack Shapiro, following the demise of their second play, confessed their errors. They had failed at collective playwriting, they had no new scripts, and they had failed to establish a permanent acting company. The Collective, therefore, inaugurated a new program of technical training for actors, directors, playwrights, and designers. To this end Lee Strasberg, Morris Carnovsky, and Cheryl

Crawford—all of the Group Theatre—were already teaching classes in acting and directing. Naturally, said Shapiro, there would be courses "in revolutionary theory and practice," but the prime purpose was to establish a highly trained acting company.[26] It would seem from the roster of part-time teachers that the Collective hoped to become a Communist version of Broadway's Group Theatre. But the new program was really no more than a reaffirmation of the Collective's original plans, and a resolution to succeed. In any event, this company resolved to leave to others the day-to-day agitational performing—in which it had never really been engaged.

This last decision angered the editors of *New Theatre*, who felt that times were too critical for any such withdrawal:

Although the Collective is necessarily a different type of theatre than the Workers' Laboratory Theatre of Action, this does not mean that the Collective can leave *all* the work of playing before mass organizations, at strike rallies, etc., to other workers' theatres. We urge that the Studio work of the Collective include short revolutionary plays and skits for public performance.[27]

Ignoring this admonition, the Theatre Collective continued according to its own plans. In September 1935 it offered a revival of scenes from *Till the Day I Die* by Clifford Odets, and once again the Communist press criticized the Collective for having spent so much time in its studios.[28] It next revived *Private Hicks* by Albert Maltz, in the spring of 1936.[29] These performances led one left-wing critic, John Gassner, to predict that this troupe would "become one of the most finished producing units of the new theatre circuit,"[30] but the Theatre Collective expired with this production.

The amateur Communist theatres thus utilized two techniques for presenting social, political, and economic doctrine. The *Proletbuehne* and the WLT introduced the stylized agitprop to their audience, while the Theatre Collective and the Theatre of Action followed the realistic tradition of the Broadway stage. Despite the many attempts at experimental forms of drama and theatre, conventional realism ultimately dominated the new theatre movement. Although the Communists favored the agitprop in the early part of the decade, they later preferred realism because they feared that their revolutionary message would get lost in the arty theatricalism of the experimental drama.

The Communists had only very few dependable amateur companies to produce the two kinds of drama, but the *Proletbuehne,* the WLT, the Theatre of Action, and the Theatre Collective all failed to fulfill the Party's hopes for a new stage. They apparently had the will and the youthful energy to succeed, but they lacked the money needed to establish permanent companies. More important, they lacked the scripts that were good enough to attract large audiences and also Marxist enough to please the Party. They settled for Marxism.

These short-lived groups made but a slight impression on their radical audience, and virtually no impression on the over-all theatrical scene in New York. Despite the Party's promises of a new theatre to help destroy capitalism, these companies failed to inspire either a political or a theatrical revolution.

Chapter 2

The Communists' League of Workers' Theatres, 1932–1934

USING personnel drawn from the WLT, the *Prolet-buehne*, and the Theatre Collective, the Communists super-imposed the League of Workers' Theatres on the flounder-ing amateur proletarian troupes in April 1932. On a political level, the new national organization was supposed

to spread the idea of the class struggle, to participate actively in the class struggle by raising funds for campaigns and for the revolutionary press, and by recruiting workers into the revolu-tionary unions and mass organizations, and especially to arouse the workers for the defense of the Soviet Union, against the com-ing imperialist attack.[1]

The League's first two official functions were thus to propa-gandize the Party's revolutionary ideas and to man the bar-ricades.

On a more theatrical level, the League's purpose was to counteract the admitted failures of the proletarian theatres before 1932. Many groups in New York and throughout the country—in Chicago, Philadelphia, and Boston—had per-formed on one or two occasions and then disappeared from the scene. Only the *Proletbuehne* and the WLT, as we have seen, exhibited any kind of staying power, but they were hardly successful either as theatres or as political propagandists.

The Communists thus understood that New York had but one or two "absolutely reliable" agitprop troupes, and they admitted that actual performances on the workers' stage were rare. In seeking to place the blame for this failure, they complained about the proletarian actors who lacked the proper political dedication, and they criticized the agitprops for being too abstract. Most of all, the Communists blamed the playwrights who were not following the correct creative process: collective dramaturgy.[2] The League of Workers' Theatres was to overcome all these defects in proletarian play production.

The League's most important purpose, however, was to overcome an even more serious shortcoming—the lack of a national organization. For the effective use of the theatre as a political weapon the Communist Party had to marshal all the amateur leftist theatres under its centralized authority. By creating and controlling a central agency of the new theatre movement, the Communists could supervise a large network of amateur companies. Thus, a small band of devoted revolutionists in control of the League could direct a vast theatrical program for political action. In theory, at least, prospects seemed rosy for the Communists.

John Bonn of the *Proletbuehne,* setting forth the entire Party line for the League, was confident about the future:

. . . this is the moment, when the workers and the working class organizations, instead of ignoring us or smiling at our attempts as they used to do, recognize us as an important factor in the revolutionary movement of the working class.[3]

Confidence was indeed in the air. When the Communist Party of New York invited the workers' stage to help in the election campaign of 1932, the League declared, in its best Soviet style, that it would "march forward as an important factor in the overthrow of the capitalist system, in the emancipation of the working class, to the glorious building of the classless society."[4] The League of Workers' Theatres would thus fight for a Soviet America.

There was some disagreement about the best methods for using the theatre as a political weapon. Should the League sponsor the mobile agitprop troupes (like the WLT) or the more conventional theatres specializing in realistic drama (like the Theatre Collective)? In 1932 the Party line was announced. The agitprop would be the primary form of the workers' stage, but realistic plays in the manner of Broadway would also be permitted, if these conventional dramas would be "as highly political in content as the agitprop type."[5] The new dramatist could thus steal bourgeois thunder as long as his play followed the Party line.

The Communists also floundered in their attitude toward the bourgeois stage of Broadway. In 1931 they had held that it was not related to the proletarian theatre at all, but by 1932 they saw it as an opponent in the class struggle. They believed that this stage reflected the decay of American capitalism and that Broadway, under the cover of art for art's sake, was really fighting to preserve a "doomed" way of life:

Just think of all the plays and movies demonstrating, explicitly or implicitly, that money does not make happy homes, that every worker in this country has a chance to become a millionaire when he starts as an obedient wage slave and rises to exploit others, that millionaires are often unhappy and always charitable, that we have to defend and to die for "our country."[6]

The League of Workers' Theatres therefore intended to expose and destroy the bourgeois stage.

Since Broadway appeared to be dying anyway, the task did not seem hard. Unemployed theatre artists—and there were many in 1932—were to be recruited into the ranks of the revolutionary theatre and thus into the ranks of the revolution.

The League of Workers' Theatres had its only success—a very minor one—in its occasional productions of "New Theatre Nights." These entertainments, produced in New York in the spring of 1934, comprised performances by various leftist theatre groups for the benefit of some revolutionary cause. The first New Theatre Night, for example, included an agitprop by the WLT, a scene by the Theatre Collective from one of its realistic dramas, a satire by actors from the Group Theatre, and songs by a group of Negro singers.[7] Since these shows spread revolutionary dogma and raised funds for the revolution, two of the League's political functions were fulfilled, albeit intermittently.

These nights also served to introduce such new playlets as *Dimitroff* by Art Smith and Elia Kazan, which was presented at the Fifth Avenue Theatre on June 3, 1934. This agitprop, consisting of eleven very brief scenes, opens with the choral singing of Communist songs offstage. Hitler, in a radio broadcast, denounces the Reds, with the result that Nazi gunfire soon stops the singing. He and Goering, having ordered the Reichstag burned, blame the Communists and bring their leaders to trial. Throughout the world the masses, led by the Communists, exert "mass pressure" by picketing German embassies, sending telegrams to the Nazi leaders, and contributing money to fight them. Dimitroff, one of the accused, defies the court by blaming Goering, but eventually wins acquittal because the masses are heard shouting slogans. Since two Communist leaders—Torgler and Thaelmann—remain in prison, however, Dimitroff addresses the theatre audience with this plea:

We have been saved by the world pressure of the revolutionary masses. But *Torgler* is still in prison and *Thaelmann* is held in chains. . . . *We must fight fascism with undiminished strength and courage. We must free our comrades. Free all class war prisoners!!!* [8]

The spectators, led by actors planted among them, repeat the last line. Then Dimitroff cries, *"Free Torgler!"* and the audience echoes the demand. Finally he shouts, *"Free Thaelmann!!"* and again the spectators respond.

Dimitroff is basically an agitprop. Like the *15 Minute Red Revue* and *Newsboy*, this episodic playlet contains choral recitations, stylized tableaux, cartoon characters, and a direct incitement to political action, but *Dimitroff* also represents a shift toward realistic drama in that historical events replace the abstract Marxist situations of its predecessors. Smith and Kazan used the agitprop not only to illustrate a political thesis but also to tell a real story.

They attempted to humanize this genre further by transforming the allegorical characters into living people. They introduced Hitler and Goering—at greater length than Novikov had presented Hearst in *Newsboy*—to replace the cartoon capitalist with his silk hat and dollar sign, and Dimitroff to replace the cartoon Communist worker with his clenched fist and red banner. While some of the scenes still consist of the old Communist slogans, other episodes contain realistic human drama.

Although *Dimitroff* is itself not a good play, it prepares the way for Odets' *Waiting for Lefty* by revealing the potentialities of merging the theatricality of the stylized agitprop with the human emotions of realistic drama. *Dimitroff*, a humanized agitprop, is the best dramatic work that the League was able to inspire.

Besides introducing new revolutionary playlets, the League's New Theatre Nights did attract professional performers from the commercial stage. For example, *Dimitroff* was written and acted by those members of the Group Theatre who sought to present plays far to the left of their

own company's efforts. Furthermore, the League could hope
to attract audiences to see these stars of the Group Theatre,
and thus secure full houses. But such successful performances were rare.

In other ways, the League failed, especially in organizing
and controlling its envisioned network of amateur theatres.
It never became a very large organization. For instance, at
the convention that created it back in 1932 there were dele-
gates from "fifty-odd dramatic groups," [9] but only 13 companies—mostly from New York—actually performed. By June
1934 only 30 affiliated groups had paid their dues, and many
of these affiliates had never even established theatres. [10] The
League thus did not become the vast network that the Party
had hoped for.

Furthermore, the affiliated groups did not always stay in
line. The best illustration of the League's failure to control
its affiliates lies in the controversy surrounding *Workers'
Theatre*, a minor magazine, which the League published in
1932 and 1933. With the first issue of 1934 this periodical
was enlarged, renamed *New Theatre,* and addressed to the
entire left, not merely to the orthodox Communists.

This change did not please the League's affiliates because
most of the articles in *New Theatre* concerned the commercial stage, not the amateur Marxist theatres. [11] One critic,
Manfred Ettinger, explained this shift by citing the "phe-
nomenal influx of prominent theatrical lights into the ranks
of 'sympathizers' with the revolutionary theatre movement."
These fellow travelers from Broadway, he noted bitterly,
were not overburdened by the hard work of the amateurs
who were running the proletarian theatres, and thus had the
time to write reports on the "decadent" commercial stage. [12]

The editors of *New Theatre,* in turn, were plainly angered
by this complaint about the dearth of publicity given to the
amateur Marxist stage. They admitted that there were short-

comings in the magazine, but they also denounced the affiliates for having failed to sell their allotted copies of *New Theatre* and, worse still, for having neglected to send the League the money for the copies they had sold. Also, since many troupes had failed even to pay their dues, the editors threatened to publish a blacklist.[13]

By withholding these funds the affiliates were perhaps anticipating the benefits of the classless society, and they must have regarded the League's financial demands as nothing less than bourgeois greed. After all, weren't they contributing their time to the new theatre movement free of charge? These petty squabbles indicated that not very much of Moscow's gold was supporting the Marxist stage in America. More importantly, they revealed that the League of Workers' Theatres did not have as much control over its little network as it had dreamed of.

Besides failing to attract many amateur theatres and failing to control those it did attract, the League could not supply its affiliates with enough good scripts. For this reason many amateur Marxist groups did not even reach the performing stage. Good plays were scarce. In 1932, for example, the Red Players, a short-lived troupe, requested some dramatic scripts that would denounce war as an inevitable part of the capitalist system,[14] but only such amateurish agit-props as Nathaniel Buchwald's *Hands Off!* were available. Two years later there was still nothing better on the same subject. The League's playwrights were apparently following the advice of J. Shapiro, the chairman of the Repertory Committee, too closely: "Make the plays short and concise and make a thorough study of the Communist Party Platform before writing them." [15]

Although the League's dramatists offered correct Marxist doctrine, they rarely wrote good drama. In 1934 the explanation arrived from Moscow. Communist plays suffered from *"too much schematism and sloganism; low artistic technique; inability to express political tasks through artistic images, etc.*" This was a fair analysis, but these failings were blamed on a "*lack of knowledge of Marxism-Leninism and consequent inability to solve problems facing revolutionary art.*"[16] The Communists expected that Marxism-Leninism, since it was a world view, could solve all problems—dramaturgic as well as social, economic, and political. If writers failed to create dramatic literature, they had not studied the Party philosophy thoroughly enough. The trouble was just the opposite—too much Marxism and too little drama.

To overcome the "schematism and sloganism" of the Marxist scripts, *New Theatre*, in 1934, advised dramatists not to write agitprops and called instead for short realistic dramas on proletarian themes.[17] Symptomatic of this shift was the conversion of the WLT to the Theatre of Action. Since most of the League's 1934 repertory consisted of agitprops, the League was left without much of a repertory and consequently had to hunt for new realistic plays.

Asserting that there were many Marxist theatre companies but a dearth of dramas, one radical playwright, Virgil Geddes, appealed for scripts.[18] But the call went unheeded, for the established playwrights with leftist sympathies continued to write for the commercial theatre, while the new playwrights who succeeded in the amateur theatre—and no one really did succeed before 1935—usually moved to the greener fields of Broadway and Hollywood.

The League, furthermore, failed to inspire professional performances of its small repertory—both agitational and realistic. Although there were such exceptions as WLT's highly praised presentation of *Newsboy*, there was a constant current of critical attack against the amateurish productions of the amateur proletarian stage. Michael Gold complained about them,[19] and Conrad Seiler, another critic, described the pitiful deficiency in "craftsmanship":

. . . there is a pronounced tendency among workers' cultural groups to present plays in a slipshod manner, with little or no consideration for anything but correct ideological content. Workers with no training and no natural aptitude . . . are urged to act; insufficient time is devoted to rehearsals; direction is bad; lines are only half mastered; plays are mounted without taste or intelligence. Too often the workers' theatre is a mere replica of some inept bourgeois group—mediocre amateurs with an implacable yearning to exhibit their mediocre "talent." [20]

A lack of money prevented these groups from renting proper lighting, scenery, and costumes, but the main fault lay with the actors themselves. Just as the belief in Marxism-Leninism was not in and of itself enough to transform Marxians into first-rate dramatists, so it did not transform bad actors into good ones.

Poor plays, poorly produced, did not please the American masses. Back in 1932 the League had warned:

We are in danger of running into blind alleys of routine repetition if we do not break through our small circles to the millions of workers that still know nothing of our activity.[21]

The 1932 audience for these plays was thus composed mostly of dedicated Communists, and in 1934 it remained the same:

The workers' theatre as now constituted, with all its gross inefficiency, may still appeal to some audiences already converted to the essential truth of proletarian ideals, but non-revolutionary audiences—the kind we must attract—are used to the smoothness of the bourgeois theatre and the films. . . .[22]

The League realized that it needed good plays and good productions to entice those spectators, but as long as its efforts remained amateurish the new and larger audience stayed away.

Because the League of Workers' Theatres attracted mainly the convinced Communists, it did not spread revolutionary propaganda very far. One critic, Harold Edgar, thought that converts did not matter, so long as the theatre encouraged believers.[23] An artistic agitprop would have succeeded in this limited goal, but good agitprops were rare. Nor did the League, unable to produce a single hit, earn large sums for revolutionary causes. A change of policy was plainly needed.

The direction of this change became evident at the League's Eastern Regional Conference held in August 1933, when two opposing views of the League's function were set forth. Ben Blake, upholding the orthodox side, said that the theatre should be used as a weapon in the fight against hunger, fascism, and war (and against the Roosevelt program, which, he said, was the cause of all three evils), and he defended the crude Marxian agitprops because they dealt with these immediate problems.

Harry Elion, upholding the new united front point of view, on the other hand, advocated "a broader conception of the revolutionary theatre," which would include *any* drama designed to destroy "reactionary prejudices."[24] Elion apparently realized that the League's plays were reaching only Party members and sympathizers, not only because the productions were so inadequate but because the scripts—both agitational and realistic—were so narrowly limited by Marxist doctrine. This organization would have to lessen its demand for complete adherence to the Party line in order to reach the American masses. In January 1935 the League, changing its course into the broader channel, rechristened itself the New Theatre League.

Chapter 3

The Communists' New Theatre League, 1935–1941

THE New Theatre League was thus the old League of Workers' Theatres with a new name and a new program:

For mass development of the American Theatre to its highest artistic and social level. For a theatre dedicated to the struggle against war, fascism, and censorship.[1]

New Theatre groups, the League asserted, could be Socialist, Farmer-Labor, liberal, or Communist, as long as they could unite on the basic program. The League also reported that "all remnants of sectarianism and the old insistence that all members agree completely with a revolutionary point of view" had been abandoned, but nothing was said about a change of personnel at the central office of the League of Workers' Theatres.[2]

The new program was vague. To the Communists, the *"highest artistic and social level"* of the American theatre meant the most efficient use of drama as a weapon in the inevitable revolution, and a replica of the Soviet Russian theatre after the establishment of a Soviet America. But to non-Communists, the highest level meant artistic plays on social themes. The program's second part, while more specific, was still vague. To the Communists, "imperialist" wars

33

were evil, but Leninist revolutions were good. To pacifists, all violence was abhorrent. To other non-Communists, only wars of aggression were unjustified. Likewise, fascism meant different things to different people. To the Marxists, it was the tyranny of a decaying capitalist state. But to the non-Marxists, fascism was simply political tyranny. There was similar disagreement about censorship. The Communists were against it only when it applied to "progressive" writers. But many non-Communists thought that all censorship was wrong. The program was thus so vague that it was potentially able to attract the broad, if fuzzy-minded, American masses. To have been against war, fascism, and censorship and for a social and artistic theatre did not necessarily make you a Communist in 1935. It all depended on the way you interpreted the key words of the League's program.[3]

Orthodox communism thus gave way to the united front in an effort to reach the vast non-Communist masses. Since the Communists had failed in their direct assault on American society and its theatre, they changed their tactics to infiltration. The New Theatre League was one cultural manifestation of the Party's united front (or popular front) strategy of creating new organizations in which all liberal and left-wing groups could participate, but over which the Communists kept strict and often secret control.

One of the earliest illustrations of this strategy was the League Against War and Fascism, which the Party had organized in October 1933. The fear of nazism drove Marxists and liberals alike into this united front. The Seventh World Congress of the Communist International, held in Moscow in August 1935, confirmed this policy.[4] During the mid-thirties the American comrades formed fronts to fight fascism in Germany and later in Spain, to organize labor unions, to support various reform measures of the New· Deal, and of course, to gain control of the theatre.

Because innocent actors and playwrights, ignorant of

Party control, could easily subscribe to the New Theatre League's seemingly moderate, idealistic program, they could be lured into this front. The Communists in the central office could control these innocents and their numerous amateur theatres—not only workers' or union groups but also theatre companies associated with churches, YMCA's, universities, and communities.[5] If all these groups could be enticed into the League and if they would then obey the national office with respect to repertory and organization, the League could become a mighty Communist weapon for political action. Once again, prospects—in theory, at least—seemed rosy for the Party. But the theory hung on the two huge "ifs."

During its first year, the new League searched for the theatrical means to fulfill its program. Speaking for the League, Mark Marvin reported that the agitprops and the supposedly realistic plays—the dramas about strikes that always ended with the conversion of the neutral worker to the revolution—would no longer do, for these "conversion" plays too often spoke the language "of the public platform and the political manual." The proposed new drama was to deal with "love, ambition, fear, and hope" as well as with strikes; the new dramas were to be realistic and, above all, "competent" and "convincing."[6] The Communists, in short, called for realism and theatrical success. So far they had had neither.

The political content of these new plays was to be sufficiently nonrevolutionary to appeal to the non-Communist masses, but the plays were to be strong enough so that the proletariat would be "precipitated into militant action" and the bourgeoisie would be "awakened to new horizons of living."[7] The League, wanting to eat its cake and have it too, thus desired nonrevolutionary plays that would incite the proletariat *and* the bourgeoisie to revolt against capitalism. The key to this paradox was subtlety; the incitement to action was to be implicit rather than explicit. A strong indictment of capitalism or war, for example, would be sufficient without an open call to a Communist revolution.

This new policy intensified a critical controversy on the left, for one critic's conception of subtlety was another's idea of reaction. Therefore, during the last half of the decade leftist critics were often divided on the merits of the political or social message of a given play. The orthodox Marxist critics favored the play with the explicit political incitement; Leon Alexander, for example, wrote that, unless the bourgeois playwright "recognizes and portrays clearly the role of the working class in changing society, his effect is that of a reactionary." [8] For these critics there was no middle ground; the playwright who was not explicitly for the revolution was against it. Dramatic excellence, they felt, would automatically follow good Marxism. They conveniently forgot that the old sectarianism had failed to produce a repertory of good plays. Although the Communists apparently realized that they would have to lower their political standards to entice new playwrights who could write good plays, the orthodox critics remained faithful to the old, rigid Party line.

Stanley Burnshaw, one of their more liberal associates, reminded them that many wavering writers could be brought into the united front and eventually into the cause if criticism were more constructive. Since these dramatists understood the decay of capitalism and the need for reform, he added, the Marxist critics could show them that communism was the only solution. Burnshaw warned the critical old guard that their unfriendly political attacks might turn these uncertain playwrights into Fascists. [9] The orthodox critics, however, contined to demand a clear revolutionary line in the drama, the popular front reviewers settled for less, and the dramatists continued to stand on their middle ground.

With luck the League at the outset of its career discovered the kind of drama it wanted. The setting for the discovery was a New Theatre Night held on January 6, 1935, at the Civic Repertory Theatre, and the play was Clifford Odets' *Waiting for Lefty*.[10]

The audience on the opening night experienced not only the excitement of an electrifying performance but also the thrill of discovering a first-rate dramatist. For the Marxist part of the audience there was the added joy in feeling the power with which Odets' Marxist point of view came across. The spectator, that first night, found himself part of the performance. The whole theatre was a union hall, and he was a union member watching his leaders conduct a meeting on the stage. He listened to his fellow members (really actors planted in the auditorium) commenting on the action, and at the end he was shouting, "Strike!" along with everyone else. The staging was brilliant.

Waiting for Lefty concerns a revolt of the rank and file of a taxi drivers' union against their corrupt officers. While waiting for Lefty, the insurgent leader, to arrive at a union meeting, militant drivers argue for a walkout. In brief flashbacks we view the personal and social motives behind their demand. First we see Edna urging Joe to strike because they are starving. Next Miller, a chemist, fired for refusing to work on poison gas for the next war, abandons chemistry and becomes a driver. Then we meet Sid, who is too poor to marry Florence.

We return to the union hall where Harry Fatt, a corrupt leader, attempts to introduce a driver to speak against a strike, but the speaker is exposed as a labor spy by his militant brother, who is sitting in the audience. In the flashbacks that follow, an unemployed actor becomes a Communist taxi driver because of the teachings of a secretary,[11] and a young intern, fired from a hospital because he is Jewish, undergoes a similar conversion. In the final scene we

again return to the union hall, where Agate calls on America
to join "the stormbirds of the working class," that is, the
Communist Party. When the news of Lefty's murder is announced, Agate, the agitator, asks the audience, "Well,
what's the answer?" The play ends with this response:

> All: STRIKE!
> Agate: LOUDER!
> All: STRIKE!
> Agate and others on stage: AGAIN!
> All: STRIKE, STRIKE, STRIKE!!! [12]

In his "Notes for Production" Odets explained that he
used "the old black-face minstrel form of chorus, end men,
specialty men and interlocutor." For example, the playwright urged the use of the strike committee as an emotional, political, and musical chorus at the climactic moments in all scenes; he suggested that the intern's episode
include an announcement that anti-Semitism is a crime
against the state in Soviet Russia.[13] Harry Fatt was undoubtedly meant to be the interlocutor from his position at the
center of the platform. Odets may have intended the individual scenes as specialty acts, and the thug—lolling at the
proscenium—as an end man with a gun to replace the tam-
bourine and bones. Perhaps Odets wanted to show an analogy between the blackface slaves of the minstrel show and
the wage slaves of *Waiting for Lefty*, but, for the most part,
the parallel seems limited to the theatrical production.

The real source of the play, however, was the agitprop.
The direct incitement of the spectators and the choral response formed the typical ending of this genre. Odets retained other stylized theatrical devices of this kind of drama.
A blackout, for example, ends each brief scene, and a spotlight immediately picks out the next, much in the manner
of *Newsboy*. Odets also used some other familiar ingredients
of the agitprop—the episodic structure, the cartoon capital-

ists, and the Marxian slogans—but he made several changes.

Continuing the trend toward realism in the left-wing theatre, Odets achieved great variety in his humanized characterizations of the cartoon worker. The drivers in *Waiting for Lefty* are basically noble, yet earthy and imperfect, unlike the idealized proletarian hero of *Dimitroff*. The secretary, although akin to the stereotyped Communist agitator, appears to be more human, with her family troubles, her wisecracks, and her charitable impulses. Even her Marxist slogans seem natural when we remember that she is a Communist. Because we see her as a psychological being we find it easier to accept her as a political creature too. Odets transformed the cartoon proletarians of the earlier agitprops into human beings with loves, hopes, fears, as well as political beliefs.

Although Odets permitted his workers to have imperfections, he did not allow Fatt, Fayette, or Grady—three versions of the top-hatted capitalist—to exhibit the slightest human virtue. Harry Fatt, the labor racketeer, runs the company union with gunmen to benefit the bosses; Fayette, the Party's conception of the industrialist, does not think beyond the profits in poison gas; and Grady, the Communists' satiric portrait of the lecherous Broadway producer, thinks of the theatre in terms of money rather than art. Because they have real names and occupations, however, these villains seem more terrifying as social menaces than their abstract ancestor.

Besides humanizing the characters Odets humanized the situations. Although all the episodes illustrate the political thesis, they are also realistic human dramas in miniature. For example, in the first flashback Joe decides to strike not because a Communist agitator has shouted slogans at him but because there are both economic *and* emotional crises in his marriage.

The dialogue and the setting also contribute to the real-

ism of *Waiting for Lefty*. The characters, for the most part
lower class New Yorkers, speak New-Yorkese—a tough, humorous, and rhythmic dialect.[14] For example, Sid explains
capitalist exploitation of the proletariat in this way:

The damn fool don't see the cards is stacked for all of us. The
money man dealing himself a hot royal flush. Then giving you
and me a phoney hand like a pair of tens or something. Then
keep on losing the pots 'cause the cards is stacked against you.
Then he says, what's the matter you can't win—no stuff on the
ball, he says to you.[15]

Odets made his Marxists sound like real New Yorkers, not
like the political tracts of the earlier agitprops. He also created a sense of realism by using the entire theatre—stage
and auditorium—as his union hall setting, thus giving the
audience the illusion of being present at an actual union
meeting.

Although the human problems loomed larger than the
political message, Odets did not ignore his thesis. As a Communist he favored his Party, but, unlike the writers of the
earliest agitprops, he did so indirectly. To lead a strike (that
is, a revolution), he metaphorically proposed the "stormbirds of the working class," that is, the elite—or the Communists. Instead of having a Party agitator recite Communist slogans, Odets had the secretary refer her "comrade,"
and the audience, to the *Communist Manifesto*. The Marxian agitation and propaganda were very clear but not quite
so open as they had been in the *15 Minute Red Revue*.

Thus, by adding realistic characters, situations, and dialogue to the nonrealistic structure of the agitprop, Odets
completed the agitprop's movement toward realistic human
drama and, because this new realism made the agitation and
propaganda seem comparatively unobtrusive, he continued
the trend toward political subtlety. He could do no more
with the agitprop without destroying it, for a further move-

ment toward realism would undoubtedly have replaced the stylized structure with the pattern of the conventional, well-made play, and a further movement toward political under-statement would have weakened the propagandistic pur-pose of the agitprop.[16]

Waiting for Lefty had a brilliant success. After five long years of trial and error the new theatre movement had its first artistic triumph. Although this play was later performed by the League's amateur affiliates, the first performance was presented by professional actors then appearing with the Group Theatre. The initial triumph belonged to the League, which sponsored the première and many performances prior to the Group's official production in late March 1935. Hav-ing awarded Odets first prize in a hastily invented play-writing contest, the League also claimed credit for his dis-covery. Although professional members of the Group The-atre actually performed *Waiting for Lefty,* the New Theatre League thus gloried in the praise for the overnight success. The League reached the height of its prominence at the start of its career.

Waiting for Lefty also became extremely popular with amateur .League groups outside New York City, for by June 1935 this play had been performed in fifty American cities.[17] These presentations afforded the League a maximum of publicity because of the many attempts at banning the play; for example, members of the New Theatre Players of Boston were arrested for acting in an "obscene" drama, the New Haven police prohibited all further performances of *Wait-ing for Lefty* following its initial production in that city, and there was trouble in Newark. All these difficulties helped the League, for here at last was the perfect opportunity to create a united front against censorship. Indeed, the Ameri-can Civil Liberties Union, Professor Walter Pritchard Eaton of Yale's School of Drama, and assorted Yale students joined with the Communists' International Labor Defense to de-

fend Odets in New Haven.[18] Many people not interested in
his revolutionary message were concerned about the curtail-
ment of his free speech.

In addition to its function as a minor *cause célèbre, Waiting for Lefty* was useful as a political weapon because it
attracted audiences. The League's high regard for the play's
power became evident when Gertrude Weil Klein wrote an
acerb review in the Socialist *New Leader,* in which she
criticized Odets for his portrayals of all non-Communist
union leaders as racketeers, for the fact that his workers
were really all professional people who happened to be
driving cabs, for his rumored view that ordinary "workers
stink," and for all the "theatrical hokum" of the script.[19]

Defending the League, Helen Sheridan wrote that, although the *New Leader* had the right to criticize the play,
it was wrong to attack such an *effective* play, for a drama
so popular with workers was obviously good. She quoted
Odets' prediction that "the working class audience" would
reply to "this cheap attempt at character-assassination," and
she reported the demand by a delegation from the Group
Theatre for a retraction from Miss Klein.[20] Like ordinary
mortals, workers in the new theatre movement worshiped
success, and in the moment of its greatest triumph the
League was piqued by this Socialist attack.

The Communist press criticized the plays' shortcomings,
but these friendly criticisms were embedded in glowing ac-
counts of the drama's merits and of its enthusiastic reception in the theatre. Nathaniel Buchwald, for example, found
fault with the loose structure, with the excessive slogans,
and with Odets' failure to confine the play to the actual
strike situation.[21] To the critics for the Communist press
the flaws were minor, however, when compared with the
general brilliance of the play and with its popular reception.
These reviewers were merely attempting to gild the first
blossom of the new theatre movement.

Waiting for Lefty deservedly made Odets famous. The search was on for a successor, but the League had no luck with its New Theatre Nights during the remainder of 1935. Several strike plays were introduced, but none lasted beyond a single showing.[22] The search ended briefly at the start of 1936 when the League discovered two short plays—*Private Hicks* by Albert Maltz and *Hymn to the Rising Sun* by Paul Green. These dramas were performed by the professional *Let Freedom Ring* Actors' Company at a New Theatre Night on January 9, 1936,[23] one year after the première of *Waiting for Lefty*.

Unlike Odets' complex narrative, the story of *Private Hicks* is set forth in the chronological sequence of conventional, realistic drama. Hicks, a private in a National Guard unit that has been activated to quell a strike in an industrial city, is arrested because he disobeyed the order to fire on the strikers and because he urged his fellow Guardsmen to lay down their weapons. As Hicks proudly goes to prison, a friendly guard promises to continue the battle against the strikebreakers.

Since the spectator had to extract his revolutionary message from *Private Hicks*, it was the more subtle, more realistic kind of drama that the League was advocating in its campaign to lure a broader audience. Likewise, the message, though quite clearly woven into the plot, was not so blatantly Marxist as the moral of *Waiting for Lefty*, for Maltz presented the Communists merely as offstage pamphleteers. This attack on strikebreaking by the National Guard was one to which the non-Communist left and the Party could both subscribe. *Private Hicks* was widely produced. In New York, for example, the Theatre Collective performed the Maltz play many times during the spring of 1936.

Hymn to the Rising Sun was a play with potentially much broader appeal than either *Waiting for Lefty* or *Private Hicks*. Paul Green depicted the brutal life of a Southern chain gang from 4 A.M. until sunrise on Independence Day. The prisoners awake, wash, and breakfast; they listen to the prescribed Fourth of July oration delivered by the Captain; they see the Captain whip a sick white prisoner; they sing "America"; they see a Negro prisoner released from the "sweat box" only after he has died "of natural causes"; and they march forth to the day's labor as the sun rises.

Paul Green made *Hymn to the Rising Sun* a conventional, realistic one-act play, very much like *Private Hicks*. Unlike Albert Maltz, however, Green managed to convey his message without having anyone on stage explicitly state it. He used no *raisonneur* comparable to Hicks, nor did he place any Communists in the background. Unlike Odets, Green created no agitator to arouse the audience. He presented a shockingly intense, yet credible, picture of life with a chain gang, but he offered no commentary on the plot other than the irony of establishing the time of the action as sunrise on Independence Day. When he depicted the Captain forcing the prisoners to sing of the "sweet land of liberty," no comment was needed.

The message was vague enough, in a political sense, to appeal to many shades of American opinion. In having the Captain report that the Governor hires the workers out to the railroad, Green was merely stating a fact. To recognize that chain gangs were exploited was not necessarily a sign of sympathy with Marxism. Since Green did not suggest a solution, the spectator could supply his own.

The Communist press, though it usually liked a more specifically Marxian message, seemed relatively happy with *Hymn to the Rising Sun*. One critic, Stanley Burnshaw, felt the urge to rebel at the picture of savagery he had witnessed; [24] perhaps he equated such rebellion with a proletarian revolution. On the other hand, the sympathetic Socialist, Democrat, or Republican might simply have desired prison reform in the South as a result of this play.

On March 14 and 15, 1936, the League introduced another successful leftist drama—*Bury the Dead,* "A Play about the War That Is to Begin Tomorrow Night" by Irwin Shaw.[25] The Shaw piece, likewise produced by professional actors, had as great a success as *Waiting for Lefty.* Not only had the League discovered a good play—it had also discovered a new dramatist. Whereas Albert Maltz and Paul Green had been established playwrights before the productions of *Private Hicks* and *Hymn to the Rising Sun,* neither Odets nor Shaw had ever had a play produced until the League gave these new dramatists their first chance. *Bury the Dead,* like *Waiting for Lefty,* was one of the League's prize-winning plays.

The action starts with a realistic episode, in which four war-weary soldiers are burying some of their dead comrades. The play turns to fantasy when the dead arise and refuse to be buried. Doctors, generals, editors, clergymen, businessmen, wives, mothers, and sweethearts, all fail to persuade the men to be buried. The risen, desiring to tell the world that they were cheated by life and war, silently march off to their mission, and the soldiers of the burial detail desert to follow them.

After the first scene Shaw used a structure as theatrically complex as that of *Waiting for Lefty.* He utilized an episodic arrangement of scenes, spotlights to pick out the action, and voices crying out of the dark in a sequence that follows the logic of the theatre and the theme rather than the conventional structure of realistic conversation. He wrote *Bury the Dead* not as a "slice of life," like *Hymn to the Rising Sun,* but rather as an explanation of life in the style of *Waiting for Lefty.*

Insofar as Irwin Shaw did not use a conventional, realistic structure, he reverted to the agitprop. He caricatured the bankers, the generals, and the priests just as the capitalists had been drawn in the old skits. Advancing beyond the agitprop, however, Shaw tried to humanize his soldiers, to present them as imperfect human beings, but he did not succeed in creating any vivid individuals as Odets had done. Shaw also made his incitement to action implicit in the dialogue; he used *raisonneurs,* but he had them speak to other characters, not directly to the audience. In this respect *Bury the Dead* was the "subtle" kind of propaganda play sought by the League.

The message, too, was broad enough to appeal to spectators of diverse political opinions. The Communists would read revolution between the lines because they believed that a proletarian uprising would automatically solve the problem of war, but the non-Communist might solve this problem by simple pacifism. The solution was left to the spectator, with the hope that the horror of war—made doubly terrifying by the play's supernatural overtones—would impel him to fight this evil.

New Theatre explained the sort of action the play was supposed to produce:

If it can draw new masses of people into the militant struggle being waged against the forces of militarism by such organizations as the American League Against War and Fascism and the American Student Union, it will have fulfilled the prime aim of its young author.[26]

Since Shaw did not urge the audience to join either of these Communist fronts, this goal was hard to reach. Perhaps the horror of *Bury the Dead* persuaded the spectator to stay out of war, but the playwright offered him no plan of organized action. When *Bury the Dead* opened a commercial run on Broadway, April 18, 1936, the *Daily Worker's* critic, S. W. Gerson, seemed happy enough, however, that the play was good propaganda to keep America out of war.[27]

The League did not find a successor to *Bury the Dead* until December 12, 1937, when Ben Bengal's *Plant in the*

Sun was presented. This one-act play, like *Private Hicks*, is a straightforward, realistic drama. Because two workers have been fired for talking about a union in the candy factory, the shipping clerks decide to strike. They chain a door open so that the other workers will see them beaten by company thugs. The strikers are beaten and carried off, but the rest of the workers decide to "sit down." *Plant in the Sun* has a simple plot, enlivened by a maximum of stage business.

Like Odets, Bengal obviously desired to create human beings instead of idealized workers, but he made the characters in *Plant in the Sun* realistic only insofar as they spoke the racy language of the Lower East Side. He distinguished the workers primarily by their national origins; he depicted the bosses and the thugs as caricatures of capitalists. This play belonged to the united front period because of the realistic style and the pro-union, but not pro-Communist, message.

This production, acted by several alumni of the old Theatre of Action, was well received by the *Daily Worker*'s critic, Eric Englander,[28] but it did not garner the extravagant praise given to *Waiting for Lefty* and *Bury the Dead*. The League arranged a series of Sunday night performances of the Bengal play during the spring of 1938, with the hope of finding a commercial backer.[29] None was found.

From 1938 through 1941 the League continued to seek significant new plays, but without success. Because of this failure, the New Theatre Nights were abandoned early in 1941. In their place the League planned to create two troupes in New York: one, "a regular producing company" for realistic plays, and the other, an agitprop unit to present "anti-war and pro-labor" dramas.[30] By 1941, however, the League had strength enough to create only the realistic theatre.

On May 18, 1941, this acting company, the New Theatre

of Manhattan, made its debut at the Transport Workers' Hall in *Zero Hour* by Albert Maltz and George Sklar. The authors had originally intended to rewrite *Peace on Earth,* their Theatre Union play of 1933, but they really wrote a new play on the same themes—anti-war, pro-labor, and anti-fascism.[31] The *Daily Worker's* critic, Ralph Warner, found Maltz and Sklar politically correct on all the issues they raised, but he condemned some of the acting and a bad lighting system.[32] The production was thus not on the professional level promised by the League. *Zero Hour* set forth its anti-war position for 12 performances.

It closed on June 21, 1941, the night before Nazi Germany invaded Soviet Russia. From August 1939 (the signing of the Nazi-Soviet Nonaggression Pact) through June 1941 (the Nazi attack on Russia) the American Communists had been extreme isolationists, in the hope that the capitalist countries in Europe would destroy each other if America did not intervene. When the Nazis invaded Russia, however, the local comrades turned into interventionists at once, in the hope that American aid would save the "Socialist fatherland." Because the anti-war message of *Zero Hour* thus became politically obsolete overnight, the play was quickly forgotten.

Despite the discovery of a few good plays—like *Waiting for Lefty*—at the New Theatre Nights from 1935 through 1941, the League had trouble keeping its affiliates supplied with scripts during this period of a little more than six years.

In 1935, with *Waiting for Lefty* already part of theatrical history, prospects for a large repertory of plays had seemed bright. Mark Marvin, head of the League's national office, predicted that the new theatre movement would "surely burst into significant maturity" in the 1935–36 season, and he urged all established playwrights to help build the League's list of plays.[33]

By September 1936, however, there was a shortage of scripts and a consequent demise of many amateur troupes. Because of a projected commercial tour of *Bury the Dead,* the production rights were temporarily withheld from most new theatre groups throughout the country. Reminding the affiliates that a great play was not written every week, Marvin urged them to follow the example of the Soviet Theatre and produce such classics as Ibsen, Gorki, Chekhov, and many others.[34]

By 1937 the repertory situation was not much better; the League's national office and the affiliates were still not satisfied. The League claimed that its officers were reading more than thirty scripts each week in the hope of discovering a new Odets, but in the meanwhile suggested productions of *Plant in the Sun* and a shortened version of the old Theatre Union play, *Black Pit* by Albert Maltz. Besides these two, the League had nothing to offer from its own files, and, abdicating its authority, it urged the affiliates to look in the *One-Act Play Magazine* and in Federal Theatre's catalogue of anti-war plays.[35]

By 1939 the repertory problem had still not been solved. The League again suggested revivals of old plays that could be modernized, such as *Peace on Earth* by Maltz and Sklar.[36] It particularly urged widespread productions of *Bury the Dead* for Armistice Day:

We have available a special brochure on BURY with an American Legion testimonial; send for the brochure and use it to approach your local Legion post and invite them to a reading with other veterans' groups and get them to sponsor you. But above All get BURY THE DEAD produced.[37]

This urgent attempt to subvert the American Legion can be attributed to the Party's isolationist line at this time.

In 1940 the League, again following this anti-interventionist line, prepared a revised version of *Private Hicks,* in which Hicks joined the National Guard as part of the national defense effort. Since the Guard was then used to fire on strikers, the moral was clear—preparedness for war was anti-labor.[88]

The League failed to secure a repertory of good, new plays because most good, liberal dramatists were not writing for the amateur left-wing theatre. There was greater fame in the commercial theatre and, more important, greater financial gain, for the royalties of a Broadway production were much larger than those of an amateur offering, and the new theatre affiliates were notoriously delinquent in paying for their scripts. New playwrights, like Odets and Irwin Shaw, once introduced to the public by the League, moved on to greater riches on Broadway and in Hollywood. In reviewing *Stage Door* by George S. Kaufman and Edna Ferber, the *Daily Worker's* critic, Charles E. Dexter, bitterly noted the accuracy with which they had drawn Keith Burgess, the proletarian playwright who makes good in Hollywood:

We may as well admit that the left theatre has been used by careerists now and again.[39]

In 1937 George Sklar, one of the leading Marxist playwrights, denied that there was a decline in the amateur new theatre movement, but he was unable to offer much evidence of activity beyond the fact that the Group Theatre and the Yiddish Artef—both professional companies—were in operation. Playwrights, Sklar felt, could write potboilers for Broadway and Hollywood as long as these dramatists aided the Party in organizational matters, money, and prestige. Sklar warned the Communists to beware the writer who would contribute only his art to the cause.[40]

By 1937, apparently, the Communist Party had decided that wealthy supporters would be more lucrative than a healthy theatre. Undoubtedly the Party would have liked both, for the Communist press persisted in pointing out deviations from Party policy in social plays. If the established writers of Broadway and Hollywood contributed time and money to the cause, however, they were forgiven for not writing Marxist dramas. The rich artist could be a more powerful weapon than his art.

Because it thus lacked a large and attractive repertory, the League failed to achieve its 1935 goal of controlling the nation's 3,200 amateur theatres. Having proclaimed itself the only organization that could supply these units "with plays and organizational advice and leadership based on years of work in this field," [41] the League offered much advice but few good plays.

A few statistics show this organizational failure. In 1936, for example, the League, lacking money and personnel, decided to limit its activities to large cities.[42] During 1936–37, its best year, the national office spent $3,000 on organizational work but received only $810 in membership dues [43] from the 32 affiliated theatres. By 1940 there was still a deficit of more than $1,500.[44] These figures expose the League for what it was—a small, financially unprofitable organization.

Nor did it enlist any professional companies, even though individual members of the Group Theatre (like Elia Kazan, J. Edward Bromberg, and Cheryl Crawford) helped the League in artistic matters.[45] It was also unable to enlist Labor Stage, the most successful of the amateur union troupes. Labor Stage did not need an unsuccessful New Theatre League.

Worst of all, the League failed to control the few amateur theatres that did join. If the affiliated units did not obey the national office at least in matters of organization and repertory, the Communist Party could not hope to control the new theatre movement. Communist domination depended on discipline, but discipline was lacking, for, in a free society, the League could not force its will on anyone. Not only were affiliates producing non-League plays, but they were also failing to pay royalties for the League dramas that they did produce. Time and again the national office warned affiliates that they were obligated to produce only League-approved plays, to credit the League in playbills, and to pay royalties. By 1940 the national office began to threaten legal action if back royalties were not paid, and *New Theatre News*, a League organ, published a "dishonor roll" of nine delinquent theatres, along with a demand for a bimonthly report from each affiliate. If these units would reform, the League declared, then

we may yet see that long desired goal—a militant, articulate chain of theatres, unified by the bonds of a common artistry and a common philosophy.[46]

This declaration is noteworthy for its political implications. By 1940 the League was no longer talking about a united front against war, fascism, and censorship. It sought instead "militant" groups with a "common philosophy," for political orthodoxy had returned to the American Communists in their isolationist phase. While the Communist Party campaigned against American intervention in the European war, the New Theatre League spent much of its time in 1940 selling "peace kits," which contained a book of anti-war sketches and a set of directions on how to organize a six-member "peace troupe."[47] The League was also busy selling Christmas seals inscribed "FOOTLIGHTS ACROSS AMERICA FOR PEACE."[48]

In December 1940 the New Theatre League proposed a change in its organization:

A decentralization of the "national" aspects of New Theatre League work is a primary consideration in determining the course of our activity today. The original concept of the New Theatre League as a closely federated chain of theatres, responsible to a New York center, was a project never fully realized. . . .[49]

Later in the same month the League's National Council ratified the proposal to decentralize control and gave theatres in Philadelphia, Chicago, Los Angeles, New York, and Nashville power over their respective regions.[50] With this decision the League ceased to exist even as a weak national organization, and the Communists' plan to control the amateur part of the new theatre movement expired.

Chapter 4

Theatre Union

THEATRE Union was founded in 1933 to offer *professional* productions of leftist dramas for the pleasure and enlightenment of the poor proletarians and their sympathetic bourgeois brothers. During the early years of the decade the technical incompetence of the amateur Communist theatres made their productions unpalatable to all but convinced radicals. The non-Communist masses preferred to get their drama from the more professional sources of Broadway and Hollywood. A few left-wing social plays had been produced on Broadway, but all had failed at the box office. The Communist Party blamed these failures on the economic structure of the commercial theatre; since workers could not afford to go to the theatre, and since the middle class did not like proletarian dramas, these productions proved unprofitable. For these economic reasons playwrights were forced to write plays to please the bourgeoisie.[1] Theatre Union was thus organized to solve the artistic problems of the amateur Communist stage and the financial ones of Broadway.

This new theatre was ostensibly a united front organization, supported not only by Communists but also by Socialists, liberals, and trade-unionists. At the start, members of the Executive and Advisory Boards included Joseph Freeman, Manuel Gomez, Paul Peters, Charles R. Walker, Liston M. Oak, Sherwood Anderson, Countee Cullen, H. W. L. Dana, John Dos Passos, Rose McClendon, John Howard Lawson, Lewis Mumford, Sidney Howard, and Elmer Rice —among others.[2]

Theatre Union thus attracted authors and theatre artists of the left. Some were interested in revolutionary politics; others were interested in "revolutionary" theatre, for a professional company devoted to proletarian drama was indeed a dramatic novelty in America.

The first principle of Theatre Union's program was broad enough, in a political sense, to attract such a popular front:

We produce plays that deal boldly with the deep-going social conflicts, the economic, emotional and cultural problems that confront the majority of the people. Our plays speak directly to this majority, whose lives usually are caricatured or ignored on the stage. We do not expect that these plays will fall into the accepted social patterns. This is a new kind of professional theatre, based on the interests and hopes of the great mass of working people.[3]

In an editorial the *New Republic*, a liberal advocate of the popular front, declared that *Peace on Earth*, the company's first production, had indeed promoted a "united front" against war.[4] Norman Thomas, the Party's erstwhile Socialist enemy, called the company "an exceedingly interesting and hopeful venture."[5]

The Communists sought to dominate every front in which they participated, and Theatre Union was no exception. Believing that the commercial stage was an effective weapon for the bourgeoisie, they sought to apply the polish of Broadway to the productions of proletarian plays and thus forge a sharper weapon for themselves. While there was a united front on the manner of production, there were many controversies over the contents of the plays, for Theatre Union, as a popular front organization, often failed to follow the Party line as specifically as the Communists desired.

This company started life with a great monetary problem: how to provide productions comparable with those of Broadway and still keep the price scale low enough to attract poor workers. In order to avoid the high rent of Broadway, this group leased the old Civic Repertory Theatre on Fourteenth Street, former home of Eva Le Gallienne's classical repertory company. Also, Theatre Union had to limit the number of actors—a serious shortcoming in a supposedly "mass" theatre; [6] in general, the productions were skimpy because there was not enough money. The audience, especially the benefit parties of various left-wing organizations, was the chief source of income, but the policy of reduced prices for these groups limited this source. Direct "contributions from interested friends," however, kept the organization alive.[7]

In order to keep its productions on the professional level, Theatre Union had to be satisfied with a united front acting company. Margaret Larkin, the executive secretary, announced that the sole criterion for choosing an actor was his acting ability. This policy, she added, was analogous to the demand of the recent Writers' Congress that revolutionary authors must first be good writers. She admitted preference for a "politically aware" cast, but a speedy start of production was more important; besides, the few nonpartisan actors could be converted later.[8]

Hoping to have a permanent company, Theatre Union organized studio groups that studied improvisation, the Stanislavsky "method" used by the Group Theatre. Theatre Union's actors improvised on such proletarian material as strikes,[9] but the lack of money prevented the growth of these acting classes into a permanent troupe.

Seeking the variety of drama that the amateur Marxist stage had failed to provide, the new company claimed that it would avoid the "stenciled dramas, each with the same slogans, the same characters in different dress, the same theatrical effects." [10] There were limits, however, to the announced variety since the plays were to be written for the working class and its sympathizers. According to Paul Peters, one of the company's dramatists, this new audience demanded four elements in "good revolutionary plays": a theme of class struggle, clear action, a "militant solution" to the struggle, and an artistic production. To ensure good plays, Peters continued, scripts were revised by a committee. When a dramatist proved too individualistic to take such collective advice, his drama was not produced.[11] Within these parochial limits Theatre Union sought variety of form and content.

The first production, *Peace on Earth* by George Sklar and Albert Maltz, opened on November 29, 1933. Essentially it is the "stenciled drama" that Theatre Union sought to avoid, for it depicts the conversion of a liberal professor from political neutrality to Marxian militancy. *Peace on Earth* reveals the persecution he must endure because of his beliefs. He is eventually hanged for a murder he did not commit. Outside the prison the masses demonstrate against war.

The opening night, according to William Gardener of *New Masses*, did not go well. There were technical troubles, especially with the lighting cues, and the bourgeois first nighters were cold because they were acting superior to the "propaganda." But after the première the proletarian spectators were loud in their applause. Indeed, he added, the production aroused them to "a fine degree of solidarity" with the cast in a display against imperialist war.[12]

The Communist press loved the play, and later the *Daily Worker* whipped up further enthusiasm by running advertisements that began:

Japan Masses Her Armies!
Hitler Defies World!
Austria Goes Fascist!
Mussolini Rattles Sabre!
U. S. Pours Millions Into
Armaments!

and concluded with the plea: "FIGHT AGAINST IMPERI-
ALIST WAR! SEE 'PEACE ON EARTH.'"[13] The drama
was a weapon, but the Party failed to realize that the emotions thus released in the theatre might better have been
released at the barricades.

Maltz and Sklar cast most of their play in the form of a
conventional, realistic drama. They wove the stereotyped
characters and the left-wing slogans into a generally realistic
plot and added many details to create the illusion that the
execution of their professor was indeed true to life in a capitalistic society. But the "bourgeois" critics regarded the play
as propaganda, and one—John Mason Brown—remarked that
Socialistic professors, far from being murdered, were being
invited to serve with the Roosevelt Administration.[14]

Although the production was realistic, the writers and the
director, Michael Blankfort, had originally wanted to introduce bits of "revolutionary" staging to match the revolutionary thesis. Blankfort had tried to insert imaginative
touches—like a policeman descending from the flies—but
these bits were abandoned because they looked silly in the
context of stage realism. Speaking for Theatre Union, Molly
Day Thacher apologized for this failure and explained that
most of the actors had been trained in the realistic tradition
of Broadway.[15] "Revolutionary" staging would have to wait.

About one month after the première of *Peace on Earth*
the *Daily Worker* reported that the play was a "smash hit"
and that Theatre Union was "salting away money for its next
workingclass play," but *Peace on Earth* had a moderate engagement of 144 performances.[16] After the play had closed,

the company admitted that it had not repaid its initial production cost.[17] The financial failure was caused by the fact that a large part of the cheering audience had been given free seats.

Theatre Union opened its second production, *Stevedore* by Paul Peters and George Sklar, on April 18, 1934. The play concerns Lonnie, an "uppity" Negro, who, partly because he had complained about being cheated by his employer, is falsely accused of raping a white woman. Lonnie escapes, pursued by a white lynch mob. Foiled many times, the mob decides to attack the Negro quarter. Lonnie, having persuaded his people to resist, is killed by the first bullet. The Negroes, continuing the fight, win with the aid of white members of the Communist union, who arrive in the proverbial nick of time. The play ends as the united forces leap over the barricades to chase the enemy.

Stevedore was realistic in both form and production, and in most of the play Peters and Sklar depicted the actual plight of many Southern Negroes. Furthermore, as a slice of life, this drama had an immediate advantage over *Peace on Earth:* Negroes were lynched more frequently than professors.

But the concluding scenes of *Stevedore*, though given the illusion of reality by both the dialogue and the production, were not true to life. The triumph of proletarian virtue over bourgeois vice was as unreal as the triumph of moral virtue had been in the traditional melodrama. Peters and Sklar presented the future, imaginary success of the Party's alliance with the Southern Negroes as if it had actually happened in New Orleans the week before. The playwrights thus inspired their comrades by treating them to the vicarious thrill of actually seeing one of the future Communist victories.

"Socialist realism" was the name given to these realistic depictions of the Party's fantasies. This kind of drama originated in Moscow in the early thirties as a reaction by the Soviet government against the "formalist," experimental productions of Meyerhold. Besides the pretense that the future was already a part of history, plays of Socialist realism were supposed to present a "definite program," to depict the characters' "cheerful readiness to struggle," and to convey a "courageous tone." [18] This literary method spread to the other arts; for example, in painting, the Soviet artist always included a tractor in pictures of collective farms, even though tractors were scarce in Russia. Socialist realism became the Party's favorite style both in the Soviet Union and in the United States.

Although Peters and Sklar clearly blamed the plight of the Negroes on capitalist exploitation, the play was not revolutionary enough for one critic. John Howard Lawson, who had just undergone his conversion to communism, zealously complained that the playwrights had failed to identify the white union that came to the aid of the Negroes as a Communist group. This failure might lead the audience to the unthinkable conclusion that the union was an AFL local. Maintaining that writers could not "write about the class struggle in *general* terms," Lawson declared that they were obliged to know the differing positions of all parties. "As for myself," Lawson said, "I do not hesitate to say that it is my aim to present the Communist position, and to do so in the most specific manner." He added that he demanded only "clarity," not orthodoxy.[19] To the Communist, however, only the Party's position was clear; every other leftist position was "confused."

Liston M. Oak of Theatre Union defended *Stevedore* and the general policies of his company. Although the organizer in the play was not called a Communist, he was called a "Red" and he was "militant." Oak added that Lawson was wrong in his worry about the AFL, inasmuch as many of its locals had come to the aid of Negroes in the past. Oak, restating the united front policy of Theatre Union, said that it would continue to present plays dealing with the "militant struggle" of the working class from the viewpoint of that class, but with the reservation that Theatre Union, unlike the agitprop troupes, would not "advance the full platform of a party." [20]

The editors of *New Theatre* added a footnote to Oak's reply. They accused Lawson of taking "a 'leftist' position," one that was "unrealistic in relationship to the united front audience." But at the same time they called for a second professional theatre—this one to express the Communist point of view.

Theatre Union was taking its united front label seriously, and Lawson wrote no more about its position. If the Party was to reach the non-Communist masses, it would have to compromise. *Stevedore* pleased the Party press and ran for 111 performances. [21] But, despite many economies, the organization was still not making a profit. [22]

On December 10, 1934, Theatre Union opened its third production, Friedrich Wolf's *The Sailors of Cattaro*, as translated by Keene Wallis and adapted for the stage by Michael Blankfort. [23] This drama recounts the historical events of an unsuccessful proletarian mutiny in an Austro-Hungarian naval squadron during the First World War. The sailors hope to end the war by gaining control of the entire fleet, but the mutiny is quelled and the leaders are shot.

Unlike *Stevedore*, *The Sailors of Cattaro* ended in defeat for the proletariat. Although Wolf offered some hope for the future at the play's end, he was unable to hide the historical fact of defeat with the curtain line, "Comrades, next time better." Nor could the director hide this fact.

Historical realism thus replaced Socialist realism at Theatre Union, and the left-wing reviewers were divided on the play's merits. Leon Alexander labeled the production "defeatist," [24] but Nathaniel Buchwald asserted that defeat could provide inspiration by showing the errors to be avoided in future revolutionary skirmishes.[25] The Party would have preferred the thrill of a stage victory to these negative lessons, but history had not been on the Communist side in the mutiny.

The Party press urged its readers to attend despite these flaws, and *The Sailors of Cattaro* ran for 96 performances. In answer to the critics who cited the play's subtlety and foreign setting as the reasons for this lack of popularity, one writer, Alfred Hayes, asserted that proletarian problems were universal and that subtlety was a sign of maturity; in addition, he cited Wolf's personal revolutionary experience in Germany as the best answer to the American critics.[26] After all, most American Communists had indulged in revolution vicariously through the Communist press and the Communist theatre.

One such "revolutionary" event occurred early on Saturday afternoon, February 9, 1935, during the run of *The Sailors of Cattaro*, when seven members of the cast and staff joined with thirty-nine other pickets in a Party-led demonstration against Ohrbach's store on East Fourteenth Street. Because mass picketing had been forbidden by an order of the State Supreme Court, twenty policemen (two on horseback) hauled the pickets (including Martin Wolfson and George Tobias) to the Mercer Street Police Station. Meanwhile at the Theatre Union on West Fourteenth Street the matinee audience waited for the curtain to rise. It didn't. Finally, Margaret Larkin, the executive secretary, told the audience what had happened, and she announced cancellation of the matinee.[27] Although it was commonplace for actors to picket during the many strikes of the Great Depression, this was the only time that the show did not go on because the actors had gone to jail. Theatre Union sent bail to the station in time for the evening performance.

Scolding the pickets, Samuel H. Friedman of Theatre

Union's board and an editor of the Socialist *New Leader*, expressed dismay that they, members of Actors' Equity, an AFL affiliate, should have been so disloyal as to help a "scab" union run "by Communists for the sake of their party, and not the workers." Friedman also reported that the players had acted on their own, not with the blessing of Theatre Union. A few weeks later Liston M. Oak, now taking a more doctrinaire position than he had in his feud with John Howard Lawson, repudiated Friedman's attack.[28] As long as the non-Communist left agreed with the Party, the united front operated harmoniously.

The fourth production, *Black Pit* by Albert Maltz, which opened on March 20, 1935, was an attempt to write a Marxian tragedy. This is the story of Joe Kovarsky, a Croatian miner in the coal fields of West Virginia. After three years in prison for union activities Joe returns to the company "patch." Unable to get either work or relief, he is forced by the needs of his pregnant wife to become a company spy. Although he plans to give no important information, he is tricked into revealing the name of the union organizer just as a strike is about to start. Outraged at Joe's betrayal, his poor but noble brother ostracizes him.

In the early advertisements *Black Pit* was subtitled the "tragedy of a stool pigeon." To the Communists, tragedy, unlike Aristotle's "bourgeois" variety, involved the *temporary* defeat of a protagonist in his struggle against the *conquerable* force of capitalism. The Marxist playwright was also obliged to arouse his spectators to further, and presumably more successful, conflict by instilling in them hatred of capitalism. Proletarian tragedy simply meant the fall of a worker, from which militant lessons could be drawn.[29]

According to this definition, Maltz had only partial success in creating a proletarian tragedy. Although he depicted a worker's defeat by the vicious power of capitalism, he failed to stress either the temporary nature of the fall or the anticapitalist propaganda. Maltz did have Joe's brother predict eventual proletarian triumph:

By God, miner gone raise head oop in sun. . . . Holler out loud "Jesus Chris' miner got blow whistle . . . not boss blow . . . miner blow" . . . Jesus Chris' I nevair gone die. . . . I gone sit here wait for dat time! [30]

Maltz did not suggest, however, how the brighter day would arrive. He did not indicate a Leninist uprising. He was more concerned with the fall than with the agitation and militant action.

Critics for the Marxist press preferred the call to revolution in *Stevedore* to the seeming defeatism of *Black Pit.* Although these reviewers agreed that the picture of the mining community was realistic, they felt that the central character was not. Joseph North, an editor of *New Masses,* was unable to believe that such an exemplary worker could have become an informer; obviously this critic wanted Socialist realism with a noble, triumphant proletariat depicted for emulation by the audience.[31] Jack Stachel, a writer for the *Daily Worker,* replied to North's criticism by defending negative lessons in drama.[32] Apologizing for his demand that Maltz write a different play, North said that he was simply suggesting more heroic plays for the future.[33]

Although the Communists were obviously afraid that the spectator might not hear the subtle call to action, they supported the play; although Maltz had omitted all direct references to "Reds" and revolution, he had exposed capitalism. In May the *Daily Worker* ran a people's publicity campaign. Kyle Crichton, a self-proclaimed miner and critic who wrote for *New Masses* under the name of Robert Forsythe, and Phil Frankfield, a critic qualified by virtue of a jail record in a mining district, attested to the play's realism.[34] Pat

Toohey, a third critic from the mines, cited the case of a real-life Joe Kovarsky and added that the play was "based upon a situation as exists now and not upon one that was or upon one we would like to see." [35] This campaign did not help very much. *Black Pit* had a modest run of 85 performances. The Communists, in their search for the correct Party line, overlooked the fact that the play was dull.

Theatre Union opened its fifth production, *Mother* by Bertolt Brecht, on November 19, 1935. The play, based on a novel by Maxim Gorki, was adapted from the German by Paul Peters. The drama consists of a series of episodes from the life of a Russian mother, Pelagea Vlassova, in the period just before the Bolshevik Revolution. She becomes a dedicated revolutionary, organizes strikes, prints and distributes Bolshevik leaflets, and sees her escaping son shot by the police. After serving a term in prison, she rises from her sickbed to aid the Party and the Revolution by carrying a red flag in a demonstration.

At last the new theatre movement had a full-length play that was "revolutionary" in both content and form, unlike the more conventional forms of realistic drama that Theatre Union had presented. *Mother* is an example of Brecht's "epic theatre"; that is, a theatre in which the direct presentation of the playwright's intellectual message is more important than the vicarious emotional experience offered by conventional plays.[36] Unlike the realistic *Black Pit*, which teaches hatred of capitalism indirectly through a succession of emotional scenes, *Mother* teaches revolutionary tactics directly by a series of illustrative episodes, choral chants, songs, and lantern slides; for example, when a sympathetic instructor starts to teach some old revolutionaries how to read and write, a chorus of workers points the moral:

> Begin! You must learn everything,
> You must be ready to take power.[37]

The spectator is not supposed to become too emotionally involved with these characters because they are presented chiefly to illustrate the idea that literacy is essential to revolution. Although the play appeals primarily to the intellect, emotion is not really omitted; for example, in the scene in the railway coach the playwright used emotion, as well as humor and suspense, to illustrate some techniques of distributing leaflets.[88]

Brecht's theatrical methods were similar to those of the agitprop, with its similar episodic form and didactic aim. The greater length of *Mother* permitted fuller development of the Marxist arguments, but, since the political doctrine of this drama was overly obvious to the leftist spectator of 1935, the increased length served only to intensify his boredom. Because Brecht had minimized emotion, for fear that it would form a wall between the spectator and the lesson,[89] he offered little dramatic interest for the spectators at Theatre Union, accustomed as they were to such emotionally charged, realistic works as *Stevedore*.

Instead of presenting a highly theatrical performance, as Brecht had intended, Victor Wolfson, the director, sought to win the American audience by subordinating the experimental theatricality to realism. In a verse letter to Theatre Union, Brecht complained that the Mother, whom he had created as a symbolic matriarch of the proletarian masses, had been reduced to a life-size, ordinary working woman, in order to gain the sympathy—not the admiration—of the spectators. He complained of all the realistic touches in the New York production, such as the smell of real cabbage being cooked on a real stove on stage.[40]

Mother, as offered by Theatre Union, was hardly an "epic" production. But Wolfson did not go far enough toward realism for Theatre Union's taste, for during the brief run of 36 performances, the play still seemed too experimental as theatre and too obvious as politics for the company's patrons.

Labor Stage reduced *Mother* to absurdity in the *Pins and Needles* sketch "Little Red Schoolhouse." The action of this skit concerns an impending strike at the La Dame Chapeau Company. One of the workers pronounces its name, spells it out, and also exhibits it on a large sign. The workers then chant about their plight. When the boss enters, one worker says:

Mr. La Dame, there's something I've been wanting to say to you for a long time, but excuse me just a minute. (He turns to the audience.) I am now about to act the part of the shop spokesman and tell the boss just how we feel about things around here. You may have come to this conclusion yourselves at one time or another, but we're not taking any chances on your intelligence.[41]

The last sentence summed up the failure of *Mother;* it insulted the intelligence of the American proletarian masses.

Although *Mother,* with its glorification of the Bolshevik Revolution, had a thoroughly Communist thesis, this production was received with some reservations by the Communist press. One critic, M. J. Olgin, liked Brecht's original concept of the drama but felt (as Brecht did) that Theatre Union's production was too realistic.[42] Another reviewer, Michael Gold, said that Theatre Union should have let Brecht direct the play.

Using his displeasure over this presentation as a starting point, Gold launched an attack on Theatre Union. Asserting that this company was supposed to produce "plays of a dynamic socialist realism, written out of proletarian American life," he asked:

Is dynamic socialist realism, the style closest to the masses of America, unworthy of the devotion of one theatre in America?

Mother, he admitted, was a good play, but it was not Theatre Union's style. Experimental plays should be done by small studio theatres.[43] Gold's pronouncement on Socialist realism reflected the Party line from Moscow,[44] but Theatre Union had never made such a parochial declaration about its aesthetic line. By producing plays of several styles, this organization was practicing its announced policy of variety.

Theatre Union did not reply to Gold's relatively mild chastisement. One week later Gold, sharpening his attack, accused the directors of "cliquism" because they produced their own plays; not only had the company ignored the "wealth" of revolutionary dramas already written, but it had also failed to develop any new American playwrights. In addition, he declared, the directors were too independent of the Communist Party:

The Theatre Union belongs to the movement. Its directors are only the trustees of the movement, as definitely as if a contract had been signed.

To remedy this deviation, Gold called for the "audiences" to share in the direction "through an open discussion." [45] He seemed sure that the Party could control any forum at Theatre Union.

Two weeks later Albert Maltz, replying for the company, denied all the charges. A group of twelve people—not the Communist Party—had created Theatre Union. If Michael Gold did not like the present policies, he should establish his own organization. Theatre Union was sufficiently revolutionary for its board, and much more revolutionary than Gold's defunct New Playwrights' Theatre of the late nineteen-twenties had been. Denying the charge of cliquism, Maltz asserted that his company produced good plays no matter who wrote them, and he added that good revolutionary dramas were extremely hard to find despite the multitude of plays that had been submitted. Maltz explained that the attack against the company had been started by disappointed playwrights, and, although he thanked Gold for bringing the accusations out into the open, he warned that slanderous onslaughts could ruin the company.[46] Gold heeded the warning, and Theatre Union went on with its activities.

The next regular production, Victor Wolfson's *Bitter Stream*, had its première on March 30, 1936. The play, based on Ignazio Silone's novel *Fontamara*, concerns some Italian peasants who form a revolutionary union to fight against the Fascist expropriation of their land and water supply. The *Daily Worker* gave the production immediate, strong support. The reviewer, Theodore Repard, was delighted that Theatre Union had returned to "the main current of the labor drama" with a play so "plain and simple and burning" that every worker could "understand and drink deeply." [47] The company had apparently taken Gold's denunciation to heart.

In the spring of 1936 *New Theatre* sent John Mullen, a "worker" who was a novelist and union organizer, to review the New York stage. Reporting that the auditorium of the Civic Repertory Theatre was not filled for this indictment of fascism, he castigated the workers who had stayed away and warned that Theatre Union would close permanently unless attendance increased at once.[48] The appeal failed, and *Bitter Stream* closed after 61 performances. The company's 1935–36 season was a flop.

The following fall, Theatre Union, abandoning the old Civic Repertory Theatre, moved its offices to West Forty-fifth Street. At this time the Board of Directors included Adelaide Walker, Liston M. Oak, Mary Fox, Albert Maltz, Margaret Larkin, George Sklar, Paul Peters, Samuel Friedman, Michael Blankfort, Victor Wolfson, Manuel Gomez, Sylvia Fenningston, Martin Wolfson, and Charles Friedman. Lem Ward replaced Charles R. Walker as general manager.[49]

New Theatre reported that this move to Broadway did not mean that either the proletarian point of view or the labor audience would be forsaken. As proof of its good intentions toward the proletariat, Theatre Union was planning to organize an agitprop troupe to perform short plays at union halls and street rallies. In journeying uptown the company was merely seeking a broader public that would include:

middle-class audiences, Broadway audiences who, three years ago, were not ready for its plays, but who are now eager for them.[50]

Theatre Union announced a subscription package of two plays—John Howard Lawson's *Marching Song* and George Sklar's *Life and Death of an American*—but no dates were set. In December the company was still seeking money to start the season. In January the Theatre Union rented the Nora Bayes Theatre, a small house on Forty-fourth Street, for the production of *Marching Song*.

This play, the seventh regular presentation, opened on February 17, 1937. *Marching Song* tells the story of a revolution in an American industrial city. A meeting to protest the sudden eviction of one blacklisted worker and his family grows into a sit-down strike by the Auto Workers' Union. The company responds by throwing a bomb and blaming the union. A committee of vigilantes and a gang of Fascists, both hired by the company, try to stop a general strike. They torture the chief union organizer to death, and they kill an innocent baby. They attack the marching workers with guns and tear gas, but the unionists win the day by seizing the city's power station.

With this stage victory Theatre Union returned to Socialist realism in an American setting, but the struggle and the victory were on a larger scale than they had been in *Stevedore*, for Lawson alluded to a multitude of injustices besides the Negro problem. It was only natural for a Communist playwright to load the case against capitalism, but Lawson, still desiring to prove the sincerity and completeness of his conversion, overloaded it by presenting the most extreme examples of both capitalist decadence and proletarian nobility. For instance, the capitalist agents murder a baby. The workers, on the other hand, arrange for emergency service for hospitals and milk plants when the power plant is seized.

Lawson added further weight to the play with his heavy-handed dialogue. When the organizer, freshly wounded, arrives on the scene, he says, "We're alright as long as we got the printing press safe." [51] Similarly, in the stage directions Lawson overloaded the drama; for example, he ordered lightning for the workers' meeting (the rising proletariat) in the abandoned factory (decaying capitalism). Lawson, who had sharply criticized other playwrights for their lack of political clarity and who had been criticized by Michael Gold on the same ground,[52] desired to exhibit his political zeal in this, his first play since his conversion to communism.

The *Daily Worker* treated the production to four excellent notices. In one of his three reviews Charles E. Dexter declared that he had been so moved at the final curtain that he wanted to raise his "clenched fist" and shout "Red Salute." [53] Critics for other Marxist publications were equally enthusiastic.[54]

Marching Song closed after 61 performances, despite these reviews and the efforts of the players to keep it running on a co-operative basis. Apparently those middle-class spectators were not so eager for proletarian plays as Theatre Union had imagined. Nor were the workers. At one performance Alexander Taylor of *New Masses* asked eight members of the audience for their reactions to the Lawson play. Of the six who liked it, he reported, four were Communists, one a Socialist, and one a Farmer-Laborite. Another, whom

Taylor judged an anarchist because he wouldn't answer personal questions, was disappointed. The last of the eight—a woman who supported the Roosevelt Administration—was indifferent to the play; she found it a series of propagandistic speeches.[55]

With the demise of *Marching Song* the company went out of existence. The promised agitprop troupe was never created.[56]

Theatre Union failed chiefly for want of funds. With an annual deficit of $15,350, the company's main problem was raising money to produce new plays and to keep current productions on the boards. Underlying the financial fiasco were the inexpensive seats and the failure to fill them at performances of good and bad plays alike.[57] Although the prices were low and the productions professional, only a tiny percentage of the New York working class attended the plays, and this percentage grew smaller during such inferior offerings as *Mother*. Theatre Union thus failed to solve the financial problems of producing left-wing dramas.

John Mullen, the union organizer turned critic, complained that the proletarians were supporting the "decadent" Broadway theatre and the "Hearst-produced movies" rather than Theatre Union,[58] and he was right. The company discovered too late, if it discovered at all, that professionalism was not the sole lure of the commercial theatre and that the low admission scale was not the only attraction of motion pictures. Apparently the masses preferred the entertainment, the glamour, the variety, and the escape of Broadway and Hollywood to the monotonous revolutionary drama in a decaying theatre on Fourteenth Street.

Furthermore, if these spectators wanted their entertainment on the stage they could, starting in the spring of 1936, patronize Federal Theatre, which invaded Broadway with professional productions of both serious and light plays, all of which were offered at movie prices or less. Theatre Union began its decline because the government's theatre began its ascent. As we shall see, the Federal Theatre helped to ruin its Marxist competitors.

Although seeking variety, Theatre Union achieved only superficial variations on a simple theme by Karl Marx. While some plays ended in success for the proletariat and others ended in defeat, they were all deadly serious presentations of the inevitable class struggle. The characters differed from play to play depending on the locale—mill, mine, or dock— but, with few exceptions, they were noble workers exploited by vicious capitalists. The tone of the dramas was uniformly lugubrious. If we judge by the box-office failure, Theatre Union gave the masses what it thought was good for them, not what they wanted. Michael Gold's accusation that the company remained aloof from its audience was true, although he would hardly have agreed to a simple spectator's innocent request for non-Marxist plays.

The company's sole dramatic experiment, Brecht's *Mother*, was treated harshly by the Communists because by 1935 they felt that a "revolutionary," that is, experimental, form of drama was no longer needed. The "new" genre —Socialist realism—had been found and had already been successfully illustrated by *Stevedore*. The Marxians were no longer interested in Brecht's arty theatricalism once they discovered that the old melodrama, with a Communist hero and a capitalist villain, was a sharper weapon for the Party.

The directors of the company had had great difficulty finding good plays of any kind about the class struggle. Michael Gold's claim that a "wealth" of such dramas existed proved untrue. Albert Maltz reported that only two of the fifty anti-Nazi scripts submitted were any good dramatically, but neither play presented the Communist belief that fascism was a political tool of the capitalists. Consequently, Theatre Union did not produce an anti-Nazi play.[59] Party hacks expounded the Party line in undramatic plays, while good playwrights wrote dramatic, but un-Marxian, dramas. Since few plays were both dramatically effective and ideologically correct, Theatre Union, like the New Theatre League, suffered from a shortage of scripts.

Who could blame the competent playwright with left-wing sympathies for avoiding the penny-pinching productions and the thought-pinching "collective" advice of Theatre Union's Board, when he could gain fame on Broadway and fortune in Hollywood? Even the Communists understood that they could not compete with this real chance for success, when in 1937 George Sklar asked playwrights for financial as well as artistic contributions to the cause.

Theatre Union also suffered from the continual critical bickering. Even after the company dissolved, Michael Gold, in a final onslaught, revealed the "inside" story of four members of the Board. "Pardon me," he began, "if I now open the door to a dark cellar and a bad smell comes forth. . . . The smell is some more of that Trotsky poison." [60] Like many Americans who had been driven toward communism by the impact of the Depression, two board members—Charles and Adelaide Walker—had become disenchanted with the Socialist fatherland; furthermore, Walker had become active in the defense of Leon Trotsky in his Mexican exile. The Walkers, Gold therefore warned, were no longer to be trusted.

Liston M. Oak and Manuel Gomez also earned the wrath of Michael Gold and the epithet of Trotskyites. Oak, Gold revealed, went to Spain and Russia "not like an 'innocent,' but like a spy to search out the land. He saw only what Charlie Walker had taught him to see," that is, the domination of the Communists in Spain. Worst of all, Oak had "used Communist Party credentials" to do his spying. [61]

The united front thus fell apart. In its life Theatre Union had often failed to follow the Party line as specifically as the Communists desired. In death the independence grew greater.

Chapter 5

Labor Stage

THE period from 1935 through 1941 saw the rise and fall of many non-Communist amateur theatres dedicated to the production of leftist plays. Some of these groups relied on the New Theatre League for their repertory; others produced their own scripts; and still others presented foreign plays in translation. Most of these groups gave one or two performances of a single script and then disbanded. Only one amateur theatre—Labor Stage—succeeded in attracting a large audience. The audience grew so large that this group later became professional.

In the fall of 1933, before the actual formation of Labor Stage, the International Ladies' Garment Workers' Union started a drama program in order to make its members aware of their social and economic environment. The union's Educational Department mimeographed two short plays, *All for One* and *In Union There Is Strength,* both by Fannia M. Cohn and Irwin Swerdlow, for presentation by amateur union dramatic groups. In the first playlet the heroine, persuaded to join the ILGWU by some of her friends, regains not only her vitality but her husband's love. The second little play concerns the enrollment of an entire family in the ILGWU and the blessings that result—better hours, higher wages, and greater happiness. The play ends with a call to action—unionism, not revolution:

75

One battle is won, but that isn't enough. We've got to push unemployment and poverty overboard. We've got to hold on to the things we won, and make more gains.[1]

Then everyone joins in singing the union's anthem. The ILGWU did not advance beyond these stilted attempts at realistic drama until the advent of Labor Stage.

Labor Stage was organized in 1936 by Louis Schaeffer, an officer in the union, as part of the ILGWU's recreational program.[2] Schaeffer, working on the premise that workers go to the theatre primarily for entertainment, decided to do a musical revue in the manner of Broadway, but with a different point of view; Labor Stage would present its satirical songs and sketches from the viewpoint of organized labor. The workingman would be educated by a strong pro-labor message, but he would first be entertained. *Pins and Needles* was designed to answer "the oft-repeated charge that labor theatres must by definition be humorless."[3]

Satire was one ingredient in the agitprop. The left-wing musical revue, itself, was at least as old as *Parade*, which had been sponsored by the Theatre Guild in 1935. Whereas earlier attempts at this form had failed because of too much message and too little wit, *Pins and Needles* struck a happy balance for the taste of the times. Labor Stage succeeded in finding that broad audience that the Communist Party and its associated leagues were seeking in vain for the entire decade. *Pins and Needles* was performed more than 1,100 times in New York City alone before it closed on June 20, 1940.[4]

At first Louis Schaeffer had trouble with some of his proletarian actors, who thought that Labor Stage should stick to the staples of the left-wing theatre: agitprops and realistic dramas—both ending with the conversion of neutral workers to a militant cause.[5] These performers regarded a Broadway revue as not sufficiently serious. After a single tryout performance of *Pins and Needles* in June 1936, the actors won out, and in January 1937 Labor Stage revived John Wexley's *Steel*, which had been seen on Broadway briefly in 1931. This realistic play, brought up to date by references to the newly formed CIO, ended according to formula with the conversion of a steelworker to the cause of unionism.[6] *Steel* was played on weekends for a total of 50 performances.[7] Labor Stage then returned to its revue.

Although two sketches by Arthur Arent and a song by Harold Rome had been performed at a New Theatre Night in 1935,[8] the New Theatre League had nothing to do with the development of *Pins and Needles* beyond offering its approval of the tryout performance given on June 14, 1936.

Ben Irwin, one of the New Theatre League's officers, was particularly happy that the show was in the tradition of the "native American review and vaudeville" because such material could reach the broad American masses—the League's target during the united front period. He was also happily surprised to find such beautiful chorus girls in a social theatre production.[9] The plain proletarian girl would surely have to yield to the American beauty if the male masses were to be lured into the united front.

Irwin was disheartened, however, by one skit—Emanuel Eisenberg's "Mother, Let Freedom Wring," which satirized such ridiculously obvious social dramas as Theatre Union's version of Bertolt Brecht's *Mother*. Although Irwin reluctantly admitted that the satire was funny, he did not like it. He consoled himself, however, with the thought that "the labor theatre was healthy enough to laugh at itself." [10] He was unwilling to face the fact that certain new theatre productions had been ridiculous. Satire on the enemies of the proletariat was always encouraged, but satire on the self-proclaimed leaders of the working class was hard to take.

In September 1937 *Pins and Needles* was produced in a revised form by the ILGWU Players for a few weekend performances at Labor Stage, the union's intimate theatre. So great was their success with both the New York critics and the public that Louis Schaeffer persuaded the actors' employers to grant the cast leave from their regular jobs in the garment industry so that *Pins and Needles* could be presented on a full-week schedule.[11] This revue continued to play to capacity audiences at Labor Stage until June 26, 1939, when it was transferred to the larger Windsor Theatre for a year's run on Broadway.[12] A second company toured the country. After the initial success the worker-actors joined Actors' Equity; Labor Stage thus turned professional.

Pins and Needles had run through several editions by the time it closed, and new songs and sketches replaced old ones as times changed. The music and lyrics were written by Harold Rome. The sketches were mostly by Joseph Schrank, sometimes with the aid of Harold Rome and also by Arthur Arent.

The 1937 edition, according to a December playbill, contained 19 numbers. Opening the show was "First Impression," in which the players identified themselves as shopworkers, not Broadway stars. The second song, "Why Sing of Stars Above!" set forth the show's point of view. Working girls wanted to hear a new kind of love song:

> Sing us a song with social significance,
> Or you can sing till you're blue.
> Let meaning shine from every line,
> Or we won't love you.[13]

Next came a sketch, "Mussolini Handicap," which satirized that dictator's policy of increasing the Italian birth rate. This skit was complemented by a song, "Public Enemy #1," the lament of an Italian woman so branded by Il Duce because she was unable to have more than one child. The fifth number was a modern dance entitled "The General Is Unveiled," which the December playbill described as follows:

The Women's Auxiliary assembles to unveil the statue of a famous general on his birthday. In the middle of a stirring address by Mr. Warmonger the general comes to life and does as he has always done: set man against man. When he resumes his granite self, he leaves behind a chastened and thoughtful group.

Next came a sketch, "We'd Rather Be Right," which satirized extremely nationalistic Americans. The seventh number was the parody of social drama with a new title—"Little Red Schoolhouse." There followed a sentimental scene and song, "Sunday in the Park," which depicted the park as the "fashionable resort" for the city's poor inhabitants. The ninth number, "Dear Beatrice Fairfax," contained the song, "Nobody Makes a Pass at Me," the lament of a girl who failed to win a man, despite her use of all the commercial products advertised as ensuring sex appeal. The first act finale, "Men Awake," was a nonpartisan call for an awakened proletariat.

The second act opened with "Lesson in Etiquette," which contained the lyric, "It's Not Cricket to Picket," as sung by a Park Avenue matron. The next song, "Vassar Girl Finds Job," satirized large department stores for their policy of hiring only college graduates as clerks. The fourteenth number, "FTP Plowed Under," was a bitter satire by Marc Blitzstein on censorship policies of the Federal Theatre Project, which had prevented the opening of *The Cradle Will Rock*, his own opera, the previous summer.[14] This skit was followed by the song, "What Good Is Love," that is, "if you have to face cold hungry days." The next song, "One Big Union for Two," was sung by a boy trying to win a girl with socially significant lyrics:

> When we have signed up and made the grade,
> We'll add a member—union made,—
> Who looks like me and like you—
> In one big union for two.

The seventeenth number, "Four Little Angels of Peace," burlesqued four "imperialists": Eden, Mussolini, a Japanese general, and Hitler:

> Four little angels of peace are we
> Reeking with odor of sanctity
> Oh we never fight
> Unless we're in the right,
> But we're always in the right you see.

As they sang they fought in slapstick fashion until they all were beaten. There followed a satire on New York aristocrats, which included "Doing the Reactionary," a song about the latest dance craze so highly favored by the best dictators and millionaires. The finale, "We've Just Begun," announced that labor intended to have a voice in the nation's future.

Pins and Needles was indeed socially significant, but it was primarily a musical revue—satiric, funny, sentimental, and sexy. In its solemn moments such as "The General Is Unveiled" and "Men Awake," *Pins and Needles* was close to the agitprop with its cartoon characters and its agitation. Even the *Daily Worker's* critic, Eric Englander, labeled these aspects of the show "phony posturing." [15] On the other hand, he and most of the other New York critics were delighted with the funny songs and sketches. For example, "Vassar Girl Finds Job" was "packed with social fact," for many department stores were hiring only college graduates during the Depression. Without bitterness Harold Rome stated the girl's situation epigrammatically:

> I used to be on the daisy chain,
> Now I'm a chain store daisy.

He enlarged the scope of satire, however, to include more eternal subjects:

> I'm selling things to fit the figure
> Make the big things small and the small things bigger.

Rome made his lyrics so amusing that the girl's plight would hardly have inspired a radical to blow up Macy's. Entertainment was more important than agitation and propaganda.

The second edition, *Pins and Needles 1939*, opened in April of that year with some new numbers [16]—"I've Got the Nerve to Be in Love," a song by Rome; "Cream of Mush," Schrank's burlesque of radio advertising; "Britannia Waives the Rules," a satire by John La Touche and Arnold Horwitt on British appeasement policies; and "Papa Lewis, Mama Green," Rome's song about the divorce in labor's family when the CIO broke away from the AFL. In "Four Little Angels of Peace," Chamberlain replaced Eden.

During the summer Labor Stage made further revisions. "The Red Mikado" by Rome and Schrank, a reflection of the popularity of the swing and hot versions of *The Mikado*, was added. This sketch mocked assorted enemies of labor:

> Three little DAR's are we,
> Reactionary as can be
> Filled to the brim with bigotry
> Three little DAR's.

Rome added a new song, "Mene, Mene, Tekel," with hand-writing on Hitler's wall; Schrank added "Paradise Mislaid," a parody on the Odets style of drama; and Rome dropped Chamberlain from the "Angels" number.

After the start of the Second World War this skit was replaced temporarily by a long announcement explaining that the rapid changes in the international situation had driven the author insane. He had been able to write only nursery rhymes:

> Little Jo Stalin
> Sat in the Kremlin
> Eating a Nazi pie.

He stuck in his thumb,
Pulled out a Polish plumb,
And cried what a smart boy am I.

A further addition was a burlesque of three reactionaries—
Father Coughlin, Fritz Kuhn, and Senator Robert Reynolds
—called "The Harmony Boys."

On November 25, 1939, *New Pins and Needles* opened
with a few major additions. There was a new version of the
old melodrama *Bertha, the Sewing Machine Girl*, with a
union man to rescue the working maiden; there was a new
allegorical song, "Stay out Sammy," sung by an American
mother who warns her child not to fight with the hoodlums
across the street unless they attack him; and there was a
new patriotic finale, "We Sing America." Most important of
all, the "Angels" number was restored as "Five Little Angels
of Peace"—Chamberlain was back and Joseph Stalin, Hitler's
new ally, was added.

This revised show was favorably received by most New
York critics, but the reviewer for the *Daily Worker*, N. C.,
had many reservations. He complained about a new song in
which a girl longed for the good old days in the shop before
she became an actress; this song, he claimed, was ridiculous
because shop conditions in a capitalist state were, by definition, never good. He complained that the radical in "Sunday in the Park" was shown offensively as a rude man. He
was most horrified that an unfavorable portrait of Stalin had
been added to the show, and he claimed that the audience
was equally shocked. He admitted that the *Bertha* skit was
funny, but he reminded his readers that, when bosses
stopped seducing working girls, they started seducing union
leaders. He said he felt as if he had seen "a friend kick his
mother downstairs." [17]

It was natural for the Communist Party to imply that it
had mothered Labor Stage, for the Party regarded itself as

the fount of all proletarian activity. Previously the Communists had claimed some credit for the creation of Labor Stage, but only in an indirect way. In 1935 they asserted that their own success in the theatre had convinced the American labor unions that the drama could be used as a weapon for labor.[18] The Communists also said that Louis Schaeffer's aim of greater variety in the social theatre paralleled the aim of the New Theatre League.[19]

At no time, however, did they deny that Labor Stage was the child of the ILGWU. In the lobby of Labor Stage the plaque inscribed "Dedicated to the Advancement of Workers' Culture"[20] was a far cry from the red banner inscribed "The Theatre Is a Weapon," which had hung over the stage of the WLT. It was true that in *Pins and Needles* Labor Stage spoke out against war, fascism, and censorship, but it did not call for a Communist revolution either directly or indirectly. During the united front period the Communists favored this theatre, but after the Nazi-Soviet Pact of 1939 killed this front, the courtship was decidedly over.

Shortly after the start of the Russo-Finnish War in November of 1939, Louis Schaeffer became the chairman of a committee of actors organized to stage benefit performances for Finland. This action, declared the Communist Party, stamped "him as the type of treacherous trade union leader who had subordinated the interests of the workers in his community to Chamber of Commerce leaders."[21] The *Daily Worker*'s critic, Ralph Warner, blamed the demise of Labor Stage on "those social-democrats who held offices in the garment industry."[22] The Communists blamed everyone but themselves for the end of the popular front, for they could not understand why the liberals and leftists, who had allowed the Party to unite with them against the menace of fascism, would no longer work with the Russians—the new friends of Nazi Germany. The Party would not understand that freedom and social reform—not the pronouncements of

Joseph Stalin—were the guides for Labor Stage and, indeed, for the entire non-Communist left.

This company elevated theatrical entertainment above doctrine and thus achieved popular success. Because its pro-union message was so entertaining, *Pins and Needles* was more successful as propaganda than were the productions of the New Theatre League. Labor Stage demonstrated that liberal ideas could be conveyed more successfully if the author did not beat or brainwash the spectator into submission. This was an ancient theatrical lesson, but the Communist leagues did not listen. For the most part they practiced the sadistic method of communicating ideas in the theatre.

Chapter 6

Federal Theatre

UNLIKE the Communist theatres that had been created as weapons against capitalism, Federal Theatre was designed primarily to alleviate the unemployment of American theatre artists during the Depression. This project, part of the Works Progress Administration (WPA), was endowed with an initial appropriation of more than six million dollars [1] and was therefore the envy of the impoverished Marxist troupes.

When Hallie Flanagan, director of the Vassar College Experimental Theatre, became national director of Federal Theatre in August 1935, the government was in show business.[2] Mrs. Flanagan envisioned her new theatre as an agency both for relief and for the rehabilitation and conservation of theatrical skills.[3] She also saw the project as a means of bringing free productions to the American people and as an incentive to the development of both native plays and original production techniques.[4] In terms of theatre art, she announced, the project would not confine itself to the "painted box set." She believed that the theatre had to experiment "with speech and rhythm forms, with dance and movement, with color and light." She also planned revivals of stage classics.[5]

Only a small percentage of the new productions would be

85

social plays. These dramas would be fully "conscious of the implications of the changing social order," for the theatre could no longer ignore the economic and social problems plaguing the United States.[6] She did not want Communist plays, that is, dramas depicting "the oversimplified collision of workers and bosses." The government's social plays would show "rather the struggle of many different kinds of people to understand the natural, social, and economic forces around them and to achieve through these forces a better life for more people."[7] The government's project, unlike the Communist theatres, was thus not primarily a social theatre.

A survey of Federal Theatre's repertory lists reveals that social drama did not, in fact, overshadow the wide variety of plays and theatricals that the government produced in New York: a revival of the morality play *Everyman;* a Negro version of *Macbeth;* the American première of T. S. Eliot's *Murder in the Cathedral;* an adaptation of Labiche's farce, *Un Chapeau de Paille d'Italie;* a swing version of Gilbert and Sullivan's *The Mikado;* as well as the socially significant living newspapers and a Communist allegory—*The Revolt of the Beavers.* Federal Theatre pleased the working class better than any of the self-styled proletarian theatres because of this diversity of drama, not to mention the project's many other entertainments such as vaudeville, marionette plays, and dance-drama. The project was primarily a theatre.

The social productions of the New York projects, though only part of the whole repertory, formed an exciting chapter. Although the percentage of social plays was small, the total number was large. We are concerned with this body of plays because of the Communists' attempt to use Federal Theatre as a propaganda agency.

The presentations of socially significant plays led inevitably to the charge that Federal Theatre was run by the Communists for purposes of spreading Marxism. There were attacks by people who equated the reforms of the New

Deal, and indeed all reform, with communism. Representative J. Parnell Thomas of New Jersey, for example, saw E. P. Conkle's *Prologue to Glory*, a politically mild drama about Abraham Lincoln, as propaganda designed "to prove that all politicians are crooked." The Congressman's charge that Lincoln's desire to debate a subject more vital than the relative value of bees and ants was "Communist talk" did not rest on solid ground.[8]

Other critics cited actual Marxist statements in certain plays as proof that the entire project was the mouthpiece of the Communist Party. Bernarr MacFadden, for instance, warned in *Liberty* that one of Federal Theatre's living newspapers would cause revolution, as certainly as Beaumarchais' *The Marriage of Figaro* had "caused" the fall of the French monarchy.[9] The attack reached the floor of the United States Senate as early as April 1936, when Senator James Davis of Pennsylvania charged that many Federal Theatre plays had spread Communist propaganda.[10] The *Saturday Evening Post* quoted the same charges in two articles and editorially accused the government's theatre of having "produced a long series of undisguisedly revolutionary plays."[11] Some of the accusations were true, for some Federal Theatre dramas did contain Marxist sentiments, but the accusers overstated their case.

Mrs. Flanagan replied to the charge of Communist propaganda with the statement that most Federal plays were either classics or native American dramas.[12] Furthermore, she had declared that the new social drama would not include "the oversimplified collision of workers and bosses," the favorite form of Communist drama. On the other hand, she naïvely failed to see anything beyond a simple fairy tale in the unmistakably Communist allegory, *The Revolt of the Beavers*.[13] A few Marxist plays were produced, but the percentage was not great enough to label all the social productions of Federal Theatre as Communist.

Similarly the accusation that the Party itself controlled Federal Theatre was exaggerated. Senator Davis, especially alarmed at the "evidence" of Mrs. Flanagan's Communist sympathies, quoted revolutionary speeches from her play, *Can You Hear Their Voices?* as well as the praise she lavished on Soviet Russia and the Russian theatre in her book, *Shifting Scenes.* If she is not a Communist, said the Senator, let her disavow her past writings.[14] Her oath to defend the Constitution obviously meant nothing to him.

Hallie Flanagan guessed that there were Communists in the New York projects, just as there were Republicans, Socialists, and Democrats; she also noted that most of the project workers belonged to the old-line stage unions, which forbade their members any connection with the Communist scab organizations.[15] She admitted that some workers carried on political activities on government time, but she believed that these activities were more concerned "with the ever-human problem of trying to get a little more money or a little more prestige" than with politics.[16] Besides, the project workers had been given legal protection by the Seventy-sixth Congress, which forbade the dismissal of anyone from relief work because of political activity.[17] If Communists were on the government's payroll, Congress was as responsible as anyone else.

The Communists, for their part, admitted that they had been active in trying to infiltrate and control Federal Theatre. Ralph Warner, a *Daily Worker* critic, declared that they had fought with the WPA personnel for a more permanent kind of governmental theatre program.[18] The Communists, usually short of cash, looked with envy and hope at the comparatively wealthy project. Here was a theatre subsidized by the government. With the Party in control, the project could become a revolutionary weapon against that government.

But Federal Theatre was a temporary organization, continually decreasing in size. This state was plainly unsatisfactory to the Communists because it reduced their opportunities for infiltration and eventual control; every time appropriations were cut, project workers had to be fired. Whatever strength the Party had in Federal Theatre was thus always in danger of reduction. That the Party failed in its attempt at control is evident from two facts: first, the majority of the productions were not socially significant; second, the Party press was not always enthusiastic about the project's social plays.

During the initial New York season, opening in the spring of 1936, Federal Theatre's series of socially significant dramas started slowly with two conventional scripts: Samuel J. Warshawsky's *A Woman of Destiny*, a simple-minded anti-war play; and Harold Clarke and Maxwell Nurnberg's *Chalk Dust*, an exposé of the sterility of American education. These productions did not attract the Party.

They were followed on March 14, 1936, by *Triple-A Plowed Under*, the first the public saw of the living newspapers, a new dramatic genre, and Federal Theatre's most significant contribution to the American social stage. This show was put together by a staff of writers supervised by Arthur Arent. The living newspaper analyzed newsworthy social problems in a highly theatrical manner. Instead of confining the analysis within the three walls of the conventional stage set, this genre presented its facts and opinions directly to the audience by means of such diverse techniques as projected diagrams, radio announcements, pantomimes, sound effects, blackout skits, and music. This rapid flow of stage pictures was a combination of the agitprop, the motion picture—especially "short subjects" like the *March of Time*—and the musical revue. The living newspaper utilized large numbers of actors and stage technicians. Although there was no conventional plot, this dramatic potpourri was unified by its theme and its theatricalism.

Triple-A was actually the second of the living newspapers mounted by Federal Theatre. The first, *Ethiopia*, performed its dress rehearsal but never gave a public performance. *Ethiopia* had been planned by Elmer Rice, the director of Federal Theatre's New York City division, not only because the Italian attack on the African kingdom was newsworthy but also because his division contained a large troupe of African singers who had been stranded in the United States.[19] Quite naturally this edition of the living newspaper portrayed both Mussolini and Haile Selassie.

Since the State Department feared that foreign countries might consider Federal Theatre an official spokesman for the American government, Jacob Baker of the WPA issued a directive forbidding the dramatic portrayal of any foreign ruler. He did permit the actors to quote speeches made by these rulers, however.[20]

Elmer Rice was naturally quite angry. Accusing the WPA of censorship, he resigned from Federal Theatre. He claimed that the WPA had not interfered with *Ethiopia* until after he had outlined a future edition of the living newspaper on the South—one that would expose the common practice of lynching Negroes and also the plight of the sharecroppers.[21] The problems encountered by *Triple-A* were minor by comparison with those of *Ethiopia*.

In twenty-six stylized scenes *Triple-A* traces the history of the agricultural depression from the inflation of the First World War through the remedies of the nineteen-thirties. We see the foreclosures of farm mortgages, the auction of a farm, the deliberate destruction of crops (while the unemployed go hungry), the drought of 1934, the organization of farmers and consumers, the creation of the Agricultural Adjustment Administration (AAA), and the resultant inflation that benefits the rich speculators and solvent farmers but hurts the poor consumers and bankrupt farmers. We watch the Supreme Court as it declares the AAA unconstitutional and the Administration as it plans the Soil Conservation Act as a substitute. Finally, we hear that state Farmer-Labor groups are organizing a new, national political party.

A typical scene illustrates how the authors established the terrible drought of 1934 with just a few words and many theatrical devices. The Voice of the Living Newspaper, a narrator, announces over the public-address system: "Summer, 1934: Drought sears the Midwest, West, Southwest." Light then reveals a farmer kneeling on his parched fields. Two voices are heard alternately over the loudspeaker, the first announcing the date in a "sharp" tone and the second reporting the weather, "fair and warmer," in a "sinister" tone. After four dates and four responses of the same report, accompanied by increasingly shrill music, the farmer rises and says "Dust!" as he lets the dry soil fall through his fingers.[22]

Although the living newspaper was founded on documented facts, the authors revealed a clear editorial sympathy for the victims of the Depression—a natural feeling because most of Federal Theatre's employees had recently been on relief.

The Communist press was delighted with *Triple-A*. Stanley Burnshaw declared in *New Masses* that "truth itself is enough to make startling and important art." [23] Facts, carefully selected by the Communists, of course, might be better weapons than slogans had been in the agitprops. Another critic, MacDonald Hall, was impressed by the collective composition and production—ideals rarely achieved in the proletarian theatres. He was also pleased with the "plain statement of the need for a Farmer-Labor Party." [24] Although this "plain statement" was really an indirect suggestion, the Communists were happy to use it to achieve their temporary political goal of utilizing this non-Communist party as a front until the time was right for the "transition" to a Soviet America.[25]

The Party was also pleased by the momentary appearance in the production of a silhouette to recite a quotation from the writings of Earl Browder. Communists in the audience applauded their leader, and other spectators joined in—in reaction to the attempt of a "patriot" to stop the performance on opening night by starting to sing "The Star-Spangled Banner" just as "Browder" began to speak.[26] It is not likely that this speech converted anyone to Marxism, inasmuch as he was merely arguing for the supremacy of Congress over the Supreme Court in the AAA case. *Triple-A* was hardly the Communist show that some critics found it to be.

A third critic, John Mullen, while praising the production of *Triple-A,* warned:

I don't think anyone should get the idea that this show, or a hundred like it spread throughout the country, will be a shortcut to the revolution.[27]

Although Mullen thought the political content was too weak, he was impressed with the *idea* of the subsidized Federal Theatre as a successor to the new theatre movement. The Communists at last recognized the potentiality of the government's project and the failure of their own theatrical efforts. *Triple-A* ran for 85 performances.

The next social production, Arthur Arent's *1935,* which opened on May 12, 1936, was another living newspaper; it was built around a single year and the theme of justice as it is applied to such groups as criminals, workers, Negroes, and politicians. The *Sunday Worker's* critic, William Lorin, urged his readers to see *1935,* despite its inferiority to *Triple-A,* and to support Federal Theatre.[28] The Communist press was apparently happy to see a social production after the government's recent right-wing "deviation" in the presentation of T. S. Eliot's "reactionary" *Murder in the Cathe-*

dral.[29] But Party support was not sufficient to increase *1935's* brief run of 34 showings.

For the remainder of its first season, Federal Theatre presented both realistic and experimental social dramas. The Communist press, though noting the political shortcomings in the productions, continued to boost the WPA stage.

Class of '29 by Orrie Lashin and Milo Hastings, which opened on May 15, 1936, was a realistic indictment of unemployment as it affected four Harvard graduates of the class of 1929. Although the playwrights offered no direct solution, the *Daily Worker's* reviewer, Inigo Ingraham, urged the American Student Union, a Communist front, to sell blocks of tickets to college students to "educate" them about conditions they would face after graduation,[30] but this drama closed after only 50 performances.

Returning to its experimental vein, Federal Theatre was even less successful with its next social play, *The Dance of Death* by W. H. Auden, which opened on May 19, 1936, in an American version prepared by Alfred Kreymborg. The play clouded behind an allegorical and poetic fog the commonplace prediction that capitalism would die. Furthermore, 'the poet pictured the death without the necessary death blow by the proletariat. Although admitting the weakness of this production, Stanley Burnshaw warned in *New Masses* that demands for technical perfection could kill the government's theatre program.[31]

In the last social drama of the first season, *Battle Hymn,* by Michael Blankfort and Michael Gold, the two strains of realism and theatricalism merged. This play, which opened on May 22, 1936, recounts in chronological order events in the career of John Brown. Preceding each of the realistic three acts the playwrights placed a stylized prologue to convey the larger social, political, and economic setting of the action to follow. In the direct manner of the living newspaper, for example, they presented information about the economic competition between North and South. They also added a nonrealistic epilogue to convey the words of John Brown and his subsequent glorification during the Civil War.

Battle Hymn, though not a pure example of Socialist realism, conformed in part to the kind of drama that Michael Gold had advocated as ideal in his attack on Theatre Union the preceding December, for the play had been "written out of proletarian American life." [32] Although the authors did not pretend that the Socialist future already existed, they did attempt to relate the historical past to the revolutionary present. Gold and Blankfort clearly implied that the freeing of Negro slaves by revolutionary violence was a necessary prelude to the emancipation of the white wage slaves of the North.[33] The dramatists thus implied that the agitational activity of John Brown was a predecessor of the current work of the Communist Party and that the Civil War was a forerunner of the coming proletarian revolution. This parallel, while not explicitly stated, was quite clear to the Communist spectators.

For, since 1934, at least, the Party had been attempting to attach itself to native revolutionary roots. On Independence Day, 1934, for instance, an editorial in the *Daily Worker* declared:

Today, the only party that carries forward the revolutionary traditions of 1776 and 1861, under the present day conditions and relationship of classes, is the Communist Party. . . .

Exactly one year later the same paper elaborated on the "parallels" of 1776 and 1935 with such items as a reprint of the Declaration of Independence, flanked by pictures of Lenin and Jefferson; a picture of Benedict Arnold, with the caption: "The W. R. Hearst of 1776"; and such headlines as "Revolution Is Never Un-American Said Founding Fathers." The Party's Platform of 1936 stated:

Communism is 20th century Americanism. The Communist Party continues the traditions of 1776, of the birth of our country; of the revolutionary Lincoln, who led the historic struggle that preserved our nation.[34]

In the nominating speech at the Party's national convention in June 1936, Earl Browder was called the John Brown of modern times.[35]

In three reviews, critics for the *Daily Worker*—Elizabeth Lawson, Howard Horstmann, and James Robie—caught the parallel between *Battle Hymn* and the events of 1936. Although there were reservations about the excess of historical details in the play, there was general praise for the revolutionary theme, especially for the novelty of interpreting history from a Communist point of view.[36] European history had been the source of such plays as *The Sailors of Cattaro*, but American history had largely been ignored before *Battle Hymn*. Michael Gold was thus attempting to use Federal Theatre to aid his Party's campaign of Americanizing Leninist revolution.

Non-Communist spectators, unacquainted with the Party's campaign, did not understand the implied parallel, however. Although there were references to such ideas as wage slavery, these contemporary allusions were incidental to the historical parts of the drama. Although violence was praised, it was violence of the past, not of the future. The editor of *Federal Theatre* magazine, Pierre de Rohan, declaring sarcastically that the project at last had convictions in advocating abolition,[37] obviously did not understand the point that Gold and Blankfort were trying to make. History was hiding the ideology for him and for the non-Communist patrons of Federal Theatre. The doctrinaire Michael Gold had failed to make his Marxist position clear to the general public. And the parallel between the Civil War and the "coming" revolution was a little silly anyway, inasmuch as

the Communists, as rebels, had to be equated with the reactionary confederate leaders.

In the socially significant productions of its second season,
Federal Theatre continued pretty much in the pattern of
the first, but offered an even wider variety of dramatic
genres and social themes. The 1936–37 group of ten social
plays opened on June 26, 1936, with *Turpentine* by J. A.
Smith and Peter Morel—a realistic drama about the unionization of Negro workers at a turpentine camp. The *Daily
Worker's* critic, Theodore Repard, liked the play but complained of ideological shortcomings.[38] This play did not
measure up to Theatre Union's *Stevedore*.

From this conventional, realistic play, Federal Theatre
shifted to another living newspaper, *Injunction Granted* by
Arthur Arent and his editorial staff. Opening on July 24,
1936, this history of American labor and its conflict with
the courts displeased Hallie Flanagan, who complained of
the distorted and "hysterical" production:

As I have repeatedly said, I will not have the Federal Theatre
used politically. I will not have it used to further the ends of
the Democratic party, the Republican party, or the Communist
party.[39]

The Communist press, for its part, found many flaws in the
production. One critic, Ben Compton, called the theme
timely but said that the script was "rambling and diffuse." [40]
Another, Alexander Taylor, complained that the playwrights, though dealing with the conflict of workers and
the state, failed to offer a solution beyond advocating the
politically inadequate CIO unionization drive. He felt that
the dramatists were being expedient in omitting the Communist cure for labor's problems.[41] Thus, while Hallie Flanagan thought the presentation too Marxist, the Communist
press thought it was not Marxist enough. The staff soon re-

vised the production, toning down some of the scenes with which Mrs. Flanagan had been displeased. *Injunction Granted* was shown 76 times.

From the heavyhanded defense of labor, Federal Theatre shifted to light social satire. On September 17, 1936, the WPA actors performed *The Path of Flowers*, a recent Soviet Russian comedy by Valentin Katayev, in an adaptation by Irving Talmadge. This play concerns the love affairs of an intellectual fellow traveler. Unhampered by the cares and conventions of Soviet Russia in the spring of 1930, he leaves his wife and lives successively with two other females. He is duly punished when he loses all his women and when his book on the society of the future is withdrawn from circulation.

Katayev was satirizing the romantic scoundrel who uses the Communist utopian ideal as a means for personal pleasure. Instead of doing the hard physical work necessary for the achievement of the classless society, this parasite merely advocates and practices the bohemian ideal of free love. In the course of the social satire Katayev wrote some very funny scenes primarily satiric of human nature. When the scoundrel is about to run off with his second mistress, for example, he insists on paying her husband for the fur coat she owns, but then tries to lower its value by ripping it and claiming it is out of fashion. Being a woman and therefore angered by this claim, she sends her lover away.

While exposing some of these human obstacles to the advance of Communist society, Katayev drew a genially satiric picture of the many imperfections of Russian life in the early nineteen-thirties—the crowded apartments and trolleys, the shortages of consumer goods, the high price of food, and the hard labor of the harvesting campaigns. For American audiences this picture of Russia, despite its geniality, was closer to the portrait painted by the Hearst press than to the one depicted by the *Daily Worker*. Katayev's play demonstrated that the millennium, contrary to the advertisements of American Communists, had not really come to Russia.

The *Daily Worker's* critic, Charles E. Dexter, hastened to explain that the play was historical rather than contemporary since it was set "in the period of the second five year plan," when, despite great strides, the perfect society remained in the future. He added that this comedy, written primarily for Moscow audiences, proved that Russia was strong enough to laugh at herself.[42] But the danger remained that Americans might also laugh at Russia during the comedy's 57 performances.

Federal Theatre became more serious in its next socially significant presentation, *It Can't Happen Here* by Sinclair Lewis and John C. Moffitt, a dramatization of the Lewis novel. Productions opened simultaneously in 21 American theatres on October 27, 1936. In New York City three companies performed the play—two in English and one in Yiddish. The project demonstrated its political courage by producing *It Can't Happen Here*, despite its rejection by Hollywood as too controversial and in the face of the voluminous criticism of the play as too radical.[43]

The preproduction controversy did not stop Federal Theatre; on the contrary, the project gained some much-needed free publicity. By opening 21 separate productions of one play in theatres across the nation, Federal Theatre also demonstrated its theatrical courage. In performing this difficult task so well, the project was challenging, in a small way, the mass distribution of motion pictures, and with a script that the film industry had turned down. *It Can't Happen Here* was performed for an amazing total of 260 weeks throughout the nation.[44] The three New York companies ran for a combined total of 314 performances.[45] The government's theatre had its first smash hit.

The drama, setting forth Lewis' vision of a Fascist America, traces the changing attitudes of Doremus Jessup, a liberal editor in a small town, toward the dictatorship. At first Jessup supports Buzz Windrip's fascism but later joins a resistance movement. In many short realistic scenes Lewis developed his thesis—fascism could happen here. Rising on the foundation of Depression-born discontents—on the unfulfilled desires of capitalists, workers, crackpots, and psychopaths—fascism would be reinforced by the support, open or tacit, of those solid, patriotic citizens like Jessup, who believe that order and security are worth more than liberty. In vivid, terrifying episodes Lewis demonstrated that only the depraved would benefit from the anarchy unleashed by a dictatorship. Capitalists are fleeced; workers are shot; even such initial supporters of Windrip as Pastor Prang (the Father Coughlin type) and Jessup are tortured and imprisoned. The bullies inherit America. The horrors of Italian and German fascism were known in this country, but Lewis made them more immediately dreadful by giving them an American setting.

Unlike the Communists, who attributed the rise of fascism solely to the capitalists, Lewis spread the guilt by blaming chiefly "the good 'citizens' who allow tyranny." [46] If these people had defended their liberty, he implied, they would not have lost it. Once fascism had come, the fight against it was just as necessary but much more difficult.

Nowhere did he suggest that the Communist Party should lead the struggle or that communism would solve anything. Although he named the underground "the People's Party," he was referring to the liberal middle class—the editors, the small businessmen, the professional people—and not to the proletarians, most of whom he depicted as dirty, lazy followers of the Fascists. American liberalism—the spirit of freedom embodied in the Bill of Rights—was the only cure that Lewis advocated.

Reviewers for the Party press, although happy that Fed-

eral Theatre had produced an anti-Fascist play, were unhappy with the un-Marxist analysis of fascism. Writing in
the *Daily Worker*, Charles E. Dexter said that Lewis should
have shown the "true" cause of fascism as the desperate
attempt of the dying capitalist class to retain its decreasing
power. Furthermore, this critic felt that the play was too
"mild" not only because Lewis failed to show any uprising
until the end but also because he suggested liberalism as a
cure for fascism. The reviewer declared that *It Can't Happen Here* should have prescribed a united front:

It should have said, sharply, clearly, forcefully . . . "On to the
People's Front! . . . Don't wait till you see the whites of his
eyes! Let him have it with both barrels! If you treasure your
democracy, be prepared to fight for it! Join hands and arms and
living bodies in a front which will retreat not one inch in the
Fascist war against liberty!" [47]

Happily the play's dialogue was not so clumsy. Sinclair
Lewis did treasure democracy and liberty, but not as catchwords out of Communist slogans.

It Can't Happen Here was followed in January by a brief
run of Conrad Seiler's *Sweet Land,* a realistic drama about
Negro sharecroppers, and in February by Arthur Arent's
Power, still another living newspaper. As with the edition
on labor, the Communist press deplored the production's
ideological weaknesses. Charles E. Dexter complained that
Arent had not treated the TVA as "merely a small step forward" and that he had failed to suggest the "short cuts to
true government ownership of power by means of political
action by the 'plain people,' the farmers and the workers of
America." [48] *Power* did not follow the Party line because
Federal Theatre was more concerned with the welfare of
the consumer than with the advancement of communism.
Power was shown 142 times.

For its next social drama the government's theatre shifted

from the Tennessee Valley of 1936 to the Nile Valley of Biblical times for an amusing costume drama. *The Sun and I* by Barrie and Leona Stavis opened on February 26, 1937, and ran for 74 performances. The first act deals with the betrayal of Joseph by his brothers and the episode with Potiphar's wife; the second act treats his attempt to plan the economy of Egypt. From his eventual defeat by the priests and populace Joseph draws three lessons: first, the goal of a unified, peaceful, and prosperous world does not justify the tyrannical means he employed; second, authority for government should reside with the governed, not with the governor; third, progress depends on popular desire for improvement.

Although the left-wing critics agreed that the spectacular and humorous portions of *The Sun and I* were entertaining, they disagreed about the value of the political lessons. Charles E. Dexter liked the recognition accorded the masses,[49] but Alexander Taylor of *New Masses* said that they were not emphasized dramatically enough. He was also annoyed because the scene showing the slaves at work was set before "a granary bearing a close, if purely fortuitous, resemblance to the tomb of Lenin."[50] If the similarity were intentional, the play might be interpreted as a genial attack on the "benevolent" despotism of *Joseph* Stalin.

The satire was so general, however, that the spectator could draw contemporary parallels according to his own beliefs. A Republican, for example, could consider the play as a satire on the social planning of the New Deal. For the nonpartisan spectator, on the other hand, *The Sun and I* was more simply an amusing and colorful variation on a Biblical theme, with incidental jabs at all authoritarian governments.

The Federal Theatre Project's next venture in social drama was a direct attack on the tyranny of Nazi Germany. Friedrich Wolf's realistic drama, *Professor Mamlock*, translated into stilted English by Anne Bromberger, opened on April 13, 1937, and was shown 76 times. Wolf recounted the story of Dr. Mamlock, a Jewish surgeon working in Berlin during Hitler's rise to power. Slowly degraded by the Nazis, the doctor commits suicide. Throughout the play Wolf implied that only the Communists were fighting the Nazis. It was only natural for him, an avowed Communist, to praise the Party, but he deviated from the Party line in recognizing that the Nazis were persecuting the Jews on grounds of race rather than class. Wolf also showed Dr. Mamlock, hardly a proletarian, as the chief victim of the terror. The playwright, however, was more interested in presenting the psychological study of a surgeon's slow awakening to the horror of totalitarian rule than in arguing the Party's pet theses—the class basis of German fascism and the Socialists' responsibility for the Nazi victory.[51] Wolf's attack on fascism was broad enough to please both liberals and Communists; indeed, the fight against fascism was one of the chief rallying points for the united front. The play was well received by Charles E. Dexter and Alexander Taylor, critics for the Communist press, despite the deviations.[52]

After a brief revival of Paul Green's *Hymn to the Rising Sun* in May, Federal Theatre turned to a socially significant fairy tale for children—the project's first and only thoroughly Communist drama. On May 20, 1937, the Children's Theatre Unit presented *The Revolt of the Beavers* by Oscar Saul and Lou Lantz. This Marxist fantasy of the nineteen-thirties concerns the adventures of two poor children in Beaverland, a country ruled by a cruel beaver chief who owns the "busy, busy" wheel on which the worker beavers turn bark into food, clothing, and shelter. The starving worker beavers are unhappy because the chief refuses to share the bark with them, but they are powerless because he threatens to replace them with the barkless beavers who have been driven from Beaverland because they had no work. Furthermore, he threatens torture and imprisonment to be administered by his generals, his army, and his gang of toughs. To the rescue of the beavers comes Oakleaf, a beaver who had been exiled because he tried to organize "a club for sad beavers to get glad." [53] Aided by the children and also a beaver professor, Oakleaf disguises himself as a polar bear, returns, and organizes both worker and barkless beavers into his club. After the beavers revolt and expel the chief and his henchmen, all the beavers work and share the bark. And so they live happily ever after in their proletarian paradise.

This allegory about the overthrow of the capitalist state by the revolutionary proletariat under the leadership of a Leninist beaver was hailed by an ecstatic reviewer for the *Daily Worker*, Mary Morrow, who asserted that the children not only loved the production but also understood the moral.[54] Although their enjoyment was undoubtedly evident, their "enlightenment" was not. The *Saturday Evening Post*, also assuming that the children comprehended the allegory, editorialized on the pernicious influence of Federal Theatre: poor children might be taught to murder rich children.[55]

The editors were overly alarmed, however. After all, the playwrights did not follow the Russian example of murdering the Czar; they merely exiled the chief to a bitter life of unemployment. Adult Marxists and Young Pioneers familiar with Communist dogma saw the parallel between Beaverland and the capitalist system, but non-Communist children saw nothing more than an entertaining show with the common ingredients of fairy tales—talking animals, triumphant heroes, and vanquished villains. Non-Communist youngsters would need further instruction. Giving four performances each week, this production ran from May 20 through June 19, 1937, but failed to incite a proletarian revolution as the Communists hoped and the *Post* feared.

During its third season, 1937–38, the Federal Theatre continued to offer a variety of social plays. Six presentations, which treated several social, political, and economic problems, were offered in various dramatic forms. The Communist Party continued to agitate for additional Marxist dramas but had to accept what it got.

The first of the social series, *Processional,* a revival of John Howard Lawson's expressionistic drama of 1925, opened on October 13, 1937, in a slightly revised version prepared by the playwright. Set in the mining district of West Virginia during a strike in the early twenties, the original play had presented American life as a violent, colorful parade of striking miners, cruel vigilantes, warmongering newspapermen, cheating capitalists, foreign-born radicals, flaming youth, and ridiculous Klansmen. In brief, the stereotypes of the jazz age marched down the aisles in a highly theatrical, experimental production. Although Lawson ridiculed the Fascists of 1925, he failed to ennoble the proletarians or to propagandize their cause.

Among his minor revisions for Federal Theatre's revival,[56] the most significant was the replacement of the stereotyped, vaudeville Negro (Rastus Jolly) by a more dignified member of his race (Joe Green). Lawson also reduced the number of vaudeville routines. Essentially, however, the play remained the same. Although Lawson had become a Communist during the thirties, his earlier picture of a stupid proletariat remained unchanged for the most part.

Having been treated to the Communist clarity of *Marching Song,* which Theatre Union had produced the preceding winter, reviewers of the left were disappointed with *Processional.* One critic, Eric Englander, was puzzled over the reason for reviving such a "dated" play, especially at a time when both Lawson and the labor movement had become so class conscious. Federal Theatre's presentation of an easily deceived working class, this critic continued, was Hearstian slander.[57] The revival ran for 81 performances.

On January 17, 1938, Federal Theatre brought forth a new edition of the living newspaper. In *One-Third of a Nation*, Arthur Arent set forth a history of the housing problems of New York City from the eighteenth century to the nineteen-thirties. He did not advocate abolition of the profit system, but he did recommend federal construction when private enterprise could not provide decent housing. Writing in the Party press, Dave Jones and Walter Ralston were in a popular front mood; they liked the production, even though it was well-documented propaganda for the New Deal housing program, and not for a Soviet America.[58] *One-Third of a Nation*, less stylized than its forerunners, achieved the longest run of the living newspapers—237 performances.

Continuing on the experimental track, on January 25, 1938, Federal Theatre offered four performances of Ernst Toller's *No More Peace*, in an English version by Edward Crankshaw and W. H. Auden. In this musical fantasy, Toller expressed his anti-war and anti-Fascist sentiments. Although he closed the play with Marx's quotation about the need for changing the world, the action of this operetta showed little hope for humanity. If the world was to be altered, Toller implied, human nature would have to be changed too.

Writing in the *Daily Worker*, John Cambridge complained that, although Toller exposed the viciousness of capitalists in wartime, he failed to show a socially conscious proletariat; the quotation from Marx at the end was merely a "sop."[59] The playwright was too pessimistic for the Marxists, who believed that the simple expedient of world revolution would end war, and too pessimistic for the liberals, who believed that man would avoid war because it was not rational. Toller knew better. That this famous German dramatist saw no hope for the future became tragically evident on May 22, 1939, when he committed suicide.

From fantasy Federal Theatre turned to a period romance, when E. P. Conkle's *Prologue to Glory* opened on March 17, 1938. This pseudo-historical account of Abraham Lincoln's days in New Salem was a love story rather than a socially significant document. Conkle did not portray "the revolutionary Lincoln," whom the Communist Party had adopted in 1936. Although they enjoyed the play, the reviewers for the Marxist press—John Cambridge and Eleanor Flexner—felt cheated by the omission of such issues as slavery and secession.[60] While this charming drama was ideologically too weak for the Communists, it was too strong for Representative J. Parnell Thomas. The public supported the play for 169 showings.

After a brief, unsuccessful run of *Trojan Incident* by Philip H. Davis, a dance-drama version of Euripides' *The Trojan Women,* Federal Theatre closed the social series of the third season in June with a brief engagement of Bernard Shaw's comedy *On the Rocks.* Set in London during the early nineteen-thirties, this play recounts the efforts of Sir Arthur Chavender, Prime Minister, to cope with the Depression by means of a program that includes nationalization of land, abolition of rates, and compulsory labor. The workers reject the plan and England remains on the rocks. As he hears the rioting masses at the end of the play, Sir Arthur vaguely prophesies the coming of a strong man who will forcibly change the social order.

Although Shaw thought that the people wanted a tyranny, he did not give them one. Although he felt that the old order had to give way to the new, he feared the "cruelty and desolation" of the actual change.[61] Shaw brought down the curtain before the rioting mob could break anything more than a few windows. He offered a penetrating and amusing analysis of a nation in economic difficulties, but he backed away from the barricades.

The Communist press was disappointed. One of its critics, John Cambridge, denounced Shaw's "degenerating political creed." Not only had this playwright advocated a Fascist tyranny, but he had committed the unpardonable sin of "slandering" the proletariat. By having the workers reject Sir Arthur's "Socialistic" program, Shaw had falsely implied that the proletariat did not want a Socialist state; Cambridge explained the fallacy—no "true" Socialist program would have abolished strikes. Nor could he understand how Shaw had the audacity to lump Lenin with such Fascists as Mussolini:

Shaw understands as well as anybody the distinction between a personal dictator and the dictatorship of the proletariat. . . .[62]

Shaw understood the "Socialist fatherland" better than the American Communists did.

Because Congress kept cutting appropriations, all the production activities of Federal Theatre were reduced during its fourth and final New York season. The small socially significant series brought forth but four dramas, but again there was a refreshing variety of theme and form.

Theodore Pratt's *Big Blow*, the first social play of the season, opened on October 1, 1938, and achieved a run of 157 performances. Pratt dramatized the conflict between a young farmer from the North and his hostile neighbors in the "cracker" district of Florida. When a hurricane strikes, he teaches his enemies a lesson in brotherhood by sheltering them in his sturdy log cabin. Writing in the *Daily Worker*, John Cambridge was disappointed because a hurricane was needed to convince people that co-operation was good.[63] The playwright was more concerned with the violent story than with the implicit social themes.

Leaving the melodrama and turning to Bernard Shaw once again, Federal Theatre produced an all-Negro version of *Androcles and the Lion,* on December 16, 1938. To the left-wing critics, Shaw's familiar tale of the persecution of Christians in ancient Rome seemed just as timely as *On the Rocks* but represented the playwright before he became a "Fascist." John Cambridge, praising this "plea for liberty," particularly liked the bit of stage business in which the Romans were shown persecuting a man who wore a sign inscribed "CHRISTIAN." [64] The analogy to the Nazi persecution of Jews was clear. The oppression of minorities was indeed a universal theme, and Shaw expressed it through universal merriment.

According to a press release distributed by Federal Theatre, this old comedy was intended to convey another contemporary conflict:

Without changing the concept of the character, the Federal Theatre . . . has brought Ferrovius to the fore by a detailed and deliberate treatment. A character beset by an inward conflict arising from his Christian philosophy of non-resistance on the one hand and his natural instinct to fight back on the other, he becomes, in this production, the symbol of that struggle between two modes of thought and action in political affairs peculiar to our time.[65]

The Communists may have understood the symbolism as specific approval of their violent ways, inasmuch as Ferrovius forgets his pacifism in the arena, but non-Communists undoubtedly failed to interpret this action so narrowly. Even H. M., the critic for *New Masses,* reported that the production was devoted to good entertainment, not to "grim political point-making." [66] This revival played 104 performances.

On April 24, 1939, Federal Theatre offered its first musical revue, *Sing for Your Supper,* which was assembled by Harold Hecht. In the tradition of *Pins and Needles,* this show was composed from the proletarian point of view, but the revue had only 60 performances, well short of the long run of Labor Stage.

The social chapter of Federal Theatre's history ended with the production of George Sklar's experimental play, *Life and Death of an American,* which opened on May 19, 1939. Subtitled "a dramatic biography," this play tells the story of Jerry Dorgan, a "typical" American, from his birth in 1900 to his death in the thirties—his childhood poverty, his interrupted education, his factory job, his war service, his marriage, his unemployment, and his death during a strike demonstration. His biography is presented against a background of the social scene—the Depression of 1907, the First World War, the boom of the twenties, and the succeeding Depression.

Although Sklar was sympathetic to the working class in his kaleidoscopic drama, he was vague about a cure for the iniquities of capitalism. Members of the chanting chorus end the play with the statement that workers will cherish the memory of Jerry Dorgan because they have become aware

> That America's destiny is their destiny
> And theirs the right to shape it.[67]

The Marxist coterie may have heard a summons to revolt, but the ordinary spectator probably understood nothing more than an appeal for greater political action by labor.

The reviewers for the Communist press—Milton Meltzer and John Cambridge—complained about the sketchiness of the play, especially the undeveloped character of the hero,[68] but they overlooked the reason for this shortcoming—Sklar had dragged too many events and too many themes into his script; for example, although he presented the hero's family as Catholic, he had some anti-Semitic children mistake the hero for a Jew because his unemployed father was a peddler.

A script covering thirty-five years was bound to be episodic, but Sklar made it more so by forcing too many issues into the script, just as he and Albert Maltz had done in *Peace on Earth* at Theatre Union six years before. *Life and Death of an American* was shown 38 times.

Federal Theatre was killed on June 30, 1939, when Congress cut off all theatre appropriations. Although those units in the project that charged admission were earning enough to pay all costs other than labor, Federal Theatre could not hope to operate without a subsidy to pay the salaries of its 7,900 employees.[69] Plays could be put on without scenery, but the stage without actors was an absurdity.

Congress had many reasons for withholding the vital funds. The project had become too controversial. Representatives Clifton Woodrum and Martin Dies spent the spring of 1939 investigating Communist influence on Federal Theatre, and, although their evidence of subversion was extremely vague, they succeeded in magnifying whatever Red threat existed.[70] The Communists, for their part, did not really help the national theatre with their frequently published protestations in its behalf.[71] Their agitated interest in the project was as helpful as a vial of poison.

Coupled with the charge of subversion was the accusation of immorality. The project was killed because it was a theatre and as such was hated by Puritans in Congress.

Hallie Flanagan believed that Congress had still other reasons for its action. Some of the legislators feared the living newspapers that had educated a large audience on such public issues as farming, power, labor, and housing; others, advocates of white supremacy, feared the opportunities that the project had provided for Negroes; still others opposed "Federal Theatre because it epitomized too vividly the New Deal theory that" the unemployed should "work at his own profession or trade, for the government."[72] She asserted also that Congress was aided in its action by the Administration's failure to fight for continuation of the project; she believed that Federal Theatre was sacrificed in order to persuade Congress to pass the major part of the WPA appropriation.[73]

To the people who had regarded the project merely as a temporary measure to relieve unemployment, the demise of Federal Theatre was not sad, for jobs were easier to find in 1939. The government had succeeded in its primary aim—the employment of theatre artists. To the people, like Hallie Flanagan, who believed that the project had also contributed to the country's culture, the end was difficult to accept. The desire for a national theatre did not die with the WPA stage.

Proponents of the new theatre movement were unhappy too. Although socially significant dramas formed only a small percentage of the project's huge and varied repertory, they constituted a larger number than the entire repertory of Theatre Union. The New York units of Federal Theatre produced 27 social plays during four theatrical seasons as compared with Theatre Union's eight during the same length of time.

Furthermore, Federal Theatre achieved a far greater variety of content and form than Theatre Union had in its meager variations on the class struggle. Although Federal Theatre produced the Communist *Revolt of the Beavers,* it also presented such liberal dramas as *It Can't Happen Here.* The project offered plays that simply exposed a social problem, dramas that advocated reform, and one play that advocated revolution. Federal Theatre offered the tragedy of *Professor Mamlock,* the fantasy of *No More Peace,* the farce of *The Path of Flowers,* the romance of *Prologue to Glory,* and the melodrama of *Big Blow.* The project also produced the realistic *Class of '29* and the experimental allegory *The Dance of Death;* the government presented plays that were well-made and plays that were unmade. And, most important, it introduced to the new theatre movement the living newspaper, a form well suited to an effective and exciting theatrical analysis of society's problems.

Federal Theatre was able to offer these diverse social dramas because it was relatively free from both financial worry and political censorship. Theatre Union, on the other hand, pressed not only by deficits but also by the surveillance of the Party's political and artistic theorists, created a much more parochial social stage. The socially significant part of the government's project, in its desire to experiment and in the diversity of its dramatic forms and political opinions, was the freest and, therefore, the best social theatre of the thirties.

It is significant that Federal Theatre presented *Life and Death of an American,* the play that was to succeed *Marching Song* at Theatre Union. As early as the fall of 1936 left-wing critics realized that the government's project had become the mainstay of the new theatre movement.[74] Indeed, Federal Theatre's success hurt the Marxist companies badly. Theatre Union was unable to produce more than one play during the 1936–37 season. The New Theatre League also was hurt by the project. The Marxists admitted that by 1938 "Federal Theatre was demanding the attention of many of our best forces in all the larger cities." [75] Since the government, unlike the League, was paying its employees, unemployed theatre artists—even Communists—undoubtedly preferred affiliation with Federal Theatre. After all, actors were unable to eat Communist praise. Little did Representatives Dies and Woodrum realize how seriously, albeit unwittingly, the project had hurt these Marxian theatres. Theatre Union and the New Theatre League would certainly have failed without the advent of the government's project, but Federal Theatre hastened their decline.

Chapter 7

The Mercury Theatre

IN the summer of 1937 John Houseman and Orson Welles, directors of Federal Theatre Project 891, broke with the mother company and organized the Mercury Theatre. They proposed to "present at popular prices great plays of all periods with a special view to their contemporary significance." This statement of purpose was broad enough to attract spectators interested in great plays as well as the audience devoted to social drama. Significantly, Houseman recognized both Eva Le Gallienne's Civic Repertory and Theatre Union among the predecessors of the new company.[1] For their first season, however, he and Welles announced a repertory consisting of such classics as *Julius Caesar* and *King John*, Dekker's *The Shoemakers' Holiday*, Webster's *The Duchess of Malfi*, and Shaw's *Heartbreak House*. This repertory was to be presented at a Forty-first Street playhouse, renamed the Mercury Theatre.

Although this program was hardly in the tradition of the new theatre movement, the Communist Party regarded the new venture with some hope, for the young producers had independently presented Marc Blitzstein's left-wing opera, *The Cradle Will Rock*.

Although Welles and Houseman had prepared this revolutionary work for Project 891 of Federal Theatre, the gov-

113

ernment canceled it at the last minute. Scenery had been
constructed, costumes had been made, and actors and musi-
cians had been rehearsed. On June 15, 1937, Federal Theatre gave a preview performance at the Maxine Elliott
Theatre.

On the next night—June 16, 1937—some 600 people gath-
ered outside the same theatre in order to attend the official
première. Shortly before curtain time, however, they were
advised that the show would not go on because the WPA
authorities in Washington had just issued a ban on all open-
ings before July 1. The government claimed that the post-
ponement was necessary because of a pending reorganiza-
tion of Federal Theatre. Many in the sidewalk audience
demanded a replacement for the postponed opera; some
saw the cancellation as censorship by the WPA.[2]

Orson Welles and John Houseman decided to open the
show without government blessing. While Houseman was
on the telephone trying to rent another theatre, Welles was
outside holding the audience. In an impromptu speech he
told them to be patient, and he introduced Will Geer, one
of the cast, to entertain them with two of the show's songs.
When Houseman succeeded in renting the Venice Theatre,
Seventh Avenue and Fifty-ninth Street, Welles invited the
crowd to journey the twenty blocks north to see the opera
that was banned.[3] The young producers left behind the sets,
the costumes, and the orchestra. Rather than face the charge
of having prevented Federal Theatre employees from returning to private industry, WPA authorities granted the
actors leaves of absence.[4]

At this point Actors' Equity refused to allow the actors to
appear on the stage because of certain union regulations.
But Welles and Houseman successfully evaded this ban on
a *stage* production by having the cast perform from the
front row of the orchestra, from the aisles, and from the
boxes. On the stage Marc Blitzstein sat in the spotlight

against a blue backdrop and played the accompaniment on a "tinny piano." Orson Welles stood near him and explained the stage action as the actors sang.[5]

Excitement ran high in the theatre that first night, as Welles, Houseman, and their associates gloried in their youthful ingenuity. Not only had they rebelled against Federal Theatre and Actors' Equity, but they had won. Here was the kind of vitality that theatre of the left worked for and advertised but so seldom achieved. Although this unusual production ran initially for only 19 performances, it became famous because of the exciting circumstances surrounding its birth. In fact, the producers advertised it as "The Show That Made the Front Pages."

Although Welles claimed in a curtain speech after the opening night performance that the opera was "not a political protest, but an artistic one," many in the audience saw the occasion as political. Even before that first performance began there were cheers from the anti-Fascist audience when an Italian flag was removed from the stage. (An Italian repertory company had been the previous tenant at the Venice Theatre.)[6] Besides, Blitzstein's subject matter was highly political.

Set in Steeltown, U.S.A., on the eve of a union drive, this opera concerns the arraignment of the local Liberty Committee on the charge of habitual prostitution for Mr. Mister, owner of the steel mill; the details are set forth in a series of flashbacks. The Rev. Salvation accepts bribes to preach peace and war, as it suits the needs of the steel industry; Editor Daily libels the union organizer; Harry Druggist, threatened with foreclosure by Mr. Mister, testifies falsely that Gus and Sadie Polak set off the explosion which killed them; Dauber, the artist, and Yasha, the violinist, join the Liberty Committee on orders from Mrs. Mister, their patron; President Prexie fires a pacifistic professor and institutes a military training program at his college so that Mr. Mister

can have a militia; Professors Mamie and Trixie support the
new militarism; Dr. Specialist is given a research appoint-
ment because he testifies that Joe Hammer, a good union
man, was drunk and "slipped" into the ladle of molten iron.
The arraignment ended, Mr. Mister tries to bribe Larry
Foreman, the organizer, to end the strike, but he refuses.
Announcing that his men are marching on the courthouse,
he warns the Liberty Committee:

> That's thunder, that's lightning,
> And it's going to surround you!
> No wonder those stormbirds
> Seem to circle around you. . . .
> Well, you can't climb down, and you can't sit still;
> There's a storm that's going to last until
> The final wind blows . . . And when the wind blows . . .
> The cradle will rock! [7]

Blitzstein explained that his opera was more concerned
with the middle class than with the proletariat. He wanted
to rescue the "intellectuals, professionals, small shopkeepers,
'little businessmen'" from the danger of joining Fascist liberty committees.[8] By showing these people the degradations
they would suffer in becoming prostitutes of capitalism, he
hoped to push them "into progressive ranks."[9] He wanted to
persuade the middle class that "allegiance only to the future" and to "honest work" was the answer to the dual threat
of capitalism and fascism.[10]

Blitzstein was a little more specific about this "future" in
his libretto. He warned that the cradle of the Liberty Committee (Mr. Mister's vicious capitalism) would fall in the
inevitable storm (Larry Foreman's militant unionism).
Blitzstein, however, did not specify a Communist revolution
as the only method for achieving the fall. Spectators could
interpret "storm" and "stormbirds" in any way they desired.

Structurally, *The Cradle* was written in the episodic tradition of the agitprop and the living newspaper. Like *Waiting for Lefty*, this opera was composed of a series of brief scenes, each illustrating a central thesis. Unlike Odets, who created emotional characters in dramatic playlets, however, Blitzstein offered caricatures in static situations. He did not permit the characters in *The Cradle* to rise above the allegorical function indicated by their names. In his use of the theatre as a classroom and his avoidance of emotional involvement between spectator and actor, Blitzstein displayed the admitted influence of Bertolt Brecht, to whom *The Cradle* was dedicated.[11]

Although music was hardly new to theatre of the left, Blitzstein's score was new because it was so completely integrated with the text. Before this production, music was limited largely to a sprinkling of songs in such presentations as Brecht's *Mother* and the Theatre Guild's revue *Parade*, or to such background accompaniment as the living newspapers utilized. Because Blitzstein set virtually his entire text to music, the new theatre movement had a novelty at the start of the 1937–38 season.

The Party press hailed the original preview of the Federal Theatre production [12] and gave the later, improvised production good publicity. As Houseman had promised, the Mercury Theatre revived the opera on December 5, 1937, for a month of Sunday night showings. On January 3, 1938, the production was transferred to the Windsor Theatre for a run of 108 performances under the joint sponsorship of the Mercury Theatre and Sam H. Grisman.[13] Writing in the *Daily Worker*, Eric Englander complained that Welles and Houseman had re-created their makeshift production.[14] Perhaps the directors hoped to re-establish the sensational atmosphere of the preceding June; perhaps they did not have the cash necessary for a full stage presentation. By resorting to a concert version, however, the producers eliminated the theatricalism inherent in the piece. *The Cradle* might have had greater success if all the technical resources of the stage had been utilized.

On November 11, 1937, before this revival, the Mercury Theatre presented a modern-dress version of *Julius Caesar*, subtitled "The Death of a Dictator." Before the opening, Houseman wrote, "The modern parallel is obvious." [15] By the use of brown uniforms and Fascist salutes, the analogy between ancient Rome and contemporary Italy was indeed clear. The *Daily Worker's* reviewer, Eric Englander, found the superficial parallel insufficient for an anti-Fascist play. He was unhappy about the display of anarchy, especially the "slanderous" picture of the masses being swayed by a demagogue.[16] He apparently felt that Shakespeare should have shown a Leninist revolution of the disciplined masses as the only solution to fascism. Unfortunately, the bard did not write that play, and the producers did not alter the plot to suit the Party line. Although Englander and his fellow critic, John Cambridge, approved the failure of Brutus, the "wavering liberal," they complained that the theme of one dictator's succeeding another was in reality a Fascist idea.[17] The public, apparently attracted by the strange theatrical production, with its weird lighting effects and its blood-red backdrop, supported *Julius Caesar* for 157 performances.

The Mercury Theatre continued its first season with Dekker's Renaissance play, *The Shoemakers' Holiday.* Although John Cambridge was pleased to report to the *Daily Worker* readers that Dekker, unlike the aristocratic Shakespeare, sympathized with the proletariat, this reviewer was displeased that the Mercury Theatre was planning nothing but revivals of old plays.[18] No successor to *The Cradle* was in the offing.

Welles and Houseman ended the season with Shaw's *Heartbreak House,* which they presented on April 29, 1938. This play concerns Captain Shotover and the weekend guests at his unusual country home. After several long conversations about civilization and war, the guests realize that they are part of a sick society, but they arrive at no specific cure. Their failure is intensified at the end when they hear bombs falling nearby. Shaw's complex analysis of English civilization and his pessimism, implicit in the falling bombs, were not satisfactory to John Cambridge.[19] The Communist Party preferred simple-minded diagnoses and sure cures in the social theatre. This production was shown only 48 times.

For its second season the Mercury Theatre managed to get only one play on the boards.[20] On November 2, 1938, Welles and Houseman presented *Danton's Death*, translated from the German of Georg Büchner by Geoffrey Dunlop. This historical drama, which Büchner had written in 1835, recounts certain events of the French Revolution from Robespierre's first attack on Danton through Danton's execution. In the conflict between the moderate Danton and the extremist Robespierre, Büchner raised a central issue of the French Revolution: how long is terror justified? Robespierre believes that it is politically necessary and morally just to stamp out his enemies. Danton, on the other hand, believes that terror, having served its purpose in overthrowing the monarchy, has become the path to dictatorship, not liberty; he feels that Robespierre's Committee of Safety is using blood instead of bread to placate the masses. Although the terror triumphs at the end of the drama, the temperate view of revolution wins the spectator's sympathy because of Büchner's sympathetic portrayal of Danton.

Shortly before the première, Manngreen, a columnist for the *Daily Worker*, urged the Mercury Theatre not to open this "distortion" of French history.[21] Although he did not explain the reasons for this epithet, he may have been disturbed by the derogatory portrait of Robespierre, some of whose brutal revolutionary methods had been employed by Lenin and were being used by Stalin. Although no such parallel may have been intended by the producers, the anti-

Communist spectator could have drawn it. Robespierre's statement, "Who makes revolutions by halves digs his own grave," was quite similar to Lenin's admonition about carrying revolution through to the end.[22]

Although the *Daily Worker's* critic, John Cambridge, urged his readers to see the production, he complained that the main conflict between the puritanical Robespierre and the lecherous Danton was personal rather than political. This reviewer also lamented that Welles had kept the masses offstage.[23] In view of the fickle, bloodthirsty specimens of the proletariat that Büchner did present, however, Cambridge should have been content with the proletarian voices coming from the wings. Büchner did not portray those noble, disciplined masses that the Communists imagined. For those who understood the play, *Danton's Death* was hardly useful to the Communist cause; for those, like Ruth McKenney, critic for *New Masses,* who were unable even to follow the plot of this choppy chronicle, the production was a total waste.[24] The play was withdrawn after 21 showings.

With the failure of *Danton's Death* Welles and Houseman abandoned their plan of repertory, their company, and their playhouse. Welles concentrated his activities on radio and motion pictures.[25]

The producers preserved the name of Mercury Theatre, however, which they used just once again when they presented *Native Son* more than two years later. In association with Bern Bernard, they opened this play by Richard Wright and Paul Green on March 21, 1941. It is the story of Bigger Thomas, a Negro youth, who murders the daughter of his white employer. The young killer is then caught, tried, and executed. *Native Son* is primarily a thrilling melodrama because of its suspenseful murder, discovery, chase, and trial.

Into this fabric of exciting theatre the playwrights embroidered designs of social significance. In the courtroom the defense counsel summarizes the principal theme: although the Negro is taught in the schools that he is free, he soon discovers that race prejudice and economic injustice keep him in slavery. The authors did not deny that Bigger had committed the murder; they did not follow the familiar pattern of the innocent Negro falsely accused, which had appeared in *Stevedore;* they did say that the American social and economic system was guilty because it denied Bigger the normal outlets for his aspiration to be a free and important man. Ironically, he does not feel free or manly until after he has killed the girl in blind revenge for the wrongs done to his race. Although the dramatists did not advocate any solution explicitly, they did imply that an end to those frustrating conditions was necessary to prevent repetitions of Bigger's crime.

Although Green and Wright were vague about the method of achieving the needed reforms, the Party press was delighted with the play. One critic, Ralph Warner, was content with the powerful attack on the economic oppression of Negroes, with the favorable presentation of the Communist who offered his help to Bigger, with the hint that the defense lawyer had spoken at Communist meetings, and with the consignment of the murdered woman to the class of "penitent rich" rather than Communist or Communist sympathizer. Although this reviewer felt that the failure to prescribe socialism as the ultimate panacea was not a weakness, he thought that the final scene would have been stronger if Bigger had realized that unity of Negroes and whites was the only cure for his suffering.[26]

The nonpartisan spectator did not see the play in the same light, however. He felt that the authors did not attack Negro persecution solely or basically on economic grounds; he saw the Communist as a rather ineffectual person; he viewed the lawyer as a reformer, not a Communist; he did not understand the subtle distinction between the "penitent rich" and the sympathizers. Although *Native Son* was an excellent thriller with a strong social message, the specific political allusions were subject to different interpretations. In view of the fact that Richard Wright, who had been a Party member in the thirties, had been expelled before this production,[27] the non-Communist impression probably coincided more closely with the author's political intention.

The praise heaped on this presentation by the Communist press, despite the earlier expulsion of Wright from the Party, can be explained not only by the unquestioned power of the play but also by the fact that *Native Son* was not anti-Communist; Wright did not turn to Red-baiting. Another reason for the Communists' delight was that Orson Welles, the director, had recently produced *Citizen Kane*, a motion picture that attacked William Randolph Hearst, one of the Party's chief enemies. Having mentioned the Welles-Hearst feud, the *Daily Worker's* critic, Ralph Warner, praised Welles for offering such an expensive production of *Native Son* for the sake of art, not profits. Such selfless nobility reminded this critic of the Socialist fatherland.[28] A higher compliment could not have been paid. *Native Son* had 114 performances.

The Mercury Theatre did not fulfill the hopes that *The Cradle Will Rock* had inspired in the Communist Party. Except for this radical opera and *Native Son* (the final production), Welles and Houseman specialized in highly theatrical revivals of old plays that were not Marxist. All the Communists could do was advise the Mercury from columns in the *Daily Worker*. Welles and Houseman ignored the advice.

Like its government parent, the Mercury Theatre was thus not exclusively a social theatre. Its socially significant productions stopped short of the revolutionary line advocated by the Communists. Welles and Houseman had, after all, tried to run a "bourgeois" repertory theatre, not a proletarian playhouse. The Mercury Theatre, for its brief life, was hardly the successor to Theatre Union.

Chapter 8

The Theatre Guild and The Playwrights' Company

UNLIKE the Marxist theatres of the nineteen-thirties, the Theatre Guild was not a child of the Depression years. Conceived as a liberal theatre that would produce "drama definitely and honestly reflecting the author's vision of life or sense of style and beauty," [1] the Guild was born on December 18, 1918—half a year before the American Communist Party was organized and more than a decade before the stock market crash. Devoted neither to drama as a weapon nor to art for art's sake, the Guild was "willing to produce a communistic play as quickly as an imperialistic play, so long as it was a good play with a definite idea to project." [2] Dramatic excellence was more important than social significance.

In the twenties the Guild produced a great variety of drama that included, among many others, Molnar's *Liliom* (a romance), S. N. Behrman's *The Second Man* (a comedy), Molnar's *The Guardsman* (a farce), Shaw's *The Devil's Disciple* (a melodrama), the Heywards' *Porgy* (a folk play), Rodgers and Hart's *The Garrick Gaieties* (a musical revue), and Toller's *Man and the Masses* (an expressionistic play of social significance).

After the crash of 1929 the Guild retained the variety, but

123

changed the pattern of production; there were fewer plays by foreign authors, fewer plays written in experimental forms, and more dramas of social significance—an increase caused by the increasing awareness of the social, political, and economic changes brought on by the Depression. The Theatre Guild was keeping up with the times.

The Communists envied the Guild's professional productions, for amateurism was hampering the new theatre movement. The Party, longing to put the Guild's theatrical craft at the service of the class struggle, tried to persuade the Guild to produce Marxist plays instead of its more usual "reformist" dramas of comparatively mild social protest. In April 1934, after the opening of *They Shall Not Die,* an unusually "strong" social drama, Michael Gold at last saw some hope for the Guild:

New York is ready to support a mature, strong, uncompromising stage that reflects the political passions and struggles of our time. The success of the Theatre Union and the host of workers' theatres proves this. There is room for the Theatre Guild also, with its remarkable technique and serious approach to stage problems.[8]

If the Guild would not become a proletarian theatre, Gold warned, "it really ought to die, and it will die." As usual, he was noisily overstating the case, for the Communist theatres were not really successful.

Although the Guild did produce some plays that pleased the Communist press, Gold's admonition was unheeded and his prediction proved untrue, for during the thirties this organization continued to present social dramas as merely a small part of its wider theatrical program.

The Communists continued their agitation against the Guild. In 1937 John Howard Lawson warned that this company could no longer remain politically neutral or merely liberal and that it ought to abandon its escapist repertory as well as its "upper-middle-class clientele"; [4] later in the same year Charles E. Dexter, the *Daily Worker* critic, prescribed "new blood" and more militancy for this sick organization; [5] and in 1940 Michael Gold branded the directors as "liberal opportunists" who had abandoned "democracy." [6]

Throughout the decade, however, the Guild followed its own artistic policy, not the Party line. The directors—Lawrence Langner, Theresa Helburn, Lee Simonson, Maurice Wertheim, Helen Westley, and Alfred Lunt—retained a healthy skepticism toward theatre of the left.

Simonson, for instance, gave some delightfully independent replies to a questionnaire, submitted by *New Theatre*, on the state of the American theatre. To a question about the place of class struggle in the drama, Simonson replied: "The theatre of class conflict can produce as many stereotypes as sentimental 'escape' dramas or sociological ones." *New Theatre* also asked, "Which outlook on life offers the greatest creative stimulation for the dramatist of today? A—Conservative? B—Fascist? C—Liberal? D—Revolutionary?" Simonson replied, "Any can be a creative stimulus to the creative dramatist." He was next asked, "Do you believe that the workers' theatre holds any promise for the future of the theatre in America?" He answered: "Only if they get over the idea that vital drama is self-produced by orthodox class dogmas." One of the last questions put to Simonson was: "To what do you attribute the tremendous vitality of the Soviet theatre?" His reply must have stunned the faithful readers of the Marxist press: "To the fact that it was a tremendously vital theatre before the Soviets." [7]

During the Depression the Guild's first five social dramas were European in origin, as a large part of the repertory had been in the preceding ten years. Two of these plays—*Red Rust* and *Roar China*—were of special interest to the local

Communist Party inasmuch as they had been originally written and produced in Soviet Russia, but they were also of interest to non-Communist theatregoers in New York who had heard many nonpartisan reports on the vitality of the Russian theatre.

The first of this group of five plays, Romain Rolland's *The Game of Love and Death*, as translated by Eleanor S. Brooks, painted what was to the Communists a heretically unpleasant picture of the French Revolution.

This short-lived production was followed by *Red Rust* by V. Kirschon and A. Ouspensky, which opened on December 17, 1929. In several columns of advance publicity the *Daily Worker* exhibited its hopes for the English version by Frank and Virginia Vernon of this Soviet Russian play, which recounts the story of a group of students in Moscow ten years after the Revolution. Their leader, a lecherous bully, torments his mistress and kills her. When his new mistress denounces him, the other students presumably liquidate him.

Red Rust was an example of Soviet self-criticism. Through the central character, who was using communism as an excuse for his personal lust, greed, and ambition, the authors hoped to expose the corruption that was destroying the new social order. Despite the numerous examples of this rust, the playwrights did not despair, for they believed that this corruption that had its origin in the old order could be eliminated.

Although this self-criticism may have aided the Soviets, it was hardly the way to win Americans to the Communist cause. Writing in the *Daily Worker*, Joseph North explained that *Red Rust* was a historical account of the "Right Danger" and asserted that these problems had been solved by the huge success of the five-year plan.[8] Local Communists could thus see the drama much as Russian Communists had seen it several years earlier, but with the additional "knowledge" that all was now well.

To those spectators who did not read the *Daily Worker*, however, the picture of corruption seemed contemporary. Although the playwrights showed the triumph of virtue, they also indicated that it succeeded because of individual students, not the state. Throughout the play, besides the emphasis on the leader's vices, the dramatists presented many gibes at such features of the Soviet life as the crowded lodgings, the red tape, the existence of beggars, the fear of government spies, the scarcity of consumer goods, and the annoyance of the public loudspeakers.

A reviewer for *New Masses*, Harold Hickerson, argued, more realistically than North, that this old example of self-criticism had been turned into counterrevolutionary propaganda. He complained that the peasants were made to appear as beasts of burden and that a backdrop of Lenin's tomb, symbolizing a dead revolution, was visible throughout the play. The only improvement on the Russian production, he said, was the singing of the "Internationale" at the end of the show.[9]

Although *Red Rust* ran for only 65 performances, Michael Gold accused the Guild of having made a profit and of planning to distort another Soviet play, *Roar China*. He threatened that *New Masses* would refuse to take Guild advertisements if this drama was to be turned into anti-Soviet propaganda.[10]

After a short run of Bernard Shaw's politically inconclusive *The Apple Cart* in the spring of 1930, the Guild produced *Roar China* by S. Tretyakov on October 27, 1930, in an English translation that Ruth Langner had fashioned from a German adaptation by Leo Lania.[11] This play, a story of imperialistic exploitation and gunboat diplomacy in China during the twenties, concerns the execution of two innocent Chinese boatmen by the evil captain of a British gunboat in revenge for the accidental drowning of an American businessman. After these murders, a noble Chinese stoker who has been telling other boatmen of the heroic Russian proletariat reveals himself as a commissar of the Canton Workers' Militia and inspires the local Chinese to unite in defiance of the imperialists.

The Marxist press complained that the Guild had once again distorted a Soviet drama. The reviewer for the *Daily Worker*, Myra Page, provided a long list of deviations from the "original text." The producers, she said, failed to refer to the Soviet Union by name; they prohibited the cast from waving a red flag in the finale; and they blurred class distinction within China.[12] The critic for *New Masses*, Leon Dennen, added that the Guild's directors had shortened the part of the Communist organizer and that they had substituted a final prophecy of world peace for the original prediction that the Chinese would soon destroy the English.[13] Despite these changes, both reviewers commended the play for its anti-imperialistic plot and for the sincere acting by the untrained Chinese cast. The sight of real Chinese proletarians on the stage was especially thrilling to Communists. If you were unable to see the original Moscow presentation, the *Daily Worker's* critic advised, the Guild's production was worth seeing in spite of its many errors. *Roar China* was performed 72 times.

The last of the five European scripts was presented on March 16, 1931, when Hans Chlumberg's anti-war fantasy, *Miracle at Verdun*, opened in a translation by Julian Leigh. On the twentieth anniversary of the start of the First World War, God sends a messenger to resurrect the dead of both sides who are buried in a small cemetery in France, with the hope that this miracle and the resultant happiness will destroy hatred and war. The living, however, refuse to accept the dead for fear of the ensuing personal, economic, and political difficulties. Hatred is intensified and preparations for war continue. *Miracle at Verdun*, with its episodic structure, its device of resurrection, and its sentiments against war, was the forerunner of Irwin Shaw's more radical drama, *Bury the Dead*. The Chlumberg fantasy had an engagement of 49 performances. The New York public apparently was not strongly attracted to the pessimistic view of war.

The Communist press ignored this bitter satire on war, probably because of Chlumberg's premise that conflict is caused by man's inherent evil, not by the capitalist system. Furthermore, Chlumberg did not assume the doctrinaire Communist position that only exploited workers were killed in the war, for among the risen dead he presented a cobbler, a farmer, a bus driver, an actor, a bookkeeper, a factory worker, and even a banker. The author depicted them as remembering their past lives with pleasant nostalgia, not with bitter enmity toward the economic system. Chlumberg's belief that nothing could be done to stop war was hardly useful to the Communists, who liked to believe that their kind of revolution could stop it.

The next six social dramas, presented by the Guild in 1932, 1933, and 1934, were all written by American dramatists, most of whom had already established their reputations on Broadway. The first of these plays, *The Good Earth*, was derived by Owen and Donald Davis from Pearl Buck's novel. The *Daily Worker's* critic, V. S., liked the presentation of corrupt landowners but bemoaned the omission of the Party's solution—collectivization of the land.[14]

The second play, *American Dream*, by the poet George O'Neil, presented a noble Communist in the last act, but another *Daily Worker* reviewer, Harold Edgar, wasn't sure whether this character's "sanity" was caused by his personality or by politics.[15] Both plays failed because they were dull, not because of the Party's reservations.

The next play in this American group succeeded. On March 6, 1933, the Guild produced Maxwell Anderson's

Both Your Houses, a play about the unsuccessful crusade of a young congressman against an omnibus appropriation bill. Favoring economy in federal spending, he overloads the bill with provisions for every special interest in the hope that the representatives will not have the nerve to pass the monstrosity. They do, and the crusader vows to take his case to the people.

Throughout the play Anderson attacked not only the grafting congressmen but also the system of government that allows and even encourages the dishonest bargaining needed to pass laws. Speaking through his protagonist in the final scene, the playwright predicted that the American people would vote themselves a new system of government that would foster honesty—a virtue impossible to achieve under parliamentary democracy. Disavowing both communism and fascism, Anderson warned that they were distinct possibilities unless American democracy was reformed.

Unfortunately, he did not specify what system, if any, would meet his requirements for honest government. Suggesting that no such system existed, he could do no more than curse both houses of Congress. Although this "solution" was hardly constructive, it did reflect the truly free American spirit of dissent, which was ever-present in the decade of the Depression. This suspenseful, humorous drama played an engagement of 120 performances and won the Pulitzer Prize, but the Communist press ignored the production.

The Guild's next socially significant presentation, John Wexley's *They Shall Not Die,* opened on February 21, 1934, to enthusiastic reviews from the left. At this date, when Albert Maltz and George Sklar were fancifully subjecting a professor to a "legal lynching" down at Theatre Union, Wexley was reporting the events of the Scottsboro case in a realistic drama. Using fictional names for both characters and organizations involved, he recounted the arrest of the nine Negro boys on charges of having raped two white women; the efforts of the Communists' National Labor Defense (the ILD), led by Rokoff (Joseph Brodsky), to free the boys after the failure of the ineffectual American Society for the Progress of Colored Persons (the NAACP); the sorrow of Lucy Wells (Ruby Bates) for her false accusation; and the trial of April 1933 with Nathan Rubin (Samuel Leibowitz) as defense attorney. Wexley brought down the curtain with the jury still deliberating.

Although the playwright did not pretend to present a completely factual account of this ugly incident in American history, he stayed close to the actual outline of events, particularly in the trial scene, in which he used many lines taken verbatim from the court transcript.[16] In episodes where no transcript existed he was free to use his imagination. In the opening act, for example, he was able to present the entire case as the deliberate frame-up of innocent Negroes by a vicious solicitor and a brutal sheriff, who used bribery, threats, and beatings to persuade the witnesses to corroborate the false accusations. There was no doubt about Wexley's feelings toward the forces of Southern law.

Despite its enthusiasm, the Party press found fault with the script. Harold Edgar declared that Wexley had failed to emphasize the correct ideological analysis of the Scottsboro situation [17] because he had merely implied the theme of economic exploitation in Rokoff's scene with the boys. Evidently realizing that the Scottsboro case was more complex than the Communists were willing to admit, Wexley also "deviated" in portraying the psychological and social fears of the Southern whites. He was apparently more concerned with the fate of the victims than with the justification of the Party's theoretical position or with the Communists' political activities.

Michael Gold also complained. Labeling the final emphasis on the bourgeois defense counsel "a most serious political blunder," this critic felt uncomfortable at the sight of a middle-class lawyer, Rubin, stealing the show. Wexley was simply reporting this fact of scene stealing. Gold, although admitting that Leibowitz had done a good job, still wanted the Scottsboro case transformed into a story of the oppressed Negro masses and of the Communist revolution that would save them. He felt that the playwright should at least have given greater emphasis to the agitational role of the Communists and the ILD, to their telegrams, and to their mass demonstrations.[18] Here, again, Wexley was more concerned with the injustice than with the Party's political activities.

Despite these serious theoretical and political errors, the Communists hoped to use *They Shall Not Die* for their own purposes since the playwright was basically sympathetic to the Party's position and since the play was exciting theatre. Despite his complaints, Michael Gold felt that the drama, by informing its audience of the frame-up, was a form of mass action.[19] Once the spectator learned of the injustice, he would contribute money to the Communists' defense funds. Any publicity given to the case, which the Party had turned into its own *cause célèbre*, could be turned into cash.

The Party did make a fortune by raising funds to defend the Scottsboro boys.[20] But it is doubtful that the Communists obtained much of this money by means of Wexley's play, because the Guild's bourgeois subscription audience was not enthusiastic. The few comrades who began supporting the show attested to this lack of enthusiasm. One who signed his name "L.A." wrote to thank Michael Gold for telling him about the drama. He said that he hadn't gone to see it because he did not want to support the Theatre Guild, but Gold induced him to go. He sat "in the front rows among the stuffed shirts and frozen mugs. But the applause from up in the balconies was heartening, particularly at the mention of the ILD and mass action." [21]

Despite many pleas issued by the Party press for more proletarian support and despite a slight reduction in the price scale, the play ran for only 62 performances. With this production the Theatre Guild turned so far left that Michael Gold tried to coax it to its "salvation."

But the Guild would not be "saved." The next play in the group of six social dramas by American playwrights was *Valley Forge*, which opened on December 10, 1934. In this pseudo-historical account of George Washington's hard winter, Maxwell Anderson debunked the Revolution by attributing its origin to the merchants' desire to protect their profits and by exposing the treachery and corruption within the Continental Congress and Army. Although Anderson was certain that all varieties of government plundered the populace, he offered a more positive point of view in *Valley Forge* than he had presented in *Both Your Houses;* Washington fought for the ideal of liberty, for the right of men to choose their government and to change it whenever it becomes corrupt. Although Anderson felt strongly that all governments decay, he preferred elective to hereditary changes. The *New Masses'* reviewer, Michael Blankfort, liked the exposé of the American Revolution but wholly misunderstood the theme. He regarded it as a summons for a Fascist dictator (like Washington) to lead America out of its Depression crisis. [22] *Valley Forge*, slowed by a contrived plot and *ersatz* Elizabethan verse, closed after 56 performances.

On December 24, 1934, the Guild presented a social drama, *Rain from Heaven*, by yet another established American playwright—S. N. Behrman. Like his preceding scripts, such as *Biography*, and his succeeding plays, such as *No Time for Comedy*, this work is a drawing-room piece with witty conversation and a love triangle. Two men— Hugo Willens, a part-Jewish refugee from Nazi Germany, and Rand Eldridge, an American aviator with Fascist be-liefs—love Lady Wyngate, a wealthy liberal. The chief dif-ference between *Rain from Heaven* and Behrman's other works lies in the motives of the characters. In this play they are motivated more by their political feelings than by their individual psyches. Taunted by Rand, Hugo de-cides to return to Germany to fight Hitler; Rand and Lady Wyngate conclude that their political creeds will keep them apart.

As the world crisis deepened, Behrman warned his audi-ence that fascism had to be fought by both active and passive liberals, by Hugo in his militant way and by Lady Wyngate in her more intellectual manner. Although Hugo denounces the catchwords of liberalism when he decides to fight, he does not join the Communist Party; throughout the play communism and fascism are equated with dicta-torship. The Marxist press, except for a belated, favorable review by John Gassner in *New Theatre*,[23] ignored the pro-duction. *Rain from Heaven* played an engagement of 99 performances. Behrman demonstrated that his comedy of manners could carry a heavy load of political significance without sinking.

Bernard Shaw had often demonstrated the same feat in his comedies, but he did not succeed with the Guild's next production—*The Simpleton of the Unexpected Isles*, a dramatic fable in which the famous playwright presented his vision of Judgment Day, not as the end of the world but rather as the beginning of human maturity. In the last act, when an angel brings judgment to the British Empire, the idle persons who have not paid their own cost to soci-ety by work simply disappear. The play ends with praise for the Life Force and for the surprises in store for the Unexpected Isles—that is, the world.

The idea of liquidating the socially useless should have

appealed to the Communists because the Soviet Russians claimed to be following that policy, but Shaw did not make the capitalists and their agents disappear and the proletarians remain; clergymen, for example, do not dissolve. The playwright's advocacy of an unexpected, insecure future ran counter to the Marxist belief that the future could be predicted and achieved scientifically. The play, beset by a disjointed plot, succumbed after 40 performances in the winter of 1935. Except for a review in *New Theatre* by John Gassner,[24] the Marxist press overlooked the work.

Because *Parade*, the Guild's next socially significant production, had originally been written by left-wing stalwarts for Theatre Union, this musical revue was eagerly awaited by the Communists. Opening on May 20, 1935, this show included songs that were sympathetic to oppressed workers and sketches that satirized enemies of the proletariat. Paul Peters and George Sklar wrote such lyrics as:

> Life could be so beautiful
> Life could be so grand for all,
> If just a few didn't own everything
> And most of us nothing at all.[25]

The sketches included "The Crisis" by Frank Gabrielson, David Lesan, and Michael Blankfort—a satiric pantomime about a capitalist who encounters many mechanical difficulties when he tries to operate his plant without the workers, who are on strike; "The Dead Cow" by Alan Baxter and Harold Johnshud—a skit in which a Hearst photographer photographs a starving American family as evidence of a famine in Russia; "Free Clinic" by Gabrielson and Lesan—an attack on the vicious incompetence of medical charity; "Home of the Brave" by Gabrielson and Lesan —a satiric vision of America under a racist dictator who despises everything un-Indian; "The Tabloid Reds" by Paul

Peters and George Sklar—a parody of the bomb-throwing radicals depicted in the Hearst press; "The Last Jackass" by Peters and Sklar—a satire on the U. S. government's policy of destroying crops and livestock; and "My Flight from the Soviets" by Peters, Sklar, and Kyle Crichton—an anti-Soviet lecture by a degenerate Russian princess.

In presenting a full-length musical revue written from a proletarian point of view, the Theatre Guild anticipated the initial tryout of *Pins and Needles* by more than a year. Unlike that brilliant show, however, *Parade* closed after only 40 performances. The lyrics lacked the sparkle of Harold Rome's lines, and the sketches lacked both the precise bite and the good humor of the Labor Stage revue. Although the script of *Parade* was frequently and openly Marxist, the *Daily Worker's* critic, Nathaniel Buchwald, charged the Guild with diluting the presentation in deference to the bourgeois subscription audience, and he blamed this weakening for the failure of the show, but at the same time he accused the company of attempting to entice proletarian spectators away from Theatre Union.[26]

If *Parade* had been produced one or two years later, the Marxist critics would undoubtedly have attributed its demise more simply to the lackluster material, for the Communists by then were themselves toning down references to the revolution in deference to the united front. Despite the failure of *Parade*, the Party kept urging new theatre groups to use the form of the musical revue as a vehicle for propaganda.[27]

For the remainder of the decade the Guild relied almost exclusively on American playwrights for its social dramas. The theme of war dominated most of these scripts, as might be expected at a time when Japan was attacking China, when Mussolini was bent on creating a new Roman Empire, and when Hitler was seeking to conquer the world.

The climate of the thirties was warlike, and before the decade was over, war itself was plaguing Europe. It was only natural for American playwrights to express their thoughts and feelings about war and about its possible consequences to the United States. The Guild and, from 1938 on, the Playwrights' Company provided the platforms for many of these expressions. The Communists, although they had strong opinions about war, rarely agreed with those set forth by the Guild's social productions from 1935 through 1941.

The first of the plays about war, *If This Be Treason* by the Rev. John Haynes Holmes and Reginald Lawrence, opened on September 23, 1935, and ran for 40 performances. This drama chronicles the efforts of a newly inaugurated American President to stop a war that his predecessor had provoked with the Japanese. Convinced that the people of both countries want peace, the President travels to Japan and ends the war. He is aided by the Japanese masses, who revolt under the leadership of a pacifist at the critical moment in the negotiations.

Holmes carried forward the wishful thinking about mass action, also exhibited by Albert Maltz and George Sklar in *Peace on Earth,* to a successful conclusion, but not quite in the way that his Marxian predecessors had envisioned. Holmes managed to end war without altering the basic structure of either American or Japanese society. The common people—not only the workers—of both countries exert pressure only to stop the conflict, not to change their otherwise happy lot. Although Holmes blamed munitions makers, stock speculators, congressmen, and military leaders for inciting war, he did not urge the destruction of the capitalist state that had produced these villains. War, said Holmes, could be stopped by the will of man with the aid of God. Just as George Sklar and Paul Peters pretended in *Stevedore* that the proletarian future had already suc-

ceeded, so Holmes pretended in his drama that the kingdom of God had already triumphed; the Guild thus offered
messianic realism instead of Theatre Union's Socialist
variety.

Although the *Daily Worker's* critic, Michael Blankfort,
liked the indictment of the warmongers, he disliked the
non-Marxist formula for stopping war; only "the united
action of the working peoples," he declared, could solve
the problem.[28] The years following 1935 demonstrated that
neither the wishes of individual persons as represented by
the diplomacy at Munich nor the Communists' united front
were strong enough to prevent war.

On March 24, 1936, the Guild presented a more pessimistic anti-war play. Robert E. Sherwood's *Idiot's Delight*
is an account of the outbreak of a second world war as it
affects a group of persons at a hotel in the Italian Alps—
especially a munitions maker who starts the conflict by persuading the Italians to bomb Paris, a pacifistic radical who
becomes a bellicose nationalist when the war starts, and an
American vaudevillian who decides to die with the industrialist's mistress when she is deserted by her lover. The
play ends with an ironic rendition of "Onward, Christian
Soldiers" sung by this couple to the accompaniment of
falling bombs.

Although the playwright accused the munitions magnate
of starting war, he also blamed the patriotic masses for
buying and using the weapons. But he did not believe that
all people were evil. Speaking through the vaudevillian,
the dramatist expressed faith in the ultimate triumph of the
meek, of the decent majority of the people—a faith he reiterated in a postscript to the play.[29] Despite the evidence
that revealed man as a creature of violence, and God as a
bored being who plays the meaningless game of Idiot's
Delight, Sherwood refused to despair. Although he depicted the bombing in the final scene in extremely ironic

terms, he also illustrated the decency of the vaudevillian in staying with the magnate's mistress. Sherwood's dark vision of the immediate future did not destroy his hope.

Idiot's Delight was the first successful anti-war play of the decade. The run of 300 performances was caused primarily by Sherwood's highly theatrical script, performed so brilliantly by Alfred Lunt as the vaudevillian and Lynn Fontanne as the mistress. The audience laughed, but it was also moved by the realistic, yet not hopeless, vision of the coming war. The success came without the aid of the Marxist press. Although one critic, Edwin Seaver, liked the many comic scenes and the laudable anti-Fascist and anti-war sentiments, he felt that the play failed in two ways: first, Sherwood did not link the munitions maker and the patriots with the declining capitalist system; and second, the playwright distorted the pacifist by converting him to chauvinism. Radicals, this reviewer predicted, would act more effectively at the start of the next conflict.[30] For the Communists, Sherwood's opposition to war was weakened by his failure to propose a solution more positive than mere hope; he had not even suggested a united front against war and fascism.

Before returning to the theme of war, the Guild presented brief runs of four socially significant productions. The first, *And Stars Remain* by Julius and Philip Epstein, which opened in October 1936, was a routine romance trimmed with jokes and mild praise for political liberalism. The second, *But for the Grace of God* by Leopold Atlas, was presented in January 1937. The *Daily Worker's* critic, Charles E. Dexter, complained that this drama, which exposed corporate profits, child labor, unemployment, and poor public health services as causes of crime, failed to recommend the revolutionary cure.[31]

The Guild's next two social dramas did deal with revolution. In February 1937 the Guild presented Maxwell Anderson's *The Masque of Kings* for an engagement of 89 performances. In this drama about Prince Rudolph—his love for Mary Vetsera, his plot to seize the Austrian throne, and his suicide at Mayerling—Anderson offered the thesis that revolution breeds the same evils it was designed to destroy, for, to retain power, revolutionaries are forced to restrict the freedom they intended to establish. But he was more concerned with a pompous verse rendition of the romantic tragedy than with this political lesson. The reviewers for the Party press, Alexander Taylor and Charles E. Dexter, disliked the play because Rudolph's revolt was bourgeois, not Marxist-Leninist.[32] These critics had more reason to dislike the play than they admitted, for Anderson's thesis was being illustrated by Joseph Stalin.

The second play about revolution—Ben Hecht's *To Quito and Back*—had a short run in October 1937. This play concerns Aleck Sterns, an American novelist, who helps the Communists seize power in Ecuador. When the Fascists counterattack and most of the Red Army desert, he advises martyrdom for the few remaining revolutionaries and joins them in death. Like Prince Rudolph, he is motivated more by love than by political beliefs; his sudden conversion from his hatred of the common people to a belief in their nobility can be explained only by his relations with his mistress. Like Anderson, Hecht was more concerned with the study of a neurotic character than with the presentation of political lessons. The *Daily Worker's* critic, Judith Reed, condemned the play because of the undignified presentation of the proletarian leaders;[33] the portrait of a Communist minister who advocates war to gain foreign markets was hard to take, especially since he had been born in Russia. Hecht wrote about the right kind of revolution, but he failed to present it from the Party's point of view.

Ruth Nelson as Edna, the starving wife who urges her husband to strike. Four shadowy union members look on. *Waiting for Lefty.* Group Theatre. First offered by New Theatre League. 1935

Militant taxi drivers, on stage and in the audience, led by Elia Kazan as Agate, raise fists in support of the strike. *Waiting for Lefty.* Group Theatre. First offered by New Theatre League. 1935

Vandamm Collection, Theatre Collection, New York Public Library

Seizing the battleship *St. George*, the proletarian sailors are about to run up the Red flag. *The Sailors of Cattaro*. Theatre Union. 1934

One of the Negroes is about to be falsely accused of rape. *Stevedore*, a play of Socialist realism. Theatre Union. 1934

Vandamm Collection, Theatre Collection, New York Public Library

Hitler" and "Stalin," two of the "Five Little Angels of Peace," in *New Pins
.nd Needles.* Labor Stage. 1939. The addition of Stalin to the group of
.ngels angered the Communist Party.

Culver Pictures, Inc.

The original, improvised production of *The Cradle Will Rock,* with composer Marc Blitzstein at the piano. Mercury Theatre. 1937

Wide World Pho

Hallie Flanagan, national director Federal Theatre from 1935 throu 1939

One of many outdoor performances by the Caravan Unit of Federal Theatre

Culver Pictures, Inc

Against the projected backdrop of the Constitution, silhouettes representing Al Smith and the Supreme Court discuss the AAA. A silhouette of Earl Browder a moment later in this scene almost caused a riot on opening night. *Triple-A Plowed Under,* a living newspaper. Federal Theatre. 1936

John Brown, Sala Straw, Jules Garfield, and Mara Alexander perform in an acting class sponsored by Theatre Union. The instructors (right) are Molly Day Thacher and Clifford Odets.

A lady garment worker portraying a Park Avenue matron sings "It's Not Cricket to Picket." *Pins and Needles.* Labor Stage. 1937

Egyptian slaves and their master in *The Sun and I.* Federal Theatre. 1937. The granary (left) offended the reviewer for *New Masses,* who saw a resemblance to Lenin's tomb.

Class war in Beaverland as the unemployed beavers (right) revolt. *The Revolt of the Beavers.* Federal Theatre. 1937

The Ku Klux Klan scene with Isabelle Bonner as Mrs. Flimmins in John Howard Lawson's 1937 revision of *Processional.* Federal Theatre.

The conflict between music and materialism. Luther Adler as Joe Bonaparte, Morris Carnovsky as his father, and Frances Farmer as Joe's girl. *Golden Boy.* Group Theatre. 1937

Billy Gaxton as John P. Wintergreen and Lois Moran as Mary Turner campaign for the Presidency in *Of Thee Sing,* the decade's first socially significant musical comedy. Produced by Sam Harris. 1931

"The Tabloid Reds," a parody of bomb-throwing Communists, set against Red-scare headlines of the Hearst press. *Parade.* Theatre Guild. 1935

In its next social drama the Guild returned to the war theme as interpreted by still another established playwright —Sidney Howard. His play, *The Ghost of Yankee Doodle*, which opened on November 22, 1937, tells the story of the Garrisons, a rich but progressive family faced with ruin some months after the start of a second world war because America's Neutrality Act prevents their selling their manufactured goods. To the rescue of this reluctant family comes a reactionary publisher who expands the recent sinking of an American ship into a campaign to get America out of the Depression and into a war. The Garrisons realize that they and their liberal beliefs are thus being sustained on the profits of bloodshed. The sister in the family understands that the Communists and jingoists seem to have more realistic solutions for the Depression, but she does not abandon her faith in the ultimate victory of liberalism and democracy.

Although Howard thus demonstrated that liberal beliefs were not sufficient to keep America at peace, he too preserved his faith in their ultimate triumph. The Garrisons have to choose between right and left for the time being, and they choose war over revolution, but after the conflict they will try once again to make the world democratic. Reviewers for the Marxist press, Michael Sayers and Eric Englander, despaired because Howard refused to prescribe communism as the only possible remedy, even though he had exposed the failures of both liberalism and capitalism.[61] Although the Guild's audience had recently welcomed a parallel oversimplification of the causes of war and a similar message of desperate hope in Sherwood's *Idiot's Delight*, the public supported Howard's rambling play for only 48 performances.

Before going on to another war drama, the Guild presented a political comedy. *Washington Jitters* by John Boruff and Walter Hart had a brief run in May 1938. The authors recounted the story of a sign painter who accidentally becomes a powerful official in the WPA but refuses to be bribed either by the Administration to support some pending legislation or by the reactionary opposition to oppose it; he exposes both parties during a nationwide broadcast and chastises the electorate for its indifference to government corruption. The playwrights' satirical jabs at both the New Deal and the Republicans did not please the Marxist press. One critic, Charles E. Dexter, complained of this nonpartisan position, especially at a time when the popular front was about to blossom forth. The dramatists, he said, should have praised the New Deal for its humanitarianism at least,[35] but he did not remind his readers of the many cartoons in the *Daily Worker* which had, a few years before, depicted Roosevelt as a lackey in the house of J. P. Morgan.

The Guild managed to produce only one social drama during the next season, 1938–39. Once again the production treated the theme of war. The play, Stefan Zweig's *Jeremiah*, opened for a short engagement in February 1939, in an acting version prepared by John Gassner and Worthington Miner from the English translation by Eden and Cedar Paul. This Biblical tragedy retells the story of Jeremiah and his failure to stop the Israelites' demand for war with the Chaldeans. Although his prophecy of doom comes true with the fall of Jerusalem and the deportation of the people, Jeremiah and the exiles retain faith in God, for physical defeat and suffering cannot conquer the Jews. This pacifistic play, originally written in 1917, was again topical in 1939, but Jeremiah's belief that the tribute of gold is better than the tribute of blood was hardly applicable to Hitler, who was demanding and obtaining both.

The critic for the *Sunday Worker*, John Cambridge, found the play "defeatist" because it declared that *all* war was both "futile" and "morally wrong." [36] Throughout the decade the Communists believed that proletarian revolution and defense of the Soviet Union were morally just. And, prompted by the Fascist successes in Ethiopia and Spain during the popular front period, 1935–1939, the Party pronounced any defense against fascism as similarly justified.[37] Had the Guild postponed *Jeremiah* until after the signing of the Nazi-Soviet pact the following August, the production would have been greeted with greater enthusiasm by the Marxist press. As it was, John Cambridge lamented that this erstwhile "progressive" company had become "decrepit." The Guild thus presented a sincerely pacifistic play, but it did not fit the Party line during the winter of that year.

One reason for the Guild's failure to produce more than the one social drama during the 1938–39 season was the formation of the Playwrights' Company. In the spring of 1938 five prominent American dramatists—Maxwell Anderson, S. N. Behrman, Sidney Howard, Elmer Rice, and Robert E. Sherwood—founded this organization for the simple purpose of producing their own plays.[38] Since these writers—except Rice—had recently provided the Guild with social dramas, the senior company was at a loss for social playwrights. After the 1938–39 season, however, the new organization often combined with the old for joint productions.

Three of the four plays of the Playwrights' first season were socially significant. Robert E. Sherwood's *Abe Lincoln in Illinois*, which opened a run of 472 performances on October 15, 1938, recounts episodes from Lincoln's life, starting with his residence in New Salem, continuing with his law practice in Springfield, and ending with his election to the Presidency. Although the drama primarily treats Lincoln's private life—his love for Ann Rutledge, his marriage to Mary Todd, and his reluctance to seek public office—such public issues as slavery and secession are raised and discussed. The first scene of the third act, for example, is devoted entirely to a semihistorical re-creation of part of the Lincoln-Douglas Debates. While secession and slavery were dead issues in

1938, such related topics as liberty and equality were vital because the Fascist powers were destroying these democratic ideals in Europe and threatening to destroy them in the New World. Lincoln's prediction that American democracy would survive reflected a more affirmative belief in the future than the mere hope Sherwood had expressed in *Idiot's Delight*.

The Party press hailed the play as a perfect drama for the united front. The *New Masses* critic, Ruth McKenney, while acclaiming the affirmation of democracy, was pleased that Sherwood had included Lincoln's defense of revolution:

Whenever they [the people] shall grow weary of the existing government, they can exercise their constitutional right of amending it, or their revolutionary right to dismember or overthrow it.[39]

This statement, a favorite with the Party since its discovery of Lincoln in 1936, together with his incidental defense of workers and strikes, made the drama seem slightly revolutionary as well as liberal. The Communists were happy with what they regarded as a link between themselves and the native American tradition of revolution. The dramatist had thus drawn the revolutionary portrait, albeit in an incidental way, that E. P. Conkle had failed to draw in Federal Theatre's *Prologue to Glory*.

Although the Communists were thus delighted with the debut of the Playwrights' Company, their hopes were almost destroyed when *Knickerbocker Holiday*, a musical comedy with a text by Maxwell Anderson and music by Kurt Weill, opened on October 19, 1938. The plot concerns the political and romantic troubles that Pieter Stuyvesant brings to New Amsterdam in 1647; as the new governor he replaces the inefficient, corrupt city council with the efficient corruption of a personal dictatorship, and he attempts to marry the fiancée of his individualistic political opponent. A rebellion forces the governor to return his power to the council and the girl to her lover.

Once again, Anderson was defending rugged individualism against the evil of government. As long as government was a necessary evil, however, he preferred a weak, amateurish democracy to a strong, professional tyranny. These views, expressed in the final scene by Stuyvesant's rival, were elaborated by Anderson in the play's preface, in which he attacked the paternalism of the New Deal by predicting that it would lead inevitably to absolute government and to the destruction of individual liberty. He warned against any change in the American system of weak, divided government run by incompetent amateurs.[40]

The Marxist press, defender of a strong central government in control of the national economy, was distressed by this grudging defense of democracy. One critic, John Cambridge, complained with some justification that Anderson's individualism was really anarchy, while another, Ruth McKenney, ignoring the earlier Communist attacks on Roosevelt, condemned the sly satire on Roosevelt's "dictatorial" methods. It was too bad, both critics agreed, that Kurt Weill's lovely music had been wasted on such a reactionary book.[41] This charming musical, delightfully escapist in its return to pre-industrial America, played an engagement of 168 performances despite the right-wing "deviations."

The Playwrights' Company turned on December 3, 1938, to a patriotic drama with fantastic overtones—*American Landscape*, Elmer Rice's story about a crisis in an old Connecticut family. Grandfather Dale decides to sell the unprofitable family business to a competitor and the ancestral home to a Nazi-American Bund, despite objections from the townspeople, the younger generation of Dales, and the ghosts of their patriotic ancestors. The grandfather's death gives the property to the grandchildren, who resolve to succeed with the factory and to keep their home out of Nazi hands. Although the material aspects of American society were changing and although the Nazis were threatening to destroy the United States, Rice felt that the "tradition of freedom and of the common rights of humanity" should be defended.[42] If he had written a less diffuse drama, one without the awkward clutter of the ghosts, his message would have been heard at many more than the 43 performances that the production had.

The Party press was divided. One reviewer, Ruth McKenney, was happy to see the organization back in the democratic (popular front) tradition of *Abe Lincoln in Illinois*,[43] but another critic, John Cambridge, while praising the anti-Fascist, pro-democratic speeches and urging his readers to hear them, complained that Rice had sidestepped the central issue of the factory's economic failure because he had not demonstrated the role of monopoly in ruining small business.[44] This critic simply wanted united front sentiments and Marxist orthodoxy in the same play.

The Playwrights' Company and the Guild turned once again to the theme of war in their next three social plays. The first two—*Key Largo* by Maxwell Anderson, which was produced by the Playwrights in November 1939, and *The Fifth Column* by Ernest Hemingway and Benjamin Glazer, which was produced by the Guild in March 1940—dealt with the Spanish Civil War, which had ended in March 1939.

Although *Key Largo* chiefly concerns the moral and intellectual problems that beset one American survivor of the conflict, the prologue, noting the dominance of Joseph Stalin in the Loyalist camp, expresses the belief that Spain will lose its freedom no matter who wins. The critic for *New Masses*, Alvah Bessie, of course, denounced this "slander" on the Spanish popular front.[45]

The Party was not much happier with *The Fifth Column*. This drama, dealing at greater length with the same civil war, concerns Philip Rawlings, an American counterespionage agent for the Loyalists, who plans to desert in order to follow a girl with whom he has fallen in love. When the Fascists advance on Madrid, he decides to remain and fight. Although the episodes deal primarily with the cloak-and-dagger adventures and with the passionate romance, Rawlings' decision to fight fascism intensifies the anti-Fascist sentiments presented throughout the play. A Loyalist officer sums up the meaning of the seemingly hopeless cause by asserting that Spain, despite its extreme backwardness, is the only European country to resist the Fascist advances; thus, the free world is given time to prepare itself for the impending attack.[46]

The Communists, then in their isolationist phase—Stalin's pact with Hitler was signed the preceding August—did not welcome *The Fifth Column*, partly because of the interventionist tone of this speech. While praising the dramatists' tribute to the heroism of the Loyalists, the reviewer for the *Daily Worker*, V. L., complained that the hero was too adventurous and bohemian and not political enough.[47] Because Ernest Hemingway and his adapter, Benjamin Glazer, did not glorify Soviet leadership of the popular front, the drama did not please the Party. Another leftist reviewer, Alvah Bessie, deploring the unpleasant pictures of some drunken Spanish people and some sadistic Loyalists, blamed the Guild and Glazer, not Hemingway, for the political failure of the play.[48] *The Fifth Column* closed after 87 performances despite its merits as an action drama, a love story, and an understated tribute to the Loyalist cause.

On April 29, 1940, the Guild and the Playwrights' Company joined forces to present another play about war—*There Shall Be No Night*, Robert E. Sherwood's account of the Russo-Finnish conflict. The plot concerns the fate of a Finnish family at the time of the Russian invasion. The father, a famous psychiatrist, forsakes his pacifistic beliefs to become an army physician and later dies as an infantryman;

the son, a ski trooper, also is killed; and the mother, an American, decides to destroy her house before the Russians arrive. Although these people know all the arguments against war, they realize that words will not stop the enslaving forces of the totalitarian powers. The Finns fight because they prefer death to slavery, and yet, believing that man will eventually understand and control his brutish nature, they hope that this war may be the last. They feel that the recognition that war is a necessity rather than a virtue may be the first achievement in the conquest of the disease.

The desperate hope that Sherwood had expressed in *Idiot's Delight* became a clear faith in this play about Finland. Warning that after the destruction of Finland (the husband and the son) the dictators would attack America (the wife), Sherwood preached against isolationism throughout the drama.

Once again the Guild and Playwrights failed to follow the Party's isolationist line, and the *Daily Worker's* critic, Ralph Warner, attacked this plea for intervention, along with Sherwood's exposé of Stalin's betrayal of the Russian Revolution.[49] The *New Masses'* reviewer, Alvah Bessie, asserting that he had been prepared to admit that the play might be dramatic despite its political errors, claimed that the dramaturgy was as bad as the ideology and concluded that no playwright could write a good drama in support of a "phony cause." [50] Good drama could thus be written only by Marxians and their allies.

The Communists, failing to admit Stalin's betrayal of both Poland and Finland, were especially upset over Sherwood's "shift" from his pro-democratic (popular front) position in *Abe Lincoln in Illinois* to his "anti-democratic" (anti-Soviet) point of view in *There Shall Be No Night*. Michael Gold accused the Guild and Sherwood of being "liberal opportunists," [51] an apt description of the Marxists themselves during the popular front period. As with their attacks on Labor Stage, the Communists blamed everyone but the Party for the demise of this union of liberals, leftists, and Marxists. *There Shall Be No Night* ran for 181 performances.

The Party's pique at the Guild was still evident in the reviews of *Love's Old Sweet Song*, William Saroyan's eccentric comedy, which opened on May 2, 1940, under the joint sponsorship of the Guild and Eddie Dowling. The main plot, about the romance of a pitchman and a spinster, was mere escapism to the Marxists. The subplot, however, was reaction, with its parodies on the Okies (taken from John Steinbeck's *The Grapes of Wrath*) and on their revolutionary reporter. In depicting the huge Yearling family (the Joads) as lazy, destructive, and lecherous, Saroyan cheerfully assaulted the Party's view that the poor and oppressed were by definition good. In presenting the sociological novelist (Steinbeck) as a nuisance to the Yearlings, the playwright attacked the belief that literary exposure of bad social conditions would improve them. Love, not revolution, was Saroyan's answer to the problems of the thirties. The *Daily Worker's* critic, Ralph Warner, denounced the comedy and its producers:

By the way, the Theatre Guild, once the stronghold of middle class liberalism in the theatre, sponsored not only this intrinsically reactionary play but also that jingoistic jetsam *There Shall Be No Night* all in one week. Of such stuff were the dreams of yesteryear's "revolutionaries of the theatre" fashioned.[52]

It was six years since the Guild's production of *They Shall Not Die* had inspired the Party's hopes. The Saroyan comedy played an engagement of 44 performances.

On December 30, 1940, the Playwrights' Company continued the social series with still another play about war—

Flight to the West by Elmer Rice. This drama, dealing with the capture of two Nazi spies aboard an airliner bound from Lisbon to New York, also treats the problems of the other passengers, principally a young American couple whose pacifistic creed has been destroyed by the fall of Paris; the husband, anticipating a Nazi invasion of America, decides to join the Army Air Corps. Like Sherwood, Rice was warning this country to defend itself against the coming attack by the insane dictators, for American democracy, though not perfectly practiced, was worth saving. The isolationist reviewers for the Communist press, of course, attacked the play for its interventionist message.[53] *Flight to the West* continued to offer its liberal speeches for 168 performances.

The Guild offered only one socially significant play, another interventionist work, during the 1940–41 season. Philip Barry's *Liberty Jones* opened on February 5, 1941, and closed after 22 showings. This confused patriotic allegory deals with the rescue of the beautiful Liberty Jones, niece of Uncle Samuel Bunting, by her husband, Commander Tom Smith of Naval Aviation, from the power of the Three Shirts (black, brown, and red) and their foreign master. Having failed to appease the enemies, Tom destroys them and thus enables Liberty to cross "the bridge over hard times." Like Sherwood and Rice, Barry warned that the military would have to save freedom in America and in the rest of the world.

The Marxian isolationists, of course, denounced the play's political message and the play itself. One critic, Alvah Bessie, declared, with justification, that the drama was on the level of a "high school pageant."[54] Another reviewer, Ralph Warner, asserting that the Guild "continues to reflect the hopeless bewilderment of its middle class audience, and its quasi-liberal directorate," concluded hopefully that the company was about to die.[55] The prediction once again proved untrue.

On October 22, 1941, the Guild and the Playwrights'

Company jointly produced *Candle in the Wind*, Maxwell Anderson's pronouncement on the theme of war. The plot concerns the efforts of an American actress to free her French lover, whom the Nazis have imprisoned for both military and political "crimes" in occupied France. The German authorities, detaining her in France when the prisoner escapes, warn that she will be arrested when Hitler attacks the United States. To this threat she replies:

Yes. We shall expect you and be ready for you. In the history of the world, there have been many wars between men and beasts. And the beasts have always lost, and men have won.[56]

Like Sherwood, Rice, and Barry, Anderson reaffirmed his belief in liberty and warned the Nazis that we would fight to defend our freedom.

Although the Marxist press had condemned the same prointervention theme in *There Shall Be No Night, Flight to the West,* and *Liberty Jones,* they welcomed Anderson's call to arms. The explanation for this shift lies in the date, not the dramaturgy, for, between the presentations of the Barry allegory and the Anderson drama, Germany had marched into Russia and thus caused the Communists to abandon isolationism in the hope of saving the Socialist fatherland. Although Anderson was now on the right political side, one leftist reviewer, Ralph Warner, complained that the play emphasized love and individualism at the expense of revolutionary politics; mass action, said this critic, would destroy Hitler, but the dramatist had ignored it.[57] *Candle in the Wind* was acted 95 times.

The Guild's last social play before Pearl Harbor, Sophie Treadwell's *Hope for a Harvest*, opened on November 26, 1941, and closed after 38 performances. This drama tells the story of a woman who has inherited a ruined ranch, which she decides to restore to its original fertility and beauty by means of hard labor. The playwright points the moral that more work could solve the problems of decaying farms and decadent farmers, but a rise in prices caused by the war helps solve the farm problem at the end of the play, thus diminishing the strength of the pro-work thesis.

The *Daily Worker's* critic, Ralph Warner, denounced this analysis of the farm situation. The decay of American farms, he asserted, was not caused by sloth and other vices, but rather by "monopoly control of markets, prices, and crop production" and by government refusal to supply mortgage relief and farm machinery.[58] The reviewer for *New Masses,* Alvah Bessie, was displeased to note that the Okies, whom the playwright depicted as lazy tramps, were introduced just for laughs.[59] Neither Miss Treadwell nor the producers had treated the exploited proletariat with sufficient solemnity. The Guild's decade of social plays ended on this note.

Of the 85 plays presented by the Theatre Guild from 1929 through 1941 and by the Playwrights' Company from 1938 through 1941, only 30 were socially significant. Like Federal Theatre, the two organizations made the social drama merely a part of their repertory. Although they were sensitive to the Depression and to the resultant social, political, and economic changes, both producing companies retained their sense of theatrical balance because they understood that entertainment was as important as didacticism, even in an unsteady decade, and also that the theatre was supposed to teach an understanding of the human heart as well as the social mind.

The Guild and the Playwrights offered variety in the social themes and dramatic forms of their productions, but not to the extent of Federal Theatre. The producing pair treated the subjects of revolution, agriculture, justice, government, and especially war from various points of view, including the rugged individualism of *Valley Forge,* the liberalism of *The Ghost of Yankee Doodle,* and the Marxism of *Parade.*

The Theatre Guild became more staid and stolid in choosing social themes as the decade wore on. After *Parade* in 1935, the organization did not offer anything that was as politically daring as that Marxist revue.

Although the Guild and the Playwrights varied their dramatic forms to include such musicals as *Knickerbocker Holiday*, such fantasies as *Miracle at Verdun*, and such eccentric comedies as *Love's Old Sweet Song*, the two companies did not have the experimental spirit that pervaded Federal Theatre's social drama or the Guild's own social productions of the twenties, such as *Processional* by John Howard Lawson and *The Adding Machine* by Elmer Rice. As the Theatre Guild grew older, the stolidity of its social themes was matched by the conventionality of its realistic form of drama. And for their social plays at least, the two organizations relied largely on reliable, established dramatists.

Although the Guild and the Playwrights did not offer the variety of Federal Theatre, their productions were much more diverse than the presentations of Theatre Union. Unlike that Marxian company, neither the Guild nor the Playwrights' Company was dedicated exclusively to the production of "strong" social dramas, and neither company interpreted public issues solely in terms of the class struggle.

In the early thirties the Guild offered four Marxist productions, all theatrical failures—*Red Rust, Roar China, They Shall Not Die,* and *Parade*. But none of these plays was welcomed without reservations by the Party press. The Playwrights' Company did not produce a single Communist drama. Although Sherwood referred to the Jeffersonian position on revolution in *Abe Lincoln in Illinois*, this dramatist emphasized his faith in liberalism and democracy, not in Leninism. The Party's attempted use of such dramas as lures for the popular front did not make these plays less liberal, less democratic, or more Marxist.

After the collapse of the united front the Guild and the

Playwrights' Company continued to preach democracy and liberty even at the cost of war, much to the displeasure of the Party. The Communists continued to envy the professional productions of the Guild and the Playwrights' Company, but these liberal, bourgeois theatres rarely utilized their theatrical skill to present the Communist Party line.

Chapter 9

The Group Theatre

THE Group Theatre has been more persistently accused of Communist control than any other Broadway theatre company of the Depression. This charge, starting in the thirties and continuing to grow even after the company's demise in 1941, received its greatest publicity in 1952, when two noted Group alumni—Clifford Odets and Elia Kazan—publicly confessed to past membership in the Party. Although the accusation of Communist control has assumed oversized proportions, it remains untrue, as this history of the company will demonstrate.

In the spring of 1931 three employees of the Theatre Guild—Harold Clurman, a playreader; Cheryl Crawford, a casting director; and Lee Strasberg, an actor—organized a company of 28 actors in order to rehearse a play for eventual presentation in New York. Besides the three directors, the members included Stella Adler, Margaret Barker, Phoebe Brand, J. Edward Bromberg, Morris Carnovsky, Walter Coy, William Challee, Virginia Farmer, Sylvia Fenningston, Friendly Ford, Paul Green, Gerrit Kraber, Lewis Leverett, Robert Lewis, Gertrude Maynard, Sanford Meisner, Paula Miller, Mary Morris, Ruth Nelson, Clifford Odets, Dorothy Patten, Herbert Ratner, Philip Robinson, Art Smith, Eunice Stoddard, Franchot Tone, Alixe Walker, and Clement Wil-

enchick.[1] During the remainder of the decade there were
frequent changes in personnel. The most important additions to the company were Luther Adler, Roman Bohnen,
Russell Collins, Elia Kazan, John Garfield, and Lee Cobb.

Aided by some theatrical "angels," including the Theatre
Guild, which contributed the script and $1,000, the new
group spent the summer of 1931 rehearsing Paul Green's
The House of Connelly on a farm in Brookfield Center,
Connecticut.[2]

By means of a permanent company of professional actors,
united by a common point of view and trained by a single
method, the directors hoped to "give the most expert and
complete dramatic expression" to plays that dealt with "the
essential moral and social preoccupations" of the times.[3]
Derived from Stanislavsky and the Moscow Art Theatre,
the training method consisted of the improvisation of scenes
and the "exercise of affective memory." In this exercise the
actor would seek to reproduce an emotion by recalling a
similar emotional experience from his own past. The emotion thus reproduced would make the actor live his part and
so make the play seem more real to the audience.[4] This
method was supposed to create greater theatrical realism
than had been possible in the previous history of the American theatre.

Under the guidance of its directors, the Group Theatre
also hoped to develop and train serious playwrights to provide suitable dramas for the permanent acting ensemble.
"A good play for us," wrote Harold Clurman, one of the
Group's directors, "is not one which measures up to some
literary standard of 'art' or 'beauty' but one which is the
image or symbol" of contemporary moral and social problems. Such problems, he felt, had to be "faced with an essentially affirmative attitude, that is, in the belief that to all of
them there may be some answer, an answer that should be
considered operative for at least the humanity of our time

and place." As long as the plays were related to life in this fashion, they could be cast in any dramatic form—in comedy, fantasy, tragedy, or farce.[5] Although the directors had a specific method for training the acting company, they had only this broad point of view for selecting plays.

Interested in moral as well as social issues, the Group was thus not organized exclusively as a social theatre. Unlike the Communist theatres, this company had no intention of using the theatre as a Party weapon or of performing primarily for proletarian spectators. On the contrary, the selection of available scripts depended on what the directors regarded as "the truest preoccupations of an intelligent American audience," [6] and the Group sought that audience on Broadway.

Financed by the Theatre Guild and some individual investors, including Franchot Tone and Eugene O'Neill, the Group's first production, Paul Green's *The House of Connelly*, opened "under the auspices of the Theatre Guild" [7] on September 28, 1931, and played an engagement of 91 performances. Set in the early years of the twentieth century, this play treats the regeneration of a Southern gentleman and his plantation through the love and work of the daughter of a tenant farmer. Green did not assume the doctrinaire position that all such tenants are hard-working laborers exploited by the aristocracy; on the contrary, most of them, both Negroes and whites, are as lazy as their landlord. The playwright was more concerned with the psychological and philosophical aspects of his story than with the social, political, or economic implications of agriculture in the South. The Party press, justifiably regarding the Group as another bourgeois theatre, ignored the production.

The Communists did notice the Group's second presentation, *1931—* by Claire and Paul Sifton, which opened under the Guild's auspices on December 10, 1931. This drama traces the degradation of Adam, a proud factory worker, who is forced into a life of poverty, sickness, and despair because of the unemployment crisis; and the decline of his sweetheart, who loses her job also and becomes diseased through a life of prostitution. Interspersed with the scenes of Adam's fall are interludes depicting in pantomime the growing anger and subsequent revolt of the unemployed masses, whom Adam and his girl join in the final episode.

In a prefatory note, the playwrights asserted that the interludes were designed to suggest "a ground swell that is bearing Adam, his group, and the audience itself, on to revolution of one sort or another." [8] Revolution, the Siftons apparently felt, would start unless the unemployed, whose plight the drama portrayed so graphically, were given the relief of jobs, not the charity of bread lines. Although the dramatists concluded the action with an uprising, they did not specify a Leninist revolution, except for the final stage direction, which calls for the chanting of a song vaguely like the "Internationale." In re-creating the horror of the Depression, the Siftons did not offer the Marxist explanation of unemployment as the inevitable result of the capitalist system, nor did they urge the Communist solution—a proletarian uprising led by the Party; the masses of *1931–* revolt without the indoctrination or the guidance of Communist agitators.

Writing in *New Masses*, Manuel Gomez, who was later a director of Theatre Union, listed this lack of "conscious leadership" as one of the play's serious shortcomings and complained also that the audience, viewing a bourgeoisie that was too vicious, might think that a more humanitarian attitude by this class would end the Depression. Despite these errors, he was thrilled by the sight of a proletarian drama being acted on Broadway, and he urged his readers to attend. [9] For the brief run of 12 performances the balcony was filled with cheering spectators, but most of the orchestra seats remained empty.[10] The middle class did not like the vicious image of itself either.

Although the production of *1931–* had aroused the Party's interest, the Communist press overlooked the Group's final production of the season, Maxwell Anderson's *Night over Taos*, which opened on March 9, 1932. This semihistorical romance, set in 1847, dramatizes the conflict between the feudal ruler of Taos, a Spanish colony in New Mexico, and his two sons. Devoid of social significance, this play did not attract radical spectators, and the brief engagement of 13 performances indicated that the Broadway audience preferred more action in their costume dramas. *Night over Taos* was important chiefly because it was the Group's first production without aid from the Theatre Guild.

In June 1932 the Group departed for Dover Furnace, New York, to prepare for a new season. Although Harold Clurman had seen no evidence of "radicalism" in the company during the first summer, he noticed a sudden interest in social, political, and economic questions during the second summer encampment, at which Group members and their many guests began to discuss Marxism enthusiastically.[11] Communist agitators and sympathizers had undoubtedly been attracted to the Group not only by the proletarian content of *1931–* but also by the technical skill with which the acting ensemble had presented all three plays of the first season. The Marxist agitation during the second summer indicated that the Communists had started a campaign to convert the Group into a revolutionary theatre. The deepening of the Depression aided them in their mission.

The details of this plot were not fully revealed until 1952, when Elia Kazan testified before the House Committee on Un-American Activities. He had joined the Group in the summer of 1932. Before he was recruited into the Party in the summer of 1934, Kazan said, a Communist cell had already been established within the Group in order to further Marxian studies, to infiltrate Actors' Equity, to support such Party fronts as the League of Workers' Theatres and the New Theatre League, and to seize control of the Group in order to transform it into a "Communist mouthpiece."

Since the Group was controlled by its three non-Communist directors (Harold Clurman, Cheryl Crawford, and Lee Strasberg) from 1931 through 1937 and by Harold Clurman alone from 1937 through 1940, Kazan continued, the Communists agitated for a more "democratic" directorate, in which the actors, especially the Communist actors, would be represented. Although an Actors' Committee was established in 1933, it served only in an advisory way. The directors retained complete authority over the organization. Kazan, who had joined the Party to fight fascism and poverty, refused to work for "democratic" control of the advisory committee and quit when a Party organizer urged him to repent this refusal.[12]

The Communists' failure to seize the Group was evident in the large amount of work that some *individual* actors did for the Party's theatrical fronts; the New Theatre League, for instance, was able to use the Group's prestige and actors, but not the Group itself. The continual agitation of the Party press for a change in the company's policies indicated also that the Communists had failed in their objective. Finally, the Group's relatively few productions with Marxian sentiments hardly qualified it as a "Red" theatre.

On September 26, 1932, the company began its second season with John Howard Lawson's *Success Story*. This play, written two years before the dramatist's conversion to communism, concerns Sol Ginsberg, a poor Jewish clerk, who abandons his radical beliefs and rises to a position of wealth as the head of an advertising agency, only to find unhappiness. Having quarreled with his wife, he seeks the love of his erstwhile sweetheart, who shoots him.

Lawson, more concerned with the psyche of Sol Ginsberg than with his role in the class struggle, displeased the Party press. The *Daily Worker*, in a very short review, praised the excellent acting but denounced the play as belonging to "the Eugene O'Neill bourgeois reactionary variety, in which the audience is asked to weep over the sexual problems of a finance-capitalist swindler." [18] Lawson's implicit theme—money does not ensure happiness—was unacceptable to the Communist have-nots, who opposed such a thesis as an invention of the rich to prevent the poor from wanting money. *Success Story*, a shocking exposé of the people in an advertising agency, ran on Broadway for 121 performances.

The Group's next presentation, Dawn Powell's *Big Night*, another exposé of individual corruption in the advertising world, opened on January 17, 1933, and closed after seven showings. The Party press did not bother to review the production. The Communists were making no headway in their attempt to get plays about the class struggle on the Group's stage.

The company's third season opened on September 26, 1933, with *Men in White*, Sidney Kingsley's tribute to the medical profession. Sidney Harmon and James R. Ullman were associate producers. This drama tells the story of Dr. Ferguson, a young intern, who must choose between an easy future as the husband of a wealthy woman and a difficult life as the assistant to a famous surgeon. The young man decides to dedicate his life to surgery. Like *Success Story* and *Big Night*, *Men in White* deals with personal problems rather than social issues. More concerned with the intern's moral choice than with the question of socialized medicine, Kingsley devoted the greater part of the drama to Dr. Ferguson's dilemma but only two brief comments to the issue of socialization. Since the dramatist preferred a community organization of medical service under the control of doctors, not politicians, this incidental bit of social significance hardly appealed to Marxists anyway.

The Party press, disappointed with the content of the play, was nevertheless impressed with the excellence of the Group's performance. Asserting that this professional company was important because it was organized as a "collective" theatre and because it had demonstrated leftist tendencies, the *Daily Worker's* critic, Harold Edgar, hoped that the Group, thus having achieved theatrical success and popular acclaim, would advance to "the drama of a classless society." [14] He was willing to let the Group enjoy its commercial success with Kingsley's highly naturalistic but socially worthless play if this company would henceforth devote its superb technique to the revolution. *Men in White,* a smash hit, enjoyed an engagement of 351 performances.

On March 22, 1934, the Group did move slightly leftward with its presentation of *Gentlewoman,*[15] John Howard Lawson's play about the romance between Gwyn Ballantine, a wealthy young widow, and Rudy Flanagan, a bohemian writer with Communist leanings. After living together for six months, the two decide to separate because her money and her love keep him from becoming a true revolutionary. He goes to Iowa to work with striking farmers. Knowing that she is doomed because of her attachment to the past, Gwyn nevertheless hopes that her coming baby will someday be unafraid to change the world.

Although Lawson, replying to the "bourgeois" critics who found the theme obscure, protested that his drama clearly illustrated the thesis that "communism" gave his characters "a new balance and reason for their lives," [16] neither Rudy nor Gwyn actually joins the Party. While both of them move toward conversion, they are too much involved in their own emotional problems to become members.

This couple did not move far enough to please the Marxist

press. Although the *Daily Worker's* critic, Melvin Levy, praised the picture of capitalist decay, he condemned the use of a bohemian fellow traveler as the gentlewoman's guide to communism. The representative of the Party, said this reviewer, should have been a strong, noble proletarian —a miner's son, for example.[17] The Group attempted to save the production by means of an advertising campaign, but *Gentlewoman,* unable to overcome the poor notices in the "bourgeois" press, closed after 12 showings.

Shortly after the demise of this drama Michael Gold attacked it. He complained that Lawson, as with his preceding plays, botched the revolutionary theme by ending the drama on an indecisive note. Since the characters were trapped in a futile struggle between the worlds of the bourgeoisie and the proletariat, Gold concluded that Lawson was himself caught between the desire to succeed in the bourgeois world and the urge to foster the revolution. Deploring the playwright's position that the hero must give up his rich mistress before he can work with strikers, Gold noted that the needy Communists would never abandon such a useful source of money. Despite the fact that *Gentlewoman* had been a financial failure, Gold attacked the Group for having followed *Men in White* with another commercial production. "What has become of all those tremendous manifestos with which" the Group "promised . . . to change the American theatre?" he asked.[18] The Group had never promised to create a politically revolutionary stage, but in Gold's narrow view change meant revolution.

The Group did not reply, but Lawson did. Admitting that most of the criticisms were correct, he explained that he did not want to preach communism until he had proved himself both as a revolutionary and as a revolutionary writer. Explaining why he had failed to achieve "revolutionary clarity" in his plays, he said that he had had no dramatic guide to follow because there was no background of American

Communist drama. He also complained that Gold's super-cilious proletarian attitude was not helpful to struggling intellectuals. But after these explanations Lawson confessed that *Gentlewoman* was confused because it did not express his true belief that communism was the only way out for the bourgeoisie. He also begged the Marxist critics to point out any deviations in his future work.[19]

Offering some advice the following week, Gold asserted that Lawson had actually hurt the movement, no matter what his intentions had been. By portraying revolutionaries as neurotics, bohemians, and social climbers, this dramatist had given the bourgeois spectators the kind of picture they wanted to see. Gold advised Lawson to create Communists who possess positive virtues.[20]

Lawson's conversion to orthodox communism soon fol-lowed. His article entitled "Towards a Revolutionary Thea-tre," which he subtitled "The Theatre—the Artist Must Take Sides," appeared in the June 1934 issue of *New Theatre*. The artist, the playwright declared, must side with the revolu-tionary proletariat.[21] Lawson's decision was perhaps based on the fact that he had proved himself as a revolutionary writer by his recent articles in the *Daily Worker* about a miners' strike in Alabama and as a revolutionary by virtue of his arrest while he was gathering the material.[22] On June 22, 1934, he appealed to all workers, farmers, and "honest" intellectuals, not "vague-minded liberals," to increase the circulation of the *Daily Worker*, the only newspaper that furnished "accurate information and revolutionary guid-ance."[23] The conversion seemed complete. Lawson became a zealously doctrinaire critic, and three years later his first revolutionary play, *Marching Song*, was presented by the Theatre Union. The Group produced no more of his plays.

On November 28, 1934, the company began its fourth season with Melvin Levy's *Gold Eagle Guy*, produced in association with D. A. Doran, Jr. This play chronicles some events in the life of Guy Button, a penniless seaman who founds the Gold Eagle Steamship Line in 1864 and becomes a millionaire. When he prays for the destruction of his enemies, God responds with the San Francisco earthquake, which destroys him. Levy painted his portrait, copied loosely from the historical figure of Robert Dollar, not only to reveal the robber baron's ruthlessness but also to display his gigantic energy and ability. Guy Button is not the Communists' simple picture of the capitalist exploiter. Levy had resigned from the Party before he wrote the play for fear that the Communists would interfere with his conception of Button, as they had interfered with his unpublished book about the imprisoned labor organizer, Tom Mooney.[24]

The controversy between the orthodox critics, who demanded a summons to revolt in all plays, and the united front critics, who were satisfied with merely "progressive" sentiments, erupted late in 1934 and thus coincided with the opening of *Gold Eagle Guy*. The Communist press was consequently divided on the merits of the play. One reviewer of the old guard, Leon Alexander, complained that Levy had eliminated the role of the exploited proletariat and all the other robber barons from his "romantic" script. According to this critic, a play that did not resolve the class struggle by revolution was hardly useful to the Party. He explained that his review was harsh because the Group had strayed from its "serious esthetic and social purposes." [25]

A popular front critic, Stanley Burnshaw, while admitting the same defects, declared that the exposé of the giant capitalist made the drama revolutionary enough.[26] The Marxian spectator could have supplied the Communist cure for Levy's evil capitalists, but the nonpartisan viewer undoubtedly felt that the drama's conflict was between Button and God, not between Button and the proletariat. The Group was still more concerned with individual psychology and morality than with class war. *Gold Eagle Guy* ran for 65 performances.

On February 19, 1935, the Group moved slightly leftward when it presented *Awake and Sing*, Clifford Odets' drama about the Bergers, a bickering Jewish family, consisting of a shrewd mother, a submissive father, a rich uncle, a Marxian grandfather, and two discontented children. The daughter deserts her illegitimate baby and her unloved husband to run away with the family's boarder; the son, Ralph, unable to marry his girl because of the Depression, is inspired by his grandfather's suicide to work for a better world. Just as Ralph's eyes are opened at the end of the play, so Odets hoped that the other Bergers and the rest of the downtrodden masses would awake from their dust and sing, as Isaiah had advised many centuries before.

Although Odets was a Party member at the time of this production, he did not specify Ralph's course of action, except to say that he would read his grandfather's books and agitate with his co-workers to get steam heat in the warehouse at which he works. Ralph idealistically hopes to change the world so that "life won't be printed on dollar bills." [27] Although the grandfather urges Ralph to act, not talk, and predicts that "in this boy's life a Red Sea will happen again," [28] Ralph does not join the Party to hasten the Red revolution. The playwright had the grandfather express Marxist sentiments throughout the drama, but Odets was more intent on creating a group of vivid characters and on depicting the comic and pathetic episodes in their lives than on propagandizing the revolution.

Since *Waiting for Lefty*, although written after *Awake and Sing*, had been presented by the New Theatre League a month earlier, Odets was already famous when the Bergers first appeared on the stage. Notwithstanding his fame and his Party membership, the Marxist press did not hesitate to criticize *Awake and Sing*. One critic, Nathaniel Buchwald, said that, despite "its sincerity and social implications," it was not a good Marxist drama because the characters were not revolutionary enough; the grandfather just read books and Ralph was too busy with his love affair for most of the drama. This reviewer blamed the play's shortcomings on the fact that *Awake and Sing* had been written two years before *Waiting for Lefty*.[29]

Another critic, Michael Blankfort, while urging his readers to see the play simply because it had been written by Odets, noted several ideological and dramatic flaws. Ralph's conversion, this critic complained, was the result of mysticism rather than Marxism, and the dialogue and characters were so unrealistic that the serious message was lost; the audience seemed more interested in the gag lines than in the propaganda.[30]

Contradicting Blankfort, Abner Biberman, a member of the Group's acting company, asserted that "the audience knew what it would take to make the Bergers really sing."[31] Blankfort held his ground, however, and said that the proletarian playwright's intentions were inconsequential unless his drama succeeded in stimulating the audience "to revolution or leftward-moving thought"; this agitation did not "have to be verbalized," but it did have to be clear. *Awake and Sing*, the reviewer reiterated, was not clear.[32] This drama, a hit despite the reservations of the Marxist press, was shown 209 times.

The Group moved closer to communism on March 26, 1935, with the official production of *Waiting for Lefty*, which was paired with *Till the Day I Die*, another short drama by Odets. Based on a letter from Germany that had appeared in *New Masses*, the latter play tells the story of a Communist agitator who is ostracized by the Party because he appears to have become an informer for the Nazis. Protesting his innocence, the tortured man explains that the

Nazis have deliberately tricked the Communists into this belief, and he begs his comrades—his brother and his sweetheart—to kill him before he really does turn informer. When they refuse, he shoots himself. Odets was not only glorifying the German Communists for their heroism but also attacking the Nazis for their brutality and sexual perversions.

The Marxist press agreed that Odets' latest play was inferior to *Waiting for Lefty*. One critic, Ralph Wittenberg, saw the portraits of ridiculous Nazis as products of wishful thought.[33] Another reviewer, Stanley Burnshaw, while complaining of the play's superficiality, liked the theme of class betrayal, even though he felt that the Broadway audience could not grasp the horror of this situation.[34] Odets' treatment of the stool pigeon theme was much more doctrinaire than that of Maltz in *Black Pit*, which Theatre Union was presenting at the same time.

With this double bill—*Waiting for Lefty* and *Till the Day I Die*—the Group surpassed Theatre Union as the most revolutionary professional theatre in New York.

After the Group's unofficial production of *Waiting for Lefty* under the auspices of the New Theatre League the preceding January, the editors of *New Theatre* had knowingly declared:

The Group is emerging from its period of groping artistic introspection. The results of four years' collective work in a sound theatrical method are here applied to express their continually maturing revolutionary convictions.[35]

When the Group officially presented its double bill in March, the *Daily Worker*'s reviewer, Leon Alexander, asserted that the audience "cheered the definite leftward step of the Group Theatre in the direction of genuine, revolutionary theatre."[36] The Communists undoubtedly thought that the Group, thus seemingly converted, would go on to bigger and better Marxist plays. The double bill was shown

136 times, and after the summer *Waiting for Lefty* was paired with *Awake and Sing* for an additional 24 performances.

The Communists liked to think that their cell within the Group and their agitation without were wholly responsible for the Marxist trend exhibited in the productions of the three Odets dramas. Such might have been the case if the three plays had no value beyond Party propaganda, but two of them at least—*Awake and Sing* and *Waiting for Lefty*—were first-rate dramas in 1935, and they still retain their wonderful balance of pathos and humor. The directors of the Group would have been fools to overlook Odets' genius just because he wrote plays with Marxist sentiments. The Group produced his plays because they were good, not because the Party demanded their production.

The Group's next presentation was not even socially significant. On November 30, 1935, the company began its fifth season with *Weep for the Virgins* by Nellise Child. The play, which concerns the frustration of a mother's plans for the material success of her daughters, deals with individual rather than social problems. Writing in the *Daily Worker*, Michael Blankfort did not like the script,[37] and Michael Gold denounced the author because, he asserted, she said that the Communists looked down on the workers.[38] *Weep for the Virgins* closed after nine showings.

The Group returned to the drama of social significance with *Paradise Lost* by Clifford Odets on December 9, 1935, but the play was ideologically fuzzy compared to *Waiting for Lefty*. The plot recounts the downfall of the Gordon family—a middle-class counterpart of the proletarian Bergers —after Mr. Gordon's partner has ruined their business by embezzlement. Despite the eviction from their home, the death of one son while participating in a robbery, and the fatal disease afflicting another son, the father suddenly realizes that, although they have lost their bourgeois paradise, they can work for a more beautiful world when men will enjoy the earth without fear of hatred or failure.

Like Ralph Berger, Leo Gordon wants a life that is not "printed on dollar bills," but he is even more vague about how to achieve it. According to his final speech, he plans to "fight" with the other men who have gained "understanding," but he does not identify either his allies or the enemy. The Marxist spectators who had seen *Waiting for Lefty* could guess that Leo Gordon would side with the Party-led proletariat in a revolution against his own class, but the text of *Paradise Lost* is not that specific. The play has no Communist *raisonneur.*

Although Leo Gordon's sudden hope makes dramatic sense, not as a political conversion but as a bit of desperate optimism voiced by a defeated man, the Group performed the script as a political allegory about the decay of the middle class.[39] Harold Clurman, the director, said that he gave the performance "a definite *line* or . . . propagandist slant";[40] for example, he interpreted the dying son who likes to play the stock market as the symbol of "an apparently normal capitalism that is dying without knowing it."[41] As a Marxian allegory, however, *Paradise Lost* is ridiculous because the downfall of the Gordons is caused by the human failings of embezzlement and disease, not by the economic failure of capitalism. Odets showed greater skill in drawing troubled human beings than in creating political symbols.

The *Daily Worker's* critic, Michael Blankfort, understanding the allegorical intention, noted that the characters were too special to be symbolic of an entire class, but he enjoyed the drama anyway.[42] Two months later the Party condemned *Paradise Lost* much more vigorously for its ideological failure; a great writer like Odets, said one of the later critics, Jay Gerlando, could do better.[43] The Party was plainly confused about this playwright. Although *Paradise Lost* was not clearly a Communist play, Odets had apparently intended to write a Marxian allegory; and, although he had recently resigned from the Party, he remained a sympathetic leftist. The Party, the playwright guessed, did not want to antagonize him, and yet wanted to warn its members of his ideological errors.[44] The play had an engagement of 73 performances.

Opening on March 13, 1936, the Group's next production, *The Case of Clyde Griffiths*, which Erwin Piscator and Lena Goldschmidt had adapted from Dreiser's *An American Tragedy*,[45] offered a Marxian thesis with deadly clarity, but not because the Party demanded such a presentation. The play had been discovered by Milton Shubert, whose family of "monopolistic" producers and theatre owners hardly met with Communist approval. Harold Clurman disliked the "schematic" arrangement of the thesis but liked the potentially novel theatricalism of the script, and Lee Strasberg thought the boy-meets-girl theme had popular appeal.[46] Such was the Party's influence on the selection of this drama.

The plot concerns Clyde Griffiths, a poor proletarian, who seduces a working girl and then drowns her so that he can marry the rich Sondra Finchley. He is tried and executed for the murder. Interspersed with the scenes that present this story are many commentaries offered by a Speaker who relates the action to the class struggle. According to this chorus, Clyde's greatest crime is the betrayal of his class; he should have worked for the emancipation of the proletariat, not for his personal gain.

Although the left-wing critics were divided on the over-all merit of this experimental production, which alternated realistic scenes with stylized episodes, these reviewers criticized the use of the Speaker, whose obvious explanations, they felt, interfered with the action and emotion of the story. John Gassner, one critic who liked the production, noted, however, that the oversimplified interpretation of society, like that in Brecht's *Mother,* would neither enlighten the Marxist audience nor convert the nonpartisan spectators.[47]

Another reviewer, John Mullen, attacked the experimental nature of the production:

. . . the less "Piscator" and other attempts on the part of the Group Theatre and Theatre Union to employ ultra-arty forms—the better. One of the reasons that thousands flocked to see *Stevedore* was because it told a simple straightforward story. . . .[48]

The Party, as indicated by the attacks on *Mother* and the praise for *Stevedore,* favored plays of Socialist realism to the "dated" experimental works that Brecht and Piscator had produced in pre-Hitler Germany. *The Case of Clyde Griffiths* was withdrawn after 19 performances because of the objections of the "bourgeois" critics, not those of the Marxist press.

The Party's agitation for control of the Group Theatre continued during the summer of 1936. Disturbed by the recent denials of Harold Clurman and Cheryl Crawford that their company had become a propaganda theatre simply because they had produced *Waiting for Lefty,*[49] a writer for *New Theatre,* Norman Stevens, asserted that the Group *was* a propaganda theatre and outlined its tasks. Declaring that this organization should not restrict itself to "plays which directly picture the working class struggle" and which end with a "call to action," he advised the Group to concentrate on dramas about the bourgeoisie:

It is possible that the richest art of our time may be developed out of the conflicts of middle-class life—the attempt of the middle class to free themselves from the fears and phobias of the past and to take their place with the workers in the struggle for a better world.

Thus, this writer really wanted plays summoning the bourgeoisie to the Communist side—dramas like *Paradise Lost,* but with more realistic conversions and greater political clarity. If the Group was to fulfill its task, he continued, the members would have to study Marxism and the company would have to be reorganized as "a really democratic collective"; that is, the socially conscious Actors' Committee would have to share control with the three directors. Furthermore, the Group would have to abandon its "dependence on motion picture or other capital" and seek financial support from the audience.[50] Norman Stevens conveniently forgot that the audience was not actually supporting Theatre Union. The Party thus clearly pointed the path to a middle-class Theatre Union, but the Group went its own "confused" way.

This political "confusion" was evident in the company's only production during the sixth season. On November 19, 1936, *Johnny Johnson,* a play by Paul Green with music by Kurt Weill, began an engagement of 68 performances. This musical fantasy tells the story of Johnny Johnson, an idealistic American private, who tries to stop the First World War because he believes that the men of both sides want peace. Having pacified the Allied military and civilian commanders with laughing gas, he obtains an order to stop the fighting, but the generals recover in time to countermand the cease fire. Arrested and returned to the United States, Johnny is committed to an insane asylum. Released after ten years, he becomes a street vendor of toys.

Paul Green was attacking war not only by satire on the Allied generals, who try to surpass each other in the numbers of casualties, but by such ironies as the declaration of war just as the monument to peace is being unveiled, the use of a statue of Jesus as a sniper's hiding place, the ratification of the "League of World Republics" by a group of lunatics, and the desire of an innocent little boy to buy a toy soldier from Johnny. Although Green illustrated the terrible gap between man's irrational nature and his rational ideals, the dramatist did not despair. Johnny does not make toy soldiers, and he does not join the parade celebrating preparedness for the next war. Although Green was depicting the seemingly hopeless quest for peace, he ended his story with a bit of hope, for Johnny retains his idealism despite his unhappy experiences in the real world.

Because Green blamed war on human nature rather than on the capitalistic system, his script disappointed the Marxist press. Calling the playwright "an idealist without a plan," one critic, Charles E. Dexter, said that Johnny should have been shown uniting with his anti-war comrades in a proletarian rebellion against the economic causes of conflict.[51] Even *Idiot's Delight*, said another reviewer, John Gassner, contained a more vigorous protest against the causes of war.[52] Despite these reservations about the theme and some complaints about the poor singing voices of the actors, these critics liked the imaginative staging and Weill's delightfully ironic music. The Group's intention of combining theatrical entertainment with a play of ideas was largely successful,[53] but the ideas were more pacifist than Marxist.

Once again the Communists began to agitate for an end to the Group's ideological "confusion" by urging that the Actors' Committee, which was controlled by the Party, be given authority in deciding Group policy.[54] This authority was being exercised exclusively by the three non-Communist directors. Although Lee Strasberg and Cheryl Crawford resigned from the company in 1937, Harold Clurman remained firmly in control,[55] and the Group did not become a "democratic collective."

On November 4, 1937, the company began its seventh season with the presentation of *Golden Boy*, in which Clifford Odets reduced the socially significant content to a minimum. This drama tells the story of Joe Bonaparte, a young violinist, who abandons his music to seek wealth and glory as a prizefighter. Nearing the apex of his career, he unintentionally kills an opponent in the ring. This mishap makes him realize that he has lost his soul in the pursuit of material wealth. Unwilling to remain a fighter and unable to return to the violin because boxing has ruined his hands, he speeds away in his car to forget his troubles—and dies in an accident.

The conflict between art and materialism—a problem that may have bothered Odets since the time of *Paradise Lost*, when he moved to Hollywood—is treated on a personal rather than a social level. Since Odets was more concerned with his characters as human beings than as symbolic products of the American social and economic system, he kept society well in the background. Although he threw a sop to the left in the minor character of Joe's brother, who, as an organizer for the CIO, fights for a nobler cause than private profit, Odets did not develop this theme. He was more interested in the moral disintegration of Joe's soul than in the success of the CIO. Ideologically, the Group had returned to the level of Lawson's *Success Story*.

The *Daily Worker's* critic, Charles E. Dexter, while admitting the excellence of Odets' dramatic technique, complained that the theme of "culture vs. commerce" was too vague because the dramatist had failed to suggest a political solution to the conflict. Since the playwright's fame stemmed from his "socially useful" *Waiting for Lefty*, this reviewer warned him not to abandon the proletarian audience.[56] Odets, always a better playwright than a propagandist, virtually abandoned the latter role in *Golden Boy*. This drama enjoyed a very successful engagement of 250 performances.

While Odets did not write a "socially useful" play, Frances Farmer and Phoebe Brand, the ladies of the cast, offered their own bit of propaganda for the united front. "The stage," said Miss Farmer, "is so often an influence on women's fashions that I am very glad . . . to make a visible example . . . about the necessity of boycotting all Japanese goods by wearing lisle stockings, instead of silk in my part in *Golden Boy*." Miss Brand added her sentiments: "The feel of lisle will become a pleasure in itself, knowing as I will that it means an economic pressure against Japan which that Fascist and murderous government is sure to feel very strongly." [57] It is difficult to imagine a more subtle example of theatrical propaganda.

The Group next produced two plays void of social significance. On February 19, 1938, *Casey Jones* by Robert Ardrey opened for a short run, but this play about the plight of a proud railroad engineer who is going blind deals with individual, not social problems.

On November 24, 1938, the company presented *Rocket to the Moon*, Clifford Odets' drama about the summer romance of a meek, married dentist. Having pushed social and economic ideas far into the background of *Golden Boy*, the playwright virtually eliminated such ideas from *Rocket to the Moon*. His characters are unhappy, but their neuroses are no longer attributed directly or indirectly to the economic system; their problems stem rather from their psyches, from their family backgrounds, or from the "nervous" times in which they live. Although admitting Odets' dramatic genius, the *Daily Worker's* reviewer, John Cambridge, accused this playwright of having deliberately suppressed the idea that the "social system" caused all the discontent.[58] *Rocket to the Moon*, Odets' deepest and best psychological study, was shown 131 times.

On January 5, 1939, the Group presented *The Gentle People* by Irwin Shaw for an engagement of 141 performances. Subtitled "A Brooklyn Fable," this play deals with Jonah and Philip, two elderly men, whose peaceful hobby of fishing near Coney Island is disturbed by Goff, a petty extortionist, who demands a weekly tribute for the "protection" of their boat. Fleeced of their life savings and beaten, the two victims, after failing to get justice in court, murder Goff and succeed in avoiding punishment. In this fable Irwin Shaw pointed the moral that gentle people must fight back when they are attacked by violent men. Since the playwright compared Goff to Hitler and Mussolini, the play became an anti-Fascist allegory; appeasement, Shaw implied, was not the way to fight Hitler.

Since Stalin and his comrades had not yet made friends with Hitler, the reviewers for the Marxist press agreed with the playwright, but they differed in their understanding of the method he was proposing. The critic for the *Daily Worker*, John Cambridge, clearly heard a summons for the German people to get rid of Hitler by the approved Communist method of revolution.[59] The reviewer for *New Masses*, H. M., on the other hand, complained that the drama presented an individual problem on an individual level. If there were an allegory, he warned, "the solution of individual direct action would have been definitely harmful." [60] The Party permitted only collective action and only under its own leadership.

Having completed the 1938–39 season with a revival of *Awake and Sing* and a production of William Saroyan's eccentric play, *My Heart's in the Highlands*, the Group began its ninth season on November 14, 1939, with *Thunder Rock*, a philosophical fantasy by Robert Ardrey. The leading character is a young, disillusioned reporter, who retreated to an ivory tower—a lighthouse on an island in Lake Michigan. After conversing with the ghosts of some people who had tried to escape the problems of their lives and times, he regains faith in himself, in mankind, and in the ultimate triumph of a benevolent destiny. Thus restored, but with no illusions that the problems can be solved easily or quickly since the Second World War has just begun, he returns to his newspaper work.

Although Ardrey's guess that a thousand years might be needed to solve all the problems of civilization was hardly a reflection of the Party line, the reviewers for the Marxist press—N. C. and Alvah Bessie—praised the play for its general optimism and for its preachment against ivory towers.[61] Furthermore, the vaguely expressed hope that America would stay out of the war was soothing to the Communists in their isolationist phase, even though the playwright inserted this hope incidentally at the end of the play.[62] *Thunder Rock* closed after 23 performances.

On February 22, 1940, the Group offered *Night Music,* a light philosophical play by Clifford Odets about the romance of Steve Takis, a brash but easily discouraged young man, and Fay Tucker, a young, aspiring actress. With the aid of Detective Rosenberger, a guardian angel, the couple gain courage to fight for their future and to enjoy the struggle despite Steve's unemployment. Steve discovers that his troubles are caused by his own lethargy and futile, destructive anger, not by capitalism or democracy; there is rather the implication that he can solve his problems because he lives in a free society. Although Odets emphasized the personal trials of the pair in this gently comic play, he was also reminding the discontented young people of America that they had the God-given ability and the power to make a happier society.

Odets thus returned to social drama, but his theme was too mild and his method was too indirect for the Party press. The critic for *New Masses,* Alvah Bessie, hinted that Odets' failure to arouse the audience to revolution was caused by the money of Hollywood. This critic, asserting that the Group was still the best hope of the American stage short of a people's theatre, urged the organization to "get down to work." [63]

But the company did not take his advice. On December 17, 1940, the Group started its tenth and final season with the presentation of Irwin Shaw's *Retreat to Pleasure*—a play about the pursuit of a young woman by several men. She accepts the proposal of a young leftist, but he, changing his mind, decides to pursue pleasure. Remembering Irwin Shaw's radical *Bury the Dead*, Alvah Bessie declared in *New Masses* that the defeatist thesis of the new play—youth should have fun before war strikes—represented the retreat of the playwright and "many another quondam leftwinger who has been unable to stand up under the pressure of present events." [64] This reviewer did not mention the fact that some of the pressure on these erstwhile leftists had been applied by the Communists, who attempted to dictate to writers, and by the recent, wild fluctuations of the Party line. The *Daily Worker's* critic, Ralph Warner, asserted that Harold Clurman had led what was "left of the Group forces down the well-worn path of retreat. . . ." [65]

When *Retreat to Pleasure* closed after 23 performances, the Group Theatre expired with it. The temperamental outbursts of members and the shortages of money and scripts plagued the organization to the end. [66]

As a social theatre of the thirties, the Group took its place between those organizations like Theatre Union, which offered nothing but socially meaningful plays, and those like Federal Theatre and the Theatre Guild, which presented social drama as a small part of their broader repertories. Of the 23 productions offered by the Group from 1931 through 1940, 13 dealt primarily with social, political, and economic problems. All the company's plays—even the social ones—dramatized individual moral questions. The Group thus remained true to its announced policy of offering scripts that dealt with both the social and the moral issues of the nineteen-thirties. Amid the social upheaval of the Depression, the Group did not forget the individual and his problems.

Of the 13 social plays, only four—*Awake and Sing, Waiting for Lefty, Till the Day I Die,* and *The Case of Clyde Griffiths*—were as clearly Marxist as the productions of Theatre Union, and of these four only one—*Waiting for Lefty*—was regarded as both an ideological and a dramatic triumph by the Party. But even with this play the Party found some fault. Although the Communists plotted to convert the Group into an agency for their propaganda, they did not succeed; four productions out of 23 hardly matched the Marxist record of Theatre Union. Besides, the Group produced these four plays because the directorate regarded them as good scripts; that is, they reflected the intellectual climate of the decade, and they all had exciting theatrical possibilities. The directors did not present these Marxist plays because the Party regarded them as effective propaganda for the revolution.

The Communists were not wholly satisfied by any of the company's social productions, not even *Waiting for Lefty*. The non-Marxist plays, like *Johnny Johnson*, displeased the Party because they were not revolutionary. Dramas that had implicit themes of class struggle, like *Gold Eagle Guy*, were rejected by the Party because they were not explicit enough. Even the openly Marxian dramas, like *Awake and Sing* and *The Case of Clyde Griffiths*, were not welcomed by the Party because they did not depict the triumphant working class necessary for Socialist realism, the pet Marxian dramatic genre. The Communists were hard to please, and the Group rarely satisfied them with its social dramas.

The Party's attempt to control the Group was doomed to fail because of the unpredictable temperaments of the actors and directors. Nearly all were nonconformists and as such were totally unsuited for the Party's political activities because the Party demanded conformity. The Group was a collective, but primarily onstage—not off; the Communists did not understand that an artistic collective was not necessarily a political one. The Group could agree on the interpretation of a particular play, but the ever-bickering membership could agree on little else. The politically disciplined Communists in the company could set forth their Party's rigid line, but their theatrically disciplined brothers could not conform because their temperaments were too individualistic.

The Group's emphasis on the individual psyche of both the actor and the character destroyed the Communists' hope of turning the company into a skillful revolutionary theatre. Because of the stress on psychology in the rehearsal methods used by the company, the performances of the social plays emphasized the personalities of the characters rather than the social issues, much to the displeasure of the Communists, who were anti-individualistic. John Howard Lawson complained about the Group's "inwardness" and "psychology." [67] More often than not, as in *Rocket to the Moon,* the Group studied the psyches of people without even considering their social, economic, or political plight. The Group was, after all, a theatre, not a spokesman for the Communist Party.

Chapter 10

Social Plays on Broadway

BESIDES the socially significant dramas presented on Broadway by the Theatre Guild, the Playwrights' Company, and the Group Theatre, there were many social plays offered by individual Broadway producers and by short-lived producing companies. Some of these managers presented only one socially significant production during the decade; a few —like Herman Shumlin, Sam Harris, and Elmer Rice—offered several plays on social themes. Although the total number of these independent productions was large, no individual manager matched the number of social dramas produced by such major theatre companies as the Guild.

The Communists understood that the commercial producers could not make money by mounting Marxist dramas because the bourgeois theatregoers would not want to see them. And yet, each season of the decade, the Party urged the production of revolutionary plays and criticized the social plays of Broadway for deviations from the Party line. The Broadway producers largely ignored the advice offered by the Communist press. More interested in the theatre as a business than in the drama as a weapon, they produced those social plays that offered hope of financial success.

During the 1929–30 season there were two plays of social significance on Broadway, both revivals of foreign plays.

182

The first was William L. Laurence's *At the Bottom,* an English adaptation of Maxim Gorki's *The Lower Depths,* which opened on January 9, 1930, under the auspices of the Leo Bulgakov Theatre Associates and played 72 performances. This drama, descriptive of life among the very poor in Czarist Russia, was ignored by the Party press despite Gorki's renown as a revolutionary writer.

The second revival was Aristophanes' *Lysistrata,* translated by Gilbert Seldes and produced in New York by the Philadelphia Theatre Association on June 5, 1930. This production was welcomed by the *Daily Worker's* critic, for, in blaming war on the desire for profits, Aristophanes had anticipated the Party line. Asserting that this ancient Greek poet had "on one or two occasions barely escaped the hired gunmen" of the "overfed and grafting parasites" of his time, the anonymous reviewer thus granted Aristophanes the posthumous honor of having been a revolutionary as well as a revolutionary writer.[1] *Lysistrata* was shown 252 times because of its hilarious emphasis on the sexual—not Marxian—method of stopping war.

The 1930–31 Broadway season saw three social dramas, all by American writers. Bela Blau presented William Bolitho's *Overture,* an anti-totalitarian drama about a German revolution, for 41 performances. Sidney Harmon offered *Precedent,* I. J. Golden's dramatization of the case of Tom Mooney, a labor organizer who was convicted of murder in a California bombing incident in 1916.[2] The play was shown 184 times.

The third, and most interesting, of these plays was DuBose Heyward's *Brass Ankle,* which opened a run of 44 performances on April 23, 1931, under the auspices of James W. Elliott. This drama was typical of the many Depression plays depicting the relations of Negroes and whites because it merely set forth the problem without advocating a solution. It tells the story of a Southern woman who discovers, on the birth of a dark son, that she has mulatto blood. Her husband, an advocate of white supremacy, kills her and the baby. Like Dion Boucicault, whose drama *The Octoroon* had been produced in 1856, DuBose Heyward merely pointed out the tragedy of the situation. The Communists, who blamed all social problems on capitalist oppression, were not interested in simple racial tensions.

During the 1931–32 season, there were five social plays. Broadway producers were apparently beginning to feel that the social theatre might be commercial. Lawrence Langner's New York Repertory Company offered a revival of Dion Boucicault's 1857 melodrama, *The Streets of New York,* which advocated alms as the solution for poverty. The play was shown 87 times. The season also saw a brief run of Barrett H. Clark's translation of Romain Rolland's *Wolves,* a play about the French Revolution. Produced by Maurice Schwartz, this drama pointed the moral that power corrupts revolutionary leaders.

The other three productions of the season were new works written by Americans. One was about labor unrest and the other two reflected the political scene. On November 17, 1931, Richard Geist presented John Wexley's *Steel,* a tale of sex and murder set against the novel background of a strike.[3] The *Daily Worker* did not review the production but ran an advertisement that described *Steel* as a "new play of REVOLT" and offered readers two tickets for the price of one.[4] Since so few of the faithful accepted the offer, the play closed after 12 performances.

It was followed by a work of political significance. *Of Thee I Sing,* a musical comedy by George S. Kaufman and Morrie Ryskind with lyrics by Ira Gershwin and music by George Gershwin, was the first American social play to become a smash hit during the Depression decade. Presented by Sam Harris on December 26, 1931, the show enjoyed an engagement of 473 performances and won the Pulitzer Prize. The plot concerns John P. Wintergreen, who is elected President of the United States on the platform of love. But he is threatened with impeachment because he has married the girl he loves and not the winner of a "Miss White House" beauty contest. The nation, however, forgives him when his wife gives birth to twins. Through this absurd plot the writers gaily satirized such political institutions as the nominating convention, the election campaign, the Vice-Presidency, and the houses of Congress. The authors and the spectators enjoyed a good laugh at American political life.

The reviewer for *Workers' Theatre,* Alfred Saxe, declared that the musical was propaganda advocating the sin of indifference to politics, but he suggested that the script could be adapted for revolutionary use by substituting Marxian mass chants for the dancing interludes between the scenes, thus making the satire "constructive." [5] Unfortunately for the Party, Kaufman, Ryskind, and the Gershwins were summoning the audience to satiric laughter, not to a "constructive" revolution. They demonstrated early in the decade that humor and music could blend perfectly with social content. *Of Thee I Sing* thus prepared the way for such socially significant shows as *Pins and Needles.*

The 1931–32 season closed with another political play, *Merry-Go-Round,* the first collaboration by Albert Maltz and George Sklar, who later wrote for Theatre Union. This drama, produced by Michael Blankfort and Walter Hart on April 22, 1932, ran for 48 performances. It exposes some policemen who protect a politically influential killer by forcing an innocent man to confess to the murder.[6]

Writing in *Workers' Theatre,* Alfred Saxe asserted that the capitalistic audience preferred its pleasant illusions to the playwrights' unpleasant realities. He illustrated his point by describing the "fat, bejeweled triple-chinned mama of the upper middle class," who sat near him. During a tense scene, she said that she couldn't stand the play and "waddled to her bridge and small prattle." [7] Play reviews were indeed vivid in *Workers' Theatre.*

The 1932–33 season saw a similar variety of social plays. Joseph K. Bickerton produced *Men Must Fight* by Reginald Lawrence and S. K. Lauren, a war play with the pessimistic —but accurate—thesis that men would fight in the next war. William J. O'Neill's Players' Theatre offered *They All Come to Moscow* by Ruth Kennell and John Washburne, an American play mildly satiric of life in Soviet Russia. The Players' Club presented *Uncle Tom's Cabin*, A. E. Thomas' version of the famous novel. These three plays were financial failures.

The other three social dramas of that season were more important because of their better-known authors: Sam and Bella Spewack, Elmer Rice, and Bertolt Brecht. The first of these three plays was the Spewacks' *Clear All Wires*, which Herman Shumlin presented on September 14, 1932, for a run of 93 showings. Shumlin was to become the leading Broadway producer of social drama during the decade.[8]

Clear All Wires recounts the difficulties created by an American correspondent in Moscow when he attempts to have a Russian prince assassinated in order to file a sensational story and thus regain favor with his publisher. Implicit in the farcical plot are two political themes connected with the Moscow setting. The first expresses the moderate idea that the American newspapers sometimes told lies about Russia. The reviewer for the *Daily Worker*, V. S., asserting that the Spewacks' reporter was typical of the "degenerate" bourgeois correspondents, wanted stronger satire on all the foreign reporters in the Soviet Union.[9] The sec-. ond theme, a good-natured satire on the new Soviet society, with its censors and secret police, was too strong for the

American Marxists, who believed that the millennium had arrived in Russia.

The Communists were even less happy over *We the People* by Elmer Rice, which he presented on January 21, 1933. In this drama about the decline of an American proletarian family, the father loses his job when the Depression starts, his savings when the bank fails, his home when the mortgage is foreclosed, and his health when he is wounded leading a parade of the unemployed. His son, forced to quit college, imprisoned for stealing coal, and falsely accused of murder while speaking at a street rally, is sentenced to death. The play ends with a mass meeting at which various speakers protest the frame-up of the young man and urge the audience to re-establish the ideals of the founding fathers—the rights to justice, life, liberty, and the pursuit of happiness.

Since the welfare of all Americans was not being promoted and since civil liberties were being curtailed, the liberal Elmer Rice urged strong reform. Unlike Albert Maltz and George Sklar, who were soon to present a similar "legal lynching" in *Peace on Earth* at Theatre Union, Rice did not suggest the revolutionary way out of the crisis.

The Marxists were angry because Rice was so near to their official position in denouncing the Depression, and yet so far from it in his liberal solution. The dramatist, said the *Daily Worker's* critic, A. J., was a "sensitive if muddled man trying to find his way out of the darkness of capitalism without the use of the compass of Marxism," [10] and another reviewer, Sender Garlin, asserted that the playwright's "fatal flaw" was his insistence on being a mere liberal.[11]

To the Communists, Elmer Rice was more than a "confused" man; he was potentially dangerous because he was stealing some of the social issues that the Party hoped to parlay into political power. Unfortunately, his attempt to cover most of the social, political, and economic questions of the thirties led to an extremely rambling and contrived drama that closed after 49 showings.

Although Bertolt Brecht was a Marxist, and not a mere liberal, his *Threepenny Opera*, as produced by Gifford Cochran and John Krimsky, displeased the American comrades. Opening on April 13, 1933, in an adaptation by Cochran and Krimsky, this 1928 show with music by Kurt Weill was based on John Gay's *The Beggar's Opera*. It retells the story of Captain Macheath, his marriage to Polly Peachum, his subsequent arrests, and his eventual pardon. In his notes on the production, Brecht carefully pointed out that Macheath and his gang were to be represented as "steady, sedate" members of the bourgeoisie, not as the conventional, lower-class robbers.[12]

True to the didactic aim of his "epic theatre," Brecht thus demonstrated his thesis that the parasitic bourgeois society survived on crime and exploitation. The Communist spectator would believe that something could be done to cure this trouble, but Brecht ironically summoned his audience merely to

> Remember all the darkness and the coldness
> The world's a vale of misery and woe.[13]

Unlike the obviously revolutionary *Mother*, which Theatre Union was to present with deadly seriousness late in 1935, the similarly experimental *Threepenny Opera* indicts capitalistic society with subtlety, irony, and humor. The anonymous reviewer for the *Daily Worker*, missing the point of Brecht's irony, objected to the outright slander on the unemployed and to the indirection with which the dramatist had hidden his proletarian point of view. This critic complained further that the script was pervaded by an un-Marxist "Greenwich Village raillery and pessimism."[14] *The Threepenny Opera*, too experimental for Broadway, closed after 12 showings.

There were eight plays of social significance during the 1933–34 season—an increase over the preceding years. Most of the productions were both artistically and financially unsuccessful. A. J. Allen presented *Legal Murder*, Dennis Donogue's dramatization of the Scottsboro case. This play was overshadowed by John Wexley's version of the case, *They Shall Not Die*, which the Theatre Guild opened less than a week later. Crosby Gaige offered *Ragged Army*, an inept drama by Beulah Dix and Bertram Millhauser, about the reconciliation of a millowner and his striking employees. Richard Aldrich and Alfred de Liagre produced *The Pure in Heart*, in which John Howard Lawson—as yet unconverted to Marxism—preached against material riches.

This season saw three more important failures—the first anti-Nazi productions of the decade. Adolf Hitler came to power on January 30, 1933, and the first American play about Nazi Germany opened on Broadway the following September, when J. J. Vincent presented *Kultur*. This play by Adolph Philip concerns the fanciful abolition of the Chancellor's anti-Semitic program after his life is saved by the skill of a part-Jewish surgeon and a transfusion of Jewish blood.[15] The *Daily Worker's* critic, Harold Edgar, denounced the playwright for having ignored the political and economic aspects of fascism.[16] *Kultur* departed after ten showings.

In November a second anti-Nazi drama appeared on Broadway when Irving Barrett and Robert Rossen presented *Birthright*, Richard Maibaum's work about the violent destruction of a German family after Hitler's rise to power.[17] The third anti-Nazi play, Leslie Reade's *The Shatter'd Lamp*, was presented the following spring by Hyman Adler. It tells the story of a German family tormented because the mother is a Jewess. She commits suicide, the son is expelled from the university and the Nazi Party, and the father is deprived of his professorship and shot.

Neither *Birthright* nor *The Shatter'd Lamp* illustrated the Communist line that Hitler was an agent of the capitalists and that he persecuted only the working class. Although the New York managers were always quick to seize upon a topical subject, and although Hitler had the added salable quality of being weird, they failed to score a hit with any of these first three plays.

During the same season the Broadway producers also showed interest in the native Fascists, but in a much more lighthearted way. On October 21, 1933, Sam Harris presented *Let 'Em Eat Cake* by the collaborators of *Of Thee I Sing:* George S. Kaufman, Morrie Ryskind, and George and Ira Gershwin. The plot again concerns John P. Wintergreen, who, having lost the Presidency in a second election, seizes the White House with the aid of his Blue Shirts and the American Army but is overthrown because he cannot pay his financial obligations. Saved from the guillotine by a revolt of the American women, who are sick of the color blue, he restores the Republic.

The playwrights were satirizing the idea of revolution and the threats made by the extremists of both the right and the left. Visible in the Union Square scene, for instance, are banners bearing such slogans as "Peace on Earth—Kill the Capitalists," "Physical Culture Is the Way Out," and "Down with Bimetalism—We Want the Single Standard." [18] Kruger, the man most closely resembling the Communists, has no program except his own advancement.

The Marxist press was, of course, unhappy about the show. One critic, Harold Edgar, protested that the playwrights were attempting to satirize revolution without understanding it and offered to send them explanatory literature.[19] Although displaying a hilarious sanity about governmental problems of the thirties, *Let 'Em Eat Cake* was unfortunately unable to match the steady brilliance of its predecessor, *Of Thee I Sing,* and so played a shorter engagement of 90 performances.

Broadway returned to a less elevated part of the American social scene on December 4, 1933, when Anthony Brown presented *Tobacco Road,* Jack Kirkland's dramatization of the Erskine Caldwell novel about the disintegration of the Lesters, a white family living on a barren Georgia farm. Although the characters behave subhumanly, they often attract sympathy as the backward victims of a changing world. The father's love for his ancestral land gives him a dignity that makes the spectator forget now and then what a lazy scoundrel he is. *Tobacco Road,* if acted in a straightforward manner, not as a burlesque, can be a moving drama.

Since the playwright neither blamed the capitalistic system for the plight of the Lester family nor suggested the revolutionary cure, the Marxist press called the play incomplete. One critic, Harold Edgar, felt that the scene in which the banker threatens eviction should have been developed into the central episode of the drama.[20] The reviewer for *New Masses,* William Gardener, saw the possibility of comparing the failure of the post-Civil War reconstruction of the South, implicit in the script, with the success of the post-Revolutionary reconstruction of the Soviet Union.[21] The dramatist, however, was more concerned with the degenerating family than with the oversimplified causes of their decline.

Tobacco Road, threatened with failure by the condemnation of the New York critics who called the play dirty, was turned into a hit by the Lebang Agency, which distributed cut-rate tickets.[22] Some spectators came to see the unromanticized picture of the South; others were attracted by the highly praised performances of Henry Hull, and later James Barton, as Jeeter Lester; but most of the audience came to peep at the erotic exhibition in the burlesqued production. In any case, *Tobacco Road* did not play 3,182 times (seven and a half years) to spectators concerned merely with the evils of capitalism or the virtues of the five-year plan of Soviet reconstruction.

The Communists saw a faint hope of penetrating the Broadway stage in three of the four social plays produced during the 1934–35 season. The one drama that offered no hope was the Margaret Hewes production of Paul Green's *Roll Sweet Chariot*, a depressing, un-Marxist account of the plight of poor Southern Negroes. This play closed after seven performances. Green's *Hymn to the Rising Sun* was not presented by the New Theatre League until the start of 1936.

When Elmer Rice moved slightly leftward in his next two socially significant dramas, and when the poet Archibald MacLeish wrote a play about the death of a capitalist, the Communists did not have accurate representations of the Party line, but they saw three productions that could—with a few key revisions—be used as propaganda.

Rice himself produced *Judgment Day* on September 12, 1934, at the Belasco Theatre, which he had leased as a showcase for his dramas of social protest. *Judgment Day*, vaguely based on the trial of Georgi Dimitroff by the Nazis, depicts the trial of George Khitov, a member of the "People's Party," who is accused of conspiring to assassinate the leader of a Fascist state in southeastern Europe. The trial ends when a liberal judge shoots the dictator. In this anti-Nazi melodrama freedom thus triumphs easily over tyranny. Although Rice called the opposition group the "People's Party," a name frequently associated with the Communists, he depicted this organization as liberal rather than Marxist; the "People" want to establish a free government, not a proletarian dictatorship.

Before the opening of *Judgment Day*, Joseph Freeman, who was a member of the Communist Party, had hopefully predicted that Elmer Rice would move from the liberalism of his earlier plays—like *We the People*—to Marxism.[23] The reviewers for the Communist press—Sender Garlin, George Willson, and Ben Blake—were unhappy with *Judgment Day,* however, because Rice did not take the correct Marxist positions. He failed to expose fascism as the last stage of decaying capitalism, and he promoted bourgeois democracy rather than a proletarian dictatorship.[24]

Had Rice produced *Judgment Day* during the united front period, a year or two later, the Communists would have been more receptive to his attacks on fascism. Rice would not then have been required to offer the entire Party line in his play. In 1934, however, only the anti-Fascists—like Art Smith and Elia Kazan, the authors of *Dimitroff*—received the Party's blessings. *Judgment Day* had 93 performances.

On October 25, 1934, Elmer Rice presented his drama *Between Two Worlds* as the second of the Belasco Theatre social series. This play, set aboard a ship sailing from New York to Europe, deals chiefly with the influence of a Soviet Russian film director on a wealthy young American couple. They decide to dedicate their lives to matters more serious than money.

The favorable portrait of the director led the reviewers for the Marxist press to praise Rice for the increased "clarity" of his social thought, but they felt that there was room for further social "enlightenment." The playwright, said Leon Alexander, still belonged to the "breed of *Nation* liberals who concede that Bolshevism may be a good thing for Russia." Although Rice exposed the capitalist system, he still failed to summon the masses to the revolution.[25] Another reviewer, Ben Blake, honoring Elmer Rice with the title of fellow traveler, urged him to continue his leftward journey. This critic was encouraged by the scene in which the Communist slaps a Russian princess.[26]

Because the "bourgeois" reviewers did not like the play,

Rice announced his retirement from the theatre even before the run of 32 performances was over.[27] The Marxists immediately began a campaign to enlist this famous playwright in their movement by promising him a large, receptive audience if he would compose Marxist dramas.[28] But Rice chose to remain a "confused" liberal. He did not return to Broadway until the Playwrights' Company produced *American Landscape* four years later.

Because Archibald MacLeish used the participants of the class struggle as characters in *Panic*, this drama had greater potential interest for the Communists than either Rice play had had. Presented on March 14, 1935, by a "Phoenix Theatre" for but two showings, this play deals with the banking panic of 1933 as it affects the stricken masses, a group of radicals led by a blind seer, and—chiefly—the country's most important banker. Warned by the radicals that fate and history are against him and stunned by the inability of his fellow bankers to help him stop the panic, this capitalist commits suicide.

The Marxists were delighted with MacLeish's "leftward turn" as evidenced by the publication of selections from the script in the March 1934 issue of *New Theatre* and by his participation in the recent Ohrbach strike. To counter Michael Gold's hasty assertion that MacLeish was unconsciously a Fascist, the *Daily Worker* published an interview in which the poet declared that he had written the play and helped in the strike in order to combat the injustices of society.[29]

MacLeish had not become a Communist, but he seemed sufficiently sympathetic to be cultivated. In a symposium that followed one of the performances of *Panic*, V. J. Jerome, the Party's literary czar, carefully explained the political errors of the drama. He informed MacLeish of Lenin's discovery that capitalists had to be killed because they did not commit suicide. Complaining also that the banker was falsely depicted as a noble character, Jerome said that the proletariat should have been the protagonist; furthermore, ignoring the literary tradition of blind seers, this critic was distressed with the blindness of the radical leader.[30] It seemed a shame that the prophet could not see the future, especially when it was so clearly on view in the Soviet Union. *Panic* was not revived. MacLeish apparently had turned as far leftward as he was going to turn.

Eight social plays were presented on Broadway during the 1935–36 season, which opened with Guthrie McClintic's production of *Winterset,* Maxwell Anderson's pompous verse drama about the aftermath of the Sacco-Vanzetti case. The play ran for 195 performances and won the New York Drama Critics' Circle Award, but it was more concerned with the eternal themes of life, love, death, and destiny than with the social issues of the case.

Arthur Hopkins' production of *Paths of Glory* followed with a very brief run. In this play Sidney Howard presented a brutally realistic picture of the unnecessary wartime slaughter caused by a psychopathic French general. Howard did not present the Marxian line on war. The Party, however, was satisfied with another war play later in the season, when Alex Yokel presented Irwin Shaw's *Bury the Dead* for a commercial run of 97 performances. This play had been discovered by the New Theatre League.

The 1935–36 season was more significant, however, for the productions of a recent comedy by a Soviet Russian dramatist, a play about the mulatto problem, a drama about the slums of New York, and some dramas that produced critical controversies.

Broadway had not seen a Soviet version of life in Russia since the Theatre Guild had offered *Red Rust* in 1929. On October 3, 1935, the Tri-Art Company offered Valentin Katayev's *Squaring the Circle,* as adapted by Dmitri Ostrov from the translation by Charles Malamuth and Eugene Lyons. The plot of this farce deals with the misalliance of two newly married couples who share the same room in Moscow. Their doubts about remedying the unhappy situation are resolved by an older Bolshevik, who advises them that an exchange of mates will not hurt the new society. Katayev was gently satirizing the Communist youth of 1928 for their excessive worry about having love conform to the Party line. The playwright also implied that there was room in the Soviet Union for people of varying temperaments and tastes—the Communist couple and the bourgeois pair. For American audiences there was the additional satire on the crowded housing conditions in the Soviet Union.

The production of this play, greeted on opening night by a mixture of cheers and boos, set off a controversy among critics of the left. Michael Gold asserted that the audience had not booed Katayev, but rather Malamuth and Lyons, the anti-Soviet translators, who had turned the play into counterrevolutionary propaganda.[81]

A few days later the critic for *New Masses*, Stanley Burnshaw, asserted that Ostrov, the director, was the real culprit. Burnshaw also reported that the production had been revised so that it seemed much less anti-Soviet. The chief trouble had been the ending; a child, symbolic of the future, who had been portrayed by an ugly midget on opening night, was replaced by a handsome boy. Furthermore, the offstage noises, symbolic of Socialist construction, which had been inaudible at the première, could be heard.

Even with these corrections the production still seemed anti-Soviet to Burnshaw because it emphasized the atypical Russian couples rather than the true Communists. Therefore, he concluded, Katayev should have given the American rights to a more "politically responsible group" that would have produced the comedy for the "limitless" audience of workers and fellow travelers, and not to Lyons,

Malamuth, and Ostrov.[32] Katayev, it would seem, had not shown sufficient loyalty to his own class, especially at a time when scripts for the few American Marxist theatres were so scarce. *Squaring the Circle* was shown 108 times.

It was followed on October 24, 1935, by Langston Hughes' *Mulatto,* which Martin Jones produced for an engagement of 373 performances. This play raised the problem of half-breeds in the South but did not offer a solution. It thus represented no social advance over *Brass Ankle,* but apparently solutions were not necessary for financial success in the social theatre.

The next important social play opened on October 28, 1935, when Norman Bel Geddes offered *Dead End* by Sidney Kingsley for a run of 687 showings. The plot deals with the death of one criminal, Baby-Face Martin, and the birth of another, Tommy MacGrath, a boy who is soon to be sent to reform school for having stabbed a man. Kingsley's story illustrated the thesis that the slums breed delinquents and the reform schools develop these "*Dead End* kids" into criminals. To intensify the squalor of the dead-end street near the river and the social injustice done to its inhabitants, the playwright added a neighboring luxury apartment house to his slum setting. Kingsley's solution to the interrelated problems of crime and slums, which he exposed so graphically and shockingly, was community housing, but this theme was implicit in the play. Kingsley seemed more interested in his realistic theatrical devices such as the real water in a tank between the audience and the stage.

Although the dramatist failed to suggest the revolutionary path to public housing, the Communists hailed the play with a burst of united front good will. Although the *Daily Worker's* critic, Michael Blankfort, hoped that Kingsley would someday preach revolution, this reviewer welcomed *Dead End* for its "sound revolutionary implication."[33] The play, added Stanley Burnshaw wishfully in *New Masses,* could lead the spectators to action even though the playwright did not specifically summon them to revolt.[34] While the Communist press still preferred explicit Marxism in the theatre, it was beginning to accept nonrevolutionary condemnations of capitalistic society.

The Party gave equally enthusiastic reviews to Albert Bein's less dramatic, more doctrinaire drama—*Let Freedom Ring*—but it lasted only 23 performances. Produced by Bein and Jack Goldsmith on November 6, 1935, this dramatization of Grace Lumpkin's novel *To Make My Bread* depicted the plight of some Carolina mountaineers who migrate to a mill town and there become involved in a strike.

This quick Broadway failure set off a loud explosion on the left. The Marxists blamed everything but the play for the fiasco. Michael Gold hastened to exculpate the Party and to blame Bein for the Broadway failure. The *Daily Worker*, said Gold, had given the production excellent publicity, but Bein had failed to organize his audience in advance by means of theatre parties. Gold hoped that the playwright would not sour on the revolution because of his unhappy experience.[35]

Bein, while reaffirming his allegiance to the movement, expressed his grievances. He was especially angry at the Group Theatre's management and Theatre Union for having rejected his masterpiece in the first place; furthermore, when he decided to produce the play himself, the revolutionary organizations refused to arrange theatre parties, and *New Masses* and *New Theatre* refused to sell tickets even though they knew where he and Miss Lumpkin "stood politically." [36] The bickering ended with a reopening at Theatre Union, where the play ran for an additional 85 showings. Bein was apparently being appeased.

The controversy over the next social drama was more physical. On January 7, 1936, the Messrs. Shubert offered *Mid-West* by James Hagan for a run of 22 performances.

Dealing with the Depression, this drama ends with the lynching of a Communist who had tried to organize a strike of farm workers.[37] Since the author sympathized with the lynchers, the *Daily Worker's* critic, Michael Blankfort, described the play as "dull, boring, lying rot." Worst of all, Herbert Kline, an official of the New Theatre League, who had expressed the same opinion by hissing throughout the first act, was hit twice by a man who had been applauding the anti-labor speeches. Since no capitalist had ever been beaten at Theatre Union, Blankfort asked rhetorically, which audience really advocated violence? [38] This incident was the closest thing to a Communist riot that the sedate American theatre of the thirties produced.

During the 1936–37 season there were eleven plays dealing with the usual Broadway variety of social themes. There were two unsuccessful exposés of the brutal life at military academies: Joseph Viertel's *So Proudly We Hail,* which was offered by James R. Ullman, and Henry Misrock's *Bright Honor,* which was produced by Jack Kirkland and Sam H. Grisman. Sam Byrd presented Samson Raphaelson's *White Man,* still another drama about the mulatto problem. There was George Abbott's *Sweet River,* another version of *Uncle Tom's Cabin.* Broadway also saw a production by Sidney Harmon and the Actors' Repertory Company, the group that had performed *Let Freedom Ring* the preceding season. The play, *200 Were Chosen* by E. P. Conkle, concerned settlers in Alaska during the Depression. There was another of Maxwell Anderson's pompous plays, *The Wingless Victory;* this one, produced by Katharine Cornell, concerned race prejudice in Massachusetts in 1800. Brock Pemberton produced Walter Charles Roberts' *Red Harvest,* still another play about the horrors of war. None of these plays was a financial success.

This season was more notable because it saw two important American playwrights—Sidney Kingsley and Lillian Hellman—move to the left. It also saw both an anti-labor drama and a Marxist allegory.

Ten Million Ghosts, produced by Sidney Kingsley himself, opened on October 23, 1936, and closed 11 performances later. This play, exposing the war-promoting activities of bankers, munitions makers, and newspaper publishers, deals with a French aviator's discovery that the mines owned by the deKruif family in both Germany and France are immune from attack. When he attempts to raid the German mines, his plane is shot down and he is killed. Some years after the war the deKruifs plan to preserve their power by installing national dictators, just as the Communists claimed world capitalism had done in Germany and Italy.

Writing in the *Daily Worker,* Charles E. Dexter hailed the play as a completely factual indictment of the munitions magnates, but complained that the ending was illogical because it did not suggest revolution as the only cure for war.[39] The Communists were delighted with Kingsley's analysis as far as it went, but they thought that it did not go far enough. *Ten Million Ghosts* offered a clear thesis but little drama. *Idiot's Delight* indicted the same capitalists in a much more entertaining fashion.

Like Sidney Kingsley, Lillian Hellman moved leftward with *Days to Come,* but not far enough to please the Party. Produced by Herman Shumlin on December 15, 1936, this play ran for only seven performances. It deals with a strike of the workers in a brush factory located in a small Ohio town. The owner imports a gang of strikebreakers who take control of the town. After a night of terror, during which a laborer's child is killed by the thugs, the workers are ready to end the strike. The owner suffers not only from the social tragedy of this bloodshed but also from the personal tragedy of his wife's infidelities. Miss Hellman offered two theses in the play: first, she indicated that the antagonists in the class struggle were moving farther and farther apart; second, she illustrated the belief that capitalism needed the support of brutal fascism.[40]

Although the critics for the Marxist press—Charles E. Dexter and Alexander Taylor—were happy with the exposé of strikebreaking, they did not like the play because there was too little emphasis on the proletarian masses and too much on the bourgeoisie.[41] Lillian Hellman, a better playwright than propagandist, seemed more intent on probing the psyches and souls of stupid capitalists than on preaching the theses or on summoning the workers to revolution. This failure to call on the audience to revolt, said John Howard Lawson, was an error, which Miss Hellman compounded by her portrayal of a passive, non-Communist organizer. Mere recognition of the class struggle, without revolutionary guidance, was not enough for Lawson.[42] It grieved the Communists to see Miss Hellman offer the proper Marxist analysis of the industrial situation without adding the accepted Communist solution.

Whereas *Days to Come* was sympathetic to the proletariat, *Tide Rising* by George Brewer, Jr., was not. Produced by Richard Aldrich and Richard Myers on January 25, 1937, this play was shown 32 times. It concerns a small-town druggist who tries to stop a strike fomented by his Communist daughter-in-law. Failing to get either side to accept a compromise settlement, this man becomes sheriff and ends the strike, but only after the rioting workers have killed his son and wrecked the drugstore. In this preachment against strikes, Brewer blamed the greed of both capital and labor for the inevitable violence.

This strike play, unusual for its accusation against labor, aroused the Party's wrath. The critic for *New Masses*, Alexander Taylor, called the drama Fascist because it raised the public interest above that of labor and because the plot supposedly proved the futility of militant action by the proletariat.[43] The *Daily Worker's* reviewer, Charles E. Dexter, was angered by the anti-Semitic sentiment inherent in the characterization of the Communist as a Jewess. He was happy to report, however, that the play was so poorly written that its rapid demise was inevitable.[44]

The playwright, for his part, was angered by the organized effort of the New Theatre League to boycott the production and to prevent both the publication and the filming of the script, but he admitted that the weak dramaturgy, not the leftist attacks, forced the early closing and prevented a sale to Hollywood.[45] The script was published by the Dramatists' Play Service in 1937, despite the League.

Although Marxist ideas were offered by several Broadway playwrights in their analyses of America's social problems, not one drama produced by the independent New York managers suggested the revolutionary solution until John C. Wilson produced *Excursion* by Victor Wolfson on April 9, 1937, for an engagement of 116 performances. Wolfson, a member of Theatre Union's Board of Directors, had already written *Bitter Stream* for that company and was thus experienced in the left-wing theatre.

Excursion is an allegory about Obediah Rich, Captain of the S.S. *Happiness,* who decides to sail his Coney Island ferry to a utopian isle in the Caribbean rather than return to Manhattan. With an assortment of discontented passengers, including two Communists, the voyage begins. These two travelers emphasize the analogy between their trip and the journey to communism. True to the Party line, these peaceful people are violently attacked by the Coast Guard (agents of capitalism) for having stolen the boat (private property). Although the Coast Guard wins the struggle, Obediah advises his passengers to keep the fighting spirit and hints that they will try the voyage again next year.

The Communists were, of course, delighted with this play, their first successful invasion of the Broadway theatre. The

Daily Worker's critic, Charles E. Dexter, was happy that the Communists were native Americans, not foreign agitators,[46] and the reviewer for *New Masses*, Alexander Taylor, was pleased that the capitalists were the instigators of the violence.[47] The Marxists enjoyed hearing the Party line amid the charming fantasy, but the nonpartisan spectators undoubtedly felt that the charm bogged down when the explanations started.

Of the four social dramas presented during the 1937–38 season, three were failures. The theatre of social significance thus did not make a good showing. Perhaps there had been too many social plays the preceding season, and the Broadway producers wanted a year's rest.

The Communists were distressed about the first of the failures—Irwin Shaw's *Siege,* which Norman Bel Geddes presented on December 8, 1937, for six showings. The play dramatizes the plight of some quarrelsome Loyalists besieged in a mountain fort.[48] Shaw, said Jack Burrows in *New Masses,* had unfortunately failed to mention the political issues of the Spanish War.[49] The *Daily Worker's* critic, Eric Englander, complained that Shaw had failed to include in the cast a single "sharp-eyed revolutionary who understands the war." [50] The Party was especially distressed because the playwright, whose *Bury the Dead* had been discovered by the New Theatre League, seemed to have outgrown his desire to please his first benefactors. The Communists became especially bitter about Irwin Shaw when the Group Theatre produced his "escapist" play, *Retreat to Pleasure,* in 1940.

The second failure was Sam Byrd's production of *Journeyman,* a dramatization of the Erskine Caldwell novel by Leon Alexander, who was a critic for the *Daily Worker,* and Alfred Hayes. The play, about depravity in the South, displeased the Communist press because it failed to explain the causes of the corruption or the revolutionary cure.[51]

Ironically, Leon Alexander had failed to write a Marxist play. The other failure was D. A. Doran's production of *Sunup to Sundown* by Francis Edwards Faragoh—a play about child labor on a tobacco farm.

The hit of the 1937–38 season was *I'd Rather Be Right* by George S. Kaufman and Moss Hart with music by Richard Rodgers and lyrics by Lorenz Hart. It was produced by Sam Harris on November 2, 1937, and had a successful run of 290 performances. The plot concerns the efforts of President Roosevelt to balance the federal budget so that two young lovers can get married. Although he fails, the boy and girl, inspired by the President's sincere desire to help the country, decide to marry anyway. Kaufman and Hart genially satirized the New Deal with its high taxes, its troubles with the Supreme Court, its expensive theatre project, and its political patronage; and such public figures as the President, his wife, his mother, the Cabinet members, and even Alf Landon, whom Roosevelt had defeated at the polls one year before. But the playwrights concluded the show with praise for American democracy.

The Communist press disliked the show. Harking back to the Party's anti-New Deal period, one critic, Eric Englander, wrote that the satire was too good-natured.[52] On the other hand, another reviewer, Jack Burrows, in the spirit of the united front, complained that the musical was part of an anti-Roosevelt plot, but then, contradicting himself, lamented the insincerity of the satire.[53] The Party was indeed hard to please.

From the Communists' point of view, the most notable event of the 1937–38 season was the development of the Theatre Arts Committee. This popular front, which the Party had created in the spring of 1937 to aid the Spanish Loyalists, expanded its activities to benefit playwrights and actors who were unable to express their leftist leanings in the politically mild fare of Broadway. Writing in the *Daily*

Worker, John Cambridge asserted that the Communist Party had no intention of turning "good writers into bad strike leaders." There were times, he continued, when artists should picket, but usually they should use their art to aid good causes. He added hastily that the TAC was "not, of course, a Communist organization." [54]

The new front created a Production Committee "to give advice to playwrights" and "to use its influence for the production of progressive plays." The committee, headed by James Proctor, included Irwin Shaw and Ben Bengal, both of whom had written plays for the New Theatre League, and also John Boruff, another dramatist. John Cambridge predicted that "progressive" playwrights would get a chance to have their dramas produced because Herman Shumlin and Jed Harris (Broadway impresarios interested in the social drama) were members of the TAC Advisory Board.[55] Other participants in the TAC were Robert Benchley, Constance Cummings, Frances Farmer, John Garfield, Lillian Hellman, Philip Loeb, and Martin Wolfson.[56] Success for this front seemed complete when Lee Shubert, of the "monopolistic" Shuberts, wrote an article in the *Sunday Worker* welcoming the new group as a defender of our democracy.[57] Just as soon as scripts were submitted, John Cambridge said, the good old days of Theatre Union would be revived—and on Broadway.[58]

The TAC did not live up to predictions because scripts that were both "progressive" and good were still hard to find. Although there were more socially significant productions during the following season, not one of them was as doctrinaire as the mildest of Theatre Union's offerings.

The TAC put most of its energies into political cabarets— midnight entertainments comprising songs, dances, and skits, performed by Broadway artists to satirize the political enemies of "progressive" ideas. The actors involved in the TAC, and indeed in most of the left-wing theatres, were probably more interested in the opportunity to perform in public than in the social message they were conveying.

The TAC lost most of its slight strength when the Nazi-Soviet Pact of 1939 destroyed the united front. The non-Communists left the organization when Louis Schaeffer, the director of Labor Stage, denounced the TAC as a Communist front and when Actors' Equity ordered its members to withdraw.[59] The TAC continued briefly as a propaganda agency against American intervention in the European war.[60]

The 1938–39 season saw ten plays of social significance, but six of them were quick failures. Three were unsuccessful anti-Nazi plays. Julien Chaqueneau presented *Waltz in Goose Step*, Oliver H. P. Garrett's exposé of the internal quarrels among Germany's depraved rulers. Oscar Hammerstein and Michael Hillman produced Norman Macowen's *Glorious Morning*, a play about the failure of a dictator to force his people to abandon religion. Four managers—Richard Aldrich, Dennis King, Sir Cedric Hardwicke, and Richard Myers—offered Jacques Deval's *Lorelei*, the story of a German-Jewish scientist who decides to return to Germany and certain martyrdom.

Writing in the *Sunday Worker*, John Cambridge attempted to explain the failure of anti-Nazi plays on Broadway. He asserted that the nonprogressive spectators did not believe that the Nazis were really evil; he claimed that the Jews did not feel comfortable seeing such dramas; and he added the usual Marxist explanation for any theatrical failure: the workers could not afford to buy tickets.[61] Cambridge overlooked the significant fact that the anti-Nazi plays had been dramatically inept.

The other unsuccessful plays included Doris Frankel's anti-Communist *Don't Throw Glass Houses*, produced by Contemporary Stage; Arnold Sundgaard's *Everywhere I Roam*, a spectacular folk pageant, offered by Marc Connelly and Bela Blau, about the development of the nation's farms; and Karel Capek's *The Mother*, another pessimistic anti-war drama, translated by Paul Selver and Miles Malleson, and presented by Victor Payne-Jennings.

The 1938–39 season was highlighted by two socially significant musicals. The first, *Sing Out the News*, was a revue composed by Harold Rome and Charles Friedman, both alumni of *Pins and Needles*. The new show, produced by Max Gordon, George S. Kaufman, and Moss Hart, opened on September 24, 1938, and ran for 105 performances—well short of the record of the Labor Stage revue.

The second was a musical comedy about Americans in the Soviet Union. *Leave It to Me* by Bella and Sam Spewack with music and lyrics by Cole Porter, was produced by Vinton Freedley on November 9, 1938. This adaptation of the Spewacks' *Clear All Wires* recounts the efforts of the newly appointed American ambassador to Soviet Russia to be recalled to the United States; he tries to make himself obnoxious by kicking the German ambassador and by shooting a Russian, but these acts make the American more popular in both the United States and Russia. He succeeds in being recalled, however, when he decides to do a good deed —he presents his plan for eliminating war by breeding the old nationalities into a single nation.

The Party press hailed the show. Although the Spewacks did "not write as Communists," said the *Daily Worker's* reviewer, John Cambridge, they were clearly on the side of "the Soviets and democracy." He was also pleased to hear the "Internationale" sung as part of the production,[62] and the critic for *New Masses*, Ruth McKenney, was especially heartened that neither Roosevelt nor Stalin was satirized.[63] The Broadway audience enjoyed *Leave It to Me* for 307 performances, but not for such highly nebulous contributions to the popular front; the spectators liked rather the clever Cole Porter songs, the comedy, and the performers—

Billy Gaxton, Victor Moore, Sophie Tucker, and especially Mary Martin, who sang that utterly un-Marxist song, "My Heart Belongs to Daddy."

The 1938–39 season also had two successful straight plays on social themes. *The American Way* had much more social significance than the Cole Porter musical. On January 21, 1939, Sam Harris and Max Gordon presented this spectacular drama by George S. Kaufman and Moss Hart. The story, tracing the career of an immigrant cabinetmaker from 1896 through 1938, depicts his rise to wealth as the owner of a furniture factory, his sorrow over the death of a son in the First World War, and his fall during the Depression. Through good times and bad he is inspired by his love of American liberty. He is killed by native Fascists as he tries to prevent his grandson from joining their ranks. Kaufman and Hart, aware of the increasing danger of fascism, were attempting to reaffirm the spectator's belief in freedom and democracy. Unlike *Life and Death of an American*, George Sklar's panorama that portrayed only the social flaws of the same period, *The American Way* presented a more balanced view.

Condemning the play as a "libel on the democracy it pretends to serve," the *Daily Worker's* critic, John Cambridge, was horrified at the depiction of a happy relationship between the workers and their employer, at the portrait of a benevolent banker, and at the omission of Sacco, Vanzetti, Mooney, and John L. Lewis; worst of all, Kaufman and Hart seemed to be enjoying their "prostitution" to the rich spectators.[64] The run of 244 performances, however, indicated that the spectators, whatever their income, were pleased by the show too.

Herman Shumlin's production of *The Little Foxes* was even more successful. Opening on February 15, 1939, this Lillian Hellman drama played an engagement of 410 showings. The plot concerns the wicked Regina Giddens, who virtually murders her husband. She also outwits her equally vicious brothers in order to get a larger share of the cotton mills that the family is planning to build. But her triumph has been won at a high price—the loss of her daughter's love.

Although the playwright omitted the working class from the drama, the critics for the Marxist press—John Cambridge and Ruth McKenney—were content that she had implicitly destroyed the myth that family fortunes were founded on sheer ability and hard work.[65] The Communist spectators saw the characters primarily as typical capitalists—just as the author seemed to suggest in her script. But the non-partisan audience saw Regina—as acted by Tallullah Bankhead—and her brothers chiefly as evil but fascinating individuals. *The Little Foxes* owed its long run to an exciting plot, brilliant characterization, and a stunning performance —not to the exposé of capitalism.

Seven dramas of social significance appeared on Broadway during the 1939–40 season, and four of them failed very quickly. The Chekhov Theatre Productions offered George Shdanoff's *The Possessed,* a series of dull conversations between moderate and extremist members of a pre-1917 subversive group in Russia. Gilbert Miller, Maurice Colburne, and Barry Jones presented *Geneva,* George Bernard Shaw's indictment of European nationalism. George Abbott produced Ayn Rand's *The Unconquered,* an anti-Communist picture of Russia in the nineteen-twenties. Guthrie McClintic presented *An International Incident,* Vincent Sheean's boring account of the awakening of an aristocratic woman to the problems of the poor after she has been beaten while observing a picket line.

The season was more significant for the first financially successful anti-Nazi play of the decade, for a comedy about free speech, and for the only commercially produced imitation of Federal Theatre's living newspaper.

On November 3, 1939, Richard Aldrich and Richard Myers produced *Margin for Error*, Clare Boothe's detective drama about the murder of a German consul in an American city. Among the suspects are the consul's wife, a doctor, and a Jewish policeman. The policeman solves the case by discovering that the consul was shot by the doctor and stabbed by the wife but that death was caused by poison accidentally drunk by the victim.

The playwright used the absurd plot as a frame for her anti-Nazi sentiments. Because of the poetically just triumph of the Jew over the Nazis and because of the playwright's sharp wisecracks, *Margin for Error* played an engagement of 264 performances, thus becoming the first anti-Nazi hit of the nineteen-thirties. Writing in *New Masses*, Agnes Day condemned the comedy.[66] The Communist Party, then in its isolationist phase, was angry because Miss Boothe included too many anti-appeasement speeches for its comfort.

The Party liked *The Male Animal* better. It did not get involved in the specific, and embarrassing problems of international politics. Presented by Herman Shumlin on January 9, 1940, this comedy by James Thurber and Elliott Nugent deals with the conflict between a professor and the reactionary trustees of a Midwestern university because he wants to read one of Vanzetti's letters as an example of English composition. He refuses to change his plan. Although the playwrights emphasized the humor of his marital trouble, they managed to convey a sincere plea for academic freedom. While the leftist reviewers—Abel Gorham and Alvah Bessie —officially favored this theme and enjoyed the comedy, they complained that the playwrights had not treated the issue of freedom at sufficient length.[67] *The Male Animal* made its point clearly, concisely, and humorously for 243 performances.

Medicine Show made its point with equal clarity, but with much less conciseness and with very little humor. This living newspaper was written by Oscar Saul (who had been one of the authors of Federal Theatre's *The Revolt of the Beavers*) and H. R. Hays. Presented by Carly Wharton and Martin Gabel on April 12, 1940, this show sought to prove that 250,000 Americans die needlessly each year because of inadequate medical attention; it blamed both the reactionary American Medical Association for preventing group health plans and the federal government for its refusal to help, and it suggested compulsory health insurance as a solution. The playwrights urged the spectators to use the democratic means of the ballot to achieve better medical care. *Medicine Show* differed from its Federal Theatre predecessors primarily in the relatively small size of its cast—a circumstance caused by the fact that the producers, not the government, were paying the actors' salaries.

The *Daily Worker*'s reviewer, Ralph Warner, praised the production as a "progressive plea for socialized medicine" but blamed the dramatists for having missed one of the chief villains—President Roosevelt, who, according to this critic, had betrayed the cause of liberalism by having run "into the impenetrable woods of reaction and war." [68] Warner was sneaking the Party's isolationist propaganda into his review.

The producers, in financial trouble five days after the opening, ran a large advertisement in the *Daily Worker*, warning that the show would close unless attendance improved at once and suggesting that the best way to "promote a national health plan" would be to support *Medicine Show*.[69] This appeal and the moderately favorable reviews by the "bourgeois" critics helped to keep the production running for 35 performances. Except for the Group Theatre's *Men in White*, *Medicine Show* was the decade's only drama about the social issue of medical care.

The 1940–41 season and the autumn of 1941 before the attack on Pearl Harbor saw six dramas of social significance.

This relatively small number of plays can be attributed in part to the end of the Depression. Also, the impending American participation in the war loomed larger for audiences and producers than the other social, political, and economic problems of the thirties. Most of the productions of this 1940–41 period at least touched on the war.

The one exception was Herman Shumlin's production of *The Corn Is Green* by Emlyn Williams, which opened on November 26, 1940, and ran for 477 performances. It was an unusual labor play in that it emphasized a single proletarian, not a whole group. The individual is a young, ignorant Welsh miner who is educated by an English schoolmistress. After many emotional and intellectual difficulties, he wins a scholarship to Oxford. Someday he will return to Wales to bring enlightenment to his fellow miners. Although Williams stressed the individual and his troubles, especially his affair with a slut, the playwright offered the slow and painful process of education as a solution for the problem of oppressed workers.

Even though Williams did not mention Marxism as part of the boy's education, the Party press liked the play. The implied thesis, Ralph Warner asserted in the *Daily Worker,* was that "oppression can end only when the workers learn the truth about the world in which they live." [70] For Marxists, "the truth" was Marxism, but "the truth" could really be anything any spectator believed in. For many in the audience, however, the glowing performance by Ethel Barrymore as the schoolmistress was far more important than the play's social message.

Praising Herman Shumlin in a second review, Ralph Warner asserted that the other Broadway impresarios had been afraid to produce the play because of its radical message. [71] Burns Mantle, on the other hand, said that several producers had indeed been frightened away—by the large advance royalties that the playwright, in the accepted capitalistic fashion, had demanded.[72]

The period of 1940–41 also saw another left-wing musical revue, *Meet the People,* assembled by Henry Myers and produced by the Hollywood Alliance for 160 performances. Edgar Selwyn presented Frederick Hazlitt Brennan's *The Wookey,* a drama about a British pacifist's acceptance of the war after Dunkirk. This play ran for 134 performances. Max Gordon produced *The Land Is Bright* by George S. Kaufman and Edna Ferber, a play about the regeneration of a robber baron's descendants. This work was shown 79 times.

Frank Ross presented *The Man with the Blond Hair,* Norman Krasna's play about the conversion of a Nazi prisoner of war to the ideals of democracy because of the kindness of a Jewish family that gives him shelter, strudel, and borsht. Krasna's wishful thinking was a little silly, and the play was withdrawn after seven showings. *The Man with the Blond Hair* did not reflect the Party line.

Lillian Hellman's *Watch on the Rhine,* produced by Herman Shumlin on April 1, 1941, was much closer to the Communists' position. The chief character is a leader of the anti-Fascist German underground who comes to America with his wife and children in order to raise funds. He hates violence but is forced to kill a Fascist agent. Although Miss Hellman preferred action against the Nazis to mere talk, she overlooked the fact that Europe had been at war since September 1939. Her kind of action was limited to the rebellious activities of an anti-Nazi group motivated by the desire for a peaceful and prosperous world. She did not even raise the question of giving aid to the brave British, who were at this time virtually alone in their battle against fascism. Miss Hellman wrote a precise, exciting drama as usual, which ran for 378 performances, but her anti-Nazi sentiments were curiously limited.

Reviewers for the Marxist press liked these hints about a

revolutionary solution to the Nazi problem. Hailing this point of view as real antifascism, the *Daily Worker's* critic, Ralph Warner, was also pleased with the references to the people who struggle for peace and prosperity—a description that the Communists often applied to themselves. He wished that Miss Hellman had been more specific, however, in naming the Party as the true leader of the fight against fascism and in identifying her protagonist as a Party member. He also felt that war should have been openly, not tacitly, rejected and that praise of the Soviet Union should have been included.[73] These additions would have made a perfect Communist drama, but Miss Hellman did not alter her script.

Writing in *New Masses,* Alvah Bessie expressed the fear that the play's unlabeled anti-Fascist sentiments would be used by those anti-Nazis who wanted to involve the United States in the war,[74] and before April was over, Ralph Warner reported in the *Daily Worker* that the "warmongering" Walter Winchell was indeed praising the play.[75] By late July, however, the Communists were no longer unhappy about the play's potential as pro-intervention propaganda, for the Party press itself began to scream for a second front in Western Europe to save the Soviet Union from the invading Nazis.

The "decade of social significance" on Broadway thus ended. Unlike the directors of Federal Theatre, the commercial managers did not experiment very much with new forms of social drama. The experimental works—*The Threepenny Opera, Panic, Bury the Dead,* and *Medicine Show*—had originated away from Broadway. Herman Shumlin, the busiest producer of social plays, invariably chose such conventional, realistic scripts as *Clear All Wires, The Male Animal, The Corn Is Green,* and the works of Lillian Hellman for production. Sam Harris, another productive impresario, was a bit more daring in presenting such socially significant variations on the conventional musical comedy as *Of Thee I Sing*, but he always ensured the success of his musical shows with a chorus line of beautiful girls.

The decade on the commercial stage was not actually one of social significance. Of the 1,500 presentations offered by the independent managers of Broadway from 1929 through 1941, only 74 treated primary themes of social, political, or economic significance.[76] The commercial producers continued to offer their "escapist" fare—their musical comedies, bedroom farces, comedies, mystery melodramas, musical revues, and psychological plays. The impresarios understood that people went to theatres to be entertained, not to be educated or converted to a political cause. Since these producers were in business and wanted to make a profit in the ordinary capitalistic manner, they had to give the customer what he wanted. Although Herman Shumlin offered many social plays, he selected works, like *The Little Foxes*, that were exceptionally exciting and therefore financially profitable in the theatre.

The social plays produced on Broadway were not dominated by Marxian presentations. Of the 74 socially significant productions only one—Victor Wolfson's *Excursion*—was a clear illustration of Marxist philosophy. Several others, like Lillian Hellman's *Watch on the Rhine*, were Marxist only by implication—a fact that exasperated the Party's orthodox critics.

Nor was the social spirit of the commercial drama anti-Marxian, although Broadway saw several explicitly anti-Communist plays, such as *Mid-West* and *Tide Rising*. The greater part of the socially meaningful productions advocated liberalism and democracy, not communism or fascism. The "reformist" plays of Elmer Rice and George S. Kaufman were thus more typical of the small spirit of social protest on Broadway than were the more doctrinaire dramas of Victor Wolfson and Lillian Hellman.

Although the Communists hoped to utilize the professionalism of Broadway to preach the revolutionary sermon, they had virtually no success, for one wholly Communist drama out of 1,500 productions was hardly an enviable record. The Party could not hope to conquer Broadway because there were too many playwrights and producers who had to be converted. The Communists tried, but the impresarios went their own way in search of theatre art and business profits.

Chapter 11

The Communist Party's Failure in the Theatre

THE Depression years have often been misnamed the "decade of social drama" because of the undue publicity given to the left-wing theatre and the notoriety that accompanied the handful of Communist plays. Although the new theatre movement offered many social productions, it did not live up to the extravagant claims made by both its friends and its enemies. It was a loud part of the New York stage but a small part.

Theatre of the left started slowly in the first part of the decade, expanded in the mid-thirties, and failed in the final years of the Depression. The years 1929 through 1933 saw relatively few socially significant productions. For example, the Group Theatre produced *1931–* by Paul and Claire Sifton; the Theatre Guild offered *Roar China*, a Soviet play; and the commercial stage of Broadway contributed Elmer Rice's *We the People*. The amateur theatre was busier with its Communist agitprops such as *Newsboy*, but the total output of this genre was neither large nor important.

The second part of the period, from 1934 through 1937, saw a much larger left-wing theatre, highlighted by the plays of Theatre Union; the most successful productions sponsored by the New Theatre League, beginning with

217

Waiting for Lefty and ending with Irwin Shaw's *Bury the Dead;* the Group Theatre's performances of plays by Clifford Odets; the Theatre Guild's production of Robert E. Sherwood's *Idiot's Delight;* the Broadway presentation of Sidney Kingsley's *Dead End;* the première of *Pins and Needles* at Labor Stage; the opening of Mercury Theatre's production of Marc Blitzstein's *The Cradle Will Rock;* and the offerings of Federal Theatre, especially the living newspapers. But even during these four peak years the New York stage was not primarily a social theatre.

The years 1938 through 1941 marked the decline of the new theatre movement. Theatre Union and the Communists' amateur troupes were dead; Federal Theatre was soon to expire; the New Theatre League searched in vain for new scripts and produced almost nothing; and the Group Theatre presented its last play in 1940. The Theatre Guild, the newly organized Playwrights' Company, and such Broadway managers as Herman Shumlin, produced the shrinking number of social plays. The new theatre movement was tired by 1937 and dead by 1941.

Contrary to Communist predictions, the New York audience—rich and poor alike—failed to patronize the social dramas. The generally short engagements of these plays can hardly match the record runs of the popular comedies. The 111 showings of *Stevedore* fell disastrously below the 835 of *Three Men on a Horse* because the Depression theatregoers preferred the escape of the Broadway farce to the serious problems of the American Negroes. The real strength of the theatre in the thirties lay in the spirit of fun, not in social significance. Theatre Union longed for the huge audience of the hit comedies—*You Can't Take It with You* and *The Man Who Came to Dinner,* for example—but had to be satisfied with its small Marxian coterie.

A few non-Communist social plays ran even longer than these popular shows, but for special reasons. *Tobacco Road* succeeded as an erotic burlesque, not as a serious play. *Pins and Needles* outdistanced the comedies because it was more entertaining, not merely because it praised unions. *Dead End* was a smash hit because its shocking naturalism, not its slight social message, titillated Broadway. *Idiot's Delight* had a long run because of the Lunts' star performances, not the anti-war message. But these plays were the exceptions to the reign of comedy during the Depression decade.

Just as the Party failed to win the spectators it failed to enlist the dramatists. The Communists did not inspire or produce a large Marxian repertoire because they insisted that the American playwright follow the twisting Party line without deviation. During the first half of the decade they demanded a parochial formula for treating all social, political, and economic themes. The problems brought on by the Depression had to be analyzed in the Marxist terms of class war and solved by means of a Marxist-Leninist revolution under the Party's leadership. Tribute to the Soviet Union, the model for a future Soviet America, was an inevitable part of the pattern.

During the second half of the decade, as the American economy began to rise from the depths of the Depression, the Communists accepted the reality of the New York theatrical and political scene by dropping the requirement for an open revolutionary message. Their rigid orthodoxy had inspired little more than a series of amateurish agitprops that, the Party admitted, had gained few converts and influenced few friends. The new Communist demand for a subtle summons to the revolution caused disagreement among the left-wing critics because personal judgment and taste were involved. Where the united front reviewers heard an implicit call to action, the old guard Marxist critics heard nothing.

Throughout the decade the Party tried to regulate the

pattern of the American social drama, but without success. The typical dramatic treatment of the major public issues of the thirties was "reformist," not revolutionary. Most social dramatists seemed to derive inspiration from the New Deal, not from the Bolsheviks' 1917 *coup d'état*. After all, the Democrats were numerous and powerful. They controlled the White House and the Congress. The Communist Party, on the other hand, though noisy, was numerically small and politically weak.

The Communists rarely saw their point of view expressed in the American theatre. On the international question of war, for example, the Party's basic belief in world revolution was implied by Albert Maltz and George Sklar in *Peace on Earth*,[1] but, except for this production and such early agitprops as Nathaniel Buchwald's *Hands Off!* the revolutionary ending did not appear in any of the decade's anti-war plays. Friedrich Wolf's *The Sailors of Cattaro* was not satisfactory to the Party because the mutiny against war ended in defeat. Other anti-war dramas such as Robert E. Sherwood's *Idiot's Delight* and Irwin Shaw's *Bury the Dead* offered the proper Marxian diagnosis of the cause of war (capitalism) but stopped short of the cure (revolution). *Johnny Johnson* was more typical of the anti-war plays of the thirties because Paul Green merely exposed the horror of conflict without offering either economic explanations or political solutions.

Even during the united front period, 1935–1939, the Communists failed to produce a wholly acceptable play about war. Without abandoning their revolutionary goal, they announced that the wars against fascism fought by Ethiopia (1935–1936) and Spain (1936–1939) were both necessary and just.[2] But not one drama about Ethiopia was actually produced. Although the Spanish War was treated in a few plays such as *The Fifth Column* by Ernest Hemingway and Benjamin Glazer, none specifically glorified the Communists' role in the Loyalist cause. *The Fifth Column* also disappointed the Communists because Glazer connected the Loyalist cause with that of the Allies in the Second World War; by March 1940, when this production opened, the conflict in Spain had ended and the Nazi-Soviet Pact had transformed the comrades into isolationists.

During this isolationist phase, too, the Party had little success with the anti-war plays. From Hitler's invasion of Poland in September 1939 until his attack on Russia in June 1941 the Communists described the new conflict as "a war between rival imperialisms for world domination" and urged the United States to stay out.[3] But Russia's invasion of Finland in 1939 was regarded by the Party as the just "defense" of the Soviet Union against the Finnish imperialist "attack," which had been inspired by the governments of Britain, France, and the United States.[4] During this isolationist period the critic for *New Masses*, Alvah Bessie, urged the production of anti-interventionist plays and asked his readers to petition Odets, Steinbeck, and Hemingway to collaborate on such a drama.[5] But these authors did not respond.

The major war plays presented during this period were as pro-interventionist as Robert E. Sherwood's *There Shall Be No Night* and Elmer Rice's *Flight to the West*. The Party had to be satisfied with its 1940 Christmas seals inscribed "FOOTLIGHTS ACROSS AMERICA FOR PEACE," which the New Theatre League distributed, and with a poor production of *Zero Hour*, a new version of *Peace on Earth* by Albert Maltz and George Sklar.

Even in 1941, when the Soviet Union joined the Allied side, the Party had small success with war plays. When Germany attacked Russia, the Communists reinterpreted the Second World War as a defense against fascism and urged the alliance of Britain, America, and the Soviet Union for the military defeat of Hitler.[6] When the Japanese attacked Pearl Harbor, the Communist Party pledged its loyalty to the United States.[7] Although the Communists would have preferred plays calling for a second front to save Russia, the Party had to be content with such non-Communist war dramas as Maxwell Anderson's *Candle in the Wind*. The American playwrights thus failed to follow the Party's tortuous policy on war.

The Party line was likewise rarely reflected in the decade's anti-Nazi dramas. Leslie Reade's *The Shatter'd Lamp*, a typical script on the subject, treated the personal tragedies of Hitler's victims, and not the Party's belief that nazism, the last stage of German capitalism, would be overthrown only by a Leninist revolution. Clifford Odets' *Till the Day I Die* and Friedrich Wolf's *Professor Mamlock* were Marxist plays, but they glorified individual Communists, not the Party line. Except for the doctrinaire agitprop *Dimitroff*, Lillian Hellman's *Watch on the Rhine* came closest to the Communists' revolutionary position, but failed to identify the Party as the leader of the underground movement. Miss Hellman was so near, and yet so far.

The Party line was reflected more frequently and successfully in those plays dealing with the social, political, and economic problems within American society. Throughout the decade the Party believed that its brand of revolution was the panacea for all local American ills. During the united front period, although the Communists played down this belief in favor of a more limited goal of social welfare, they did not abandon their hope for a Communist revolution leading to a Soviet America. They, of course, protested that *they* would not use violence in this "transition" to the Socialist state. If blood were shed, the capitalists' violent counterrevolution would be to blame.

Among the plays dealing with native American problems, the most popular theme of the new theatre movement was the class war between the workers and their bosses, but most dramas on this subject failed to offer the Communist solution. Such plays usually showed direct sympathy for the workers by depicting their plight as the Siftons had done in *1931-*, but a few plays—Lillian Hellman's *Days to Come* and *The Little Foxes,* for example—were indirectly sympathetic by exposing vicious capitalists.

Still other plays about class war offered something more positive than mere sympathy for the proletariat. In *We the People,* for instance, Elmer Rice tried to settle the conflict by means of liberalism and democracy; in *Tide Rising* George Brewer suggested compromise by both sides as the way out; and in *Injunction Granted* the Federal Theatre writers advocated the unionization drive of the CIO.

Several playwrights prescribed more revolutionary cures for class war—for example, Clifford Odets in *Waiting for Lefty,* Lou Lantz and Oscar Saul in *The Revolt of the Beavers,* John Howard Lawson in *Marching Song,* Marc Blitzstein in *The Cradle Will Rock,* and Victor Wolfson in *Excursion.* Although these plays were clearly Marxist, the use of allegory as in *The Revolt of the Beavers* or metaphor as in *The Cradle Will Rock* made them seem less revolutionary than such directly Communist agitprops as the *15 Minute Red Revue.* The Party had its greatest success with the labor plays because they treated the primary Marxist conflict.

Still another domestic issue—the social injustice endured by the American minorities—was often treated by dramatists of the thirties, but rarely in accord with the Communist position. The Party, officially opposed to all discrimination, concentrated its propaganda on the Negroes. The Marxists maintained that the Negro, victimized by economic exploitation, not racial prejudice, could gain his full citizenship only by joining with them in a proletarian revolution. During the first half of the decade the Party platform called not only for "equal rights for the Negroes" but also for "self-determination for the Black Belt." [8] During the second half of the decade this implied promise of a Negro People's Republic in the Deep South was quietly dropped.[9]

Of the many plays dealing with the Negro problem *Stevedore* was the most successful illustration of the Party's position because Paul Peters and George Sklar analyzed the persecution in economic terms and depicted a violent resolution by the unified forces of the Negroes and the Communists. These playwrights did not, however, call for self-determination. Although John Wexley explained the Scottsboro case in *They Shall Not Die* as an example of economic suppression of the Negroes, he failed to suggest a revolution or even to glorify the mass pressure that the Communists claimed they were applying. In *Native Son* Richard Wright and Paul Green merely included poverty among the many reasons that explained why one Negro committed a murder. Paul Green's *Hymn to the Rising Sun* and DuBose Heyward's *Brass Ankle* were more typical plays on the minority problem because they raised the issue without establishing a simple cause or prescribing a simple cure.

Of the few plays treating another domestic issue—the plight of the American farmer—not one clearly expressed the Party's belief that collective farming—to be established by revolution—would end the agricultural crisis.[10] Although Hallie Flanagan and Margaret Ellen Clifford presented sympathetic references to the Communists throughout *Can You Hear Their Voices?* these playwrights did not specifically urge revolution.[11] The writers of *Triple-A Plowed Under*, Federal Theatre's graphic account of the agricultural Depression, suggested that the farmers join with the workers to apply political—not revolutionary—pressure on the government. *Tobacco Road* simply established the fact that some Southern farmers were in trouble. The Party thus had to be satisfied with comparatively mild treatments of this important theme of agriculture.

There were even fewer productions dealing with the issues

of medical care, housing, and power. None of the plays on these questions of public health and welfare advocated the revolutionary remedy or even the Party's united front program of complete government control during the "transition" to "socialism." Except for Sidney Kingsley's incidental references to the need for better medical care for the poor in *Men in White,* this problem did not receive full treatment until Oscar Saul and H. R. Hays urged the relatively mild program of national health insurance in *Medicine Show.*

On the question of shelter for the American poor, Sidney Kingsley exposed the slums of *Dead End* as incubators for criminals and vaguely suggested community housing as the answer; Arthur Arent, offering an equally graphic exposé in *One-Third of a Nation,* advocated a government slum-clearance program. On the issue of public power, Arent defended the TVA in *Power* but did not urge a program of complete nationalization of power plants—to the despair of his Marxist critics.

Few playwrights treated the theme of government, particularly whether democracy was a suitable political system for critical times. In advocating a proletarian dictatorship the Communists believed that bourgeois democracy was inadequate, but during the united front period they paid lip service to this political system. They hailed Robert E. Sherwood's *Abe Lincoln in Illinois* not because of its extended defense of democracy but for his reference to Lincoln's reiteration of the Jeffersonian position that the people have the right to revolt. Maxwell Anderson's bitter satire on Congress in *Both Your Houses,* for example, could not satisfy the Party because of the playwright's anarchistic point of view; he had failed to advocate communism as the only alternative to democracy. Most of the productions about government were such genially satiric musical comedies as *I'd Rather Be Right,* which upheld democracy.

Theatrical reproductions of the great experiment in the

"Socialist fatherland" never matched the utopian fantasies of the American Communists. The Spewacks' *Clear All Wires* was typical because it was mildly satiric of living conditions in the Soviet Union. Even such imported Russian plays as *Red Rust* and *The Path of Flowers* were too satiric for the taste and faith of the loyal comrades. Dramas like *Class of '29* by Orrie Lashin and Milo Hastings, which complimented the Soviets, did so incidentally. Except for such agitprops as the *15 Minute Red Revue,* no drama was devoted entirely to the glorification of the Soviet Union.

The Party's revolutionary beliefs and program were thus rarely set forth by the social dramatists of the thirties. The Communists can be credited with influence on the left-wing drama to the extent that they publicized the issues of the decade, but such success was not great. We can be sure that Roosevelt's fireside chats reached a much larger audience than did the Party's publications and agitprops. We can also be sure that sensitive playwrights were able to see the Depression without the Party's aid. As Clifford Odets told the House Committee on Un-American Activities, he learned his hatred of poverty from experience, not from communism.[12] The American spirit of radicalism would have made itself heard in the theatre even if the Communist Party had never existed. American reform—not Communist revolution —was the majority movement of the thirties, despite the Marxists' loud proclamations to the contrary.

The Communists had even smaller success in establishing new dramatic forms to convey the Party line. During the early thirties the Marxists favored the agitprop because it used a direct method of preaching Marxism and inciting revolution and because this kind of theatre could be produced by the Party's mobile shock troupes both in union halls and on street corners. The Party abandoned this dramatic form in 1934 because its Communist slogans and stereotyped characters were not winning converts. Ironically, the only artistically successful agitprop was not produced until 1935, when Odets added realism to the forsaken structure to create *Waiting for Lefty.*

For the remainder of the decade the Communists were ambivalent toward the experimental forms of drama. They accepted the living newspapers because these Federal Theatre productions successfully used documented facts to illustrate the limited thesis that American society had shortcomings. Local comrades, on the other hand, rejected the experimental works of Bertolt Brecht (*Mother*) and Erwin Piscator (*The Case of Clyde Griffiths*) because their Marxist lessons were too obvious for the relatively sophisticated American worker and because these productions were theatrical failures. The Party's views on experimental forms of drama thus depended more on the ideological content and the theatrical success than on the structure and style of the play itself. A popular play with the "right" message meant more to the Party than a "new" genre.

From 1934 on, the Communists preferred what seemed to be the perfect form of drama—the realistic well-made play of Broadway, but with different subject matter. Each drama told essentially one story—the inevitable success of the Party. In plays such as *Marching Song* a nonpartisan worker was always converted to communism and the Communists always succeeded in besting the bosses. The name given to this combination of the realistic form and the optimistic Marxist content was Socialist realism.

The Communists theorized that such plays of Socialist realism would win more converts than the agitprop had because the realistic form would give the spectators the illusion that they were watching live characters in true situations. The spectators could identify more easily with these "real" characters than with the slogan-spouting cartoons in the agitprop. For example, the spectator, identifying himself with a "real" character who becomes a Communist, would likewise be inspired to join the Party.

The problem of the Marxist playwright, therefore, was to depict credible conversions in all genres. Since conversion seemed extreme to non-Communists in real life, the dramatist had the difficult, but not impossible, task of persuading the audience that communism was the only way out for the characters in his play. In *Waiting for Lefty* Clifford Odets succeeded in convincing his spectators that the drivers had to choose this extreme solution. In his more conventional plays—*Awake and Sing* and *Paradise Lost*—however, the decisions for Marx seemed unreal because they occurred so suddenly. In *Stevedore,* within the framework of the conventional, realistic play, Paul Peters and George Sklar managed to create a believable picture of the passive Negroes as they united with the Red unionists.

Odets, Peters, and Sklar may have convinced the audience that their characters had to choose communism, but whether these playwrights persuaded the spectator to join the Party is open to question. The answer depended on the personality and the prejudices of the spectator, not on the plight of a "realistic" character. *Waiting for Lefty* and *Stevedore* may have helped the fellow traveler into the Party, but these plays did not start a stampede of the general public to Communist headquarters. On the contrary, by offering the vicarious experience of fighting injustice, these productions relieved the spectator's latent indignation at the wrongs of society. The emotional catharsis induced by the drama made the theatre a less satisfactory weapon than the Party theorists had imagined. Apparently they had never read Aristotle's *Poetics*.

There is no question that the Communist Party sought to direct the new theatre movement and, indeed, the entire

New York stage. The Communists succeeded in controlling those minor theatres that they themselves had organized as amateur theatrical fronts—the *Proletbuehne,* the WLT (later named the Theatre of Action), and the Theatre Collective. These groups, as the Marxists admitted, succeeded only in preaching to the convinced comrades.

The Party's attempt to create a large network of Marxist theatres by organizing amateur dramatic groups into the League of Workers' Theatres and the New Theatre League also failed. The Communists were unable to supply the promised repertory of good "progressive" plays to the few groups that did join. The affiliates, for their part, failed to produce competent performances of the authorized scripts and often performed unauthorized dramas. The Party ran the central offices of both Leagues, but it never achieved either financial or ideological control over the many undisciplined members. Artistic success came to the New Theatre League only when it sponsored professional performances of *Waiting for Lefty, Hymn to the Rising Sun,* and *Bury the Dead* at the New Theatre Nights of 1935 and 1936.

The Communists had their most successful outlet in Theatre Union, but the productions of this professional company were not all satisfactory to the Party's doctrinaire critics. Although the scripts were clearly Marxist, they were often not sufficiently blatant in their doctrine to suit the Communist Party. Theatre Union, created as a united front organization, often exhibited an appropriately mild independence, which exasperated the Party. The Communists would have preferred a larger repertory and longer engagements, for seven scripts spread over four seasons (an average run of 85 performances for each) did not indicate the kind of success that the Party regarded as historically inevitable. Although Theatre Union was more successful than the other Communist theatrical enterprises, it was, nevertheless, a failure by the practical standards of Broadway.

The Party's efforts to supplement the productions of its own companies by gaining control of the comparatively wealthy Federal Theatre and the technically expert Group Theatre did not succeed. Although there were Communists in both of these organizations, the Party was unable to control the management of either. Nor did the other professional theatres—the Theatre Guild, the Playwrights' Company, the Mercury Theatre—or the independent impresarios of the commercial stage heed the continual agitation and advice offered by the Party press. Labor Stage, the only successful union company of the thirties, likewise followed its own inspiration, not the Party's dictates. The few Marxist dramas produced on the non-Communist stage were presented because of their dramatic value, not because of their ideological merit. The Communist plan to turn the bourgeois theatre into a proletarian weapon was a failure.

The Communists failed to control the new theatre movement because they were unable to control either the playwrights or the audience. The Party, taking its cue from Lenin, demanded from its writers absolute conformity with the Communist line,[13] but the playwrights, living in a free society, refused to conform. After the production of *Waiting for Lefty* Clifford Odets wandered from Marxism, and after the presentation of *Bury the Dead* Irwin Shaw likewise strayed. The Party was unable to stop the new gold rush to California, for the left-wing playwrights, like good American capitalists, preferred the gold of Hollywood to the glory of Moscow. The Party sought its share of the claim in 1937 when George Sklar warned his comrades to beware the artist who would contribute only his art to the movement.

Just as the Communists failed to control the supply of Marxist drama, they failed to control the demand of the American "mass" audience. In the first issue of *New Theatre* the Marxist critics identified themselves:

. . . In our ranks stand longshoremen, clerks, coal miners, doctors, cooks, poets, laundresses, professional reviewers, steel puddlers, lawyers, starving idle people. . . .

We take the prerogative as the courts of last resort. And we mean to use it, in these columns and in the theatre. Our seal of approval and our roar of censure shall mark the fate of the future American drama. Perhaps you will listen to us, brothers Producer, Director, Actor, Playwright, Designer. We take our rightful place as an integral part of the theatre. We are the Audience.[14]

Brother producer listened to his audience as he always had done—through the box office, and not through the columns of a short-lived Marxist periodical. The Communists' greatest failure was their inability to train the spectators to demand the kind of drama that the Party thought they inevitably ought to demand.

The contradiction between the desires of the masses and the plans of the self-appointed leaders was evident throughout the decade, especially in the tremendous growth of the motion-picture industry. Just as the playwrights escaped to Hollywood, so the masses—the longshoremen, the clerks, and the cooks—escaped vicariously to the same world of wealth and glamour. Metro-Goldwyn-Mayer grew rich while Theatre Union went broke, for the American people preferred the Hollywood escape from their problems to *Mother*'s revolutionary cure. The American woman preferred to identify herself with the Celluloid Cinderella, and not with a Bolshevik matriarch; the American man wanted to be Prince Charming, not a union organizer. Clark Gable, Jean Harlow, and Shirley Temple had box-office appeal, but the actors at Theatre Union did not. The American spectator hoped to have a little of Hollywood's gold and glamour rub off on him. He was too tired to submit to the Party's agitation and propaganda.

The theatrical history of the new theatre movement proved that the roar of the Marxists did not indeed determine the destiny of the American theatre. John Howard Lawson's 1936 prediction that the drama without social significance would be a rarity within a few years did not come true,[15] for the social drama had begun to decline before the decade was over. After Lawson's *Marching Song* in 1937, the story of the left-wing stage was anticlimactic. The new theatre movement was dying.

Although plays of social significance were still written and produced, the playwrights' urge to protest and the spectator's desire to listen grew weaker as the nation grew stronger. As the symptoms of the economic disorder began to disappear toward the end of the thirties, the playwrights' prescriptions seemed more and more superfluous. The more spectacular return of American prosperity, brought on by the start of the wartime boom, destroyed the remaining theatrical aspirations of the American Communists. The new theatre movement was dead. Drama had not been a good weapon.

NOTES

The following abbreviations are used in the notes and bibliography:

DW—*Daily Worker* (References are to the New York City editions, for the most part.)

NM—*New Masses*

NT—*New Theatre*

NT and F—*New Theatre and Film*

NTN—*New Theatre News*

NYPL, Thea Coll—New York Public Library, Theatre Collection

SW—*Sunday Worker*

WT—*Workers' Theatre*

HCU-AA—House Committee on Un-American Activities

The abbreviation p. 2-3-3 refers to Act 2, Scene 3, page 3 of a play typescript.

NOTES TO INTRODUCTION

1. The term was often used. See, for instance, Bosley Crowther, "Theatre of the Left," *New York Times*, April 14, 1935, Sec. 9, p. 2.

2. The Workers' Drama League produced a single play in 1926, and the New Playwrights' Theatre (1926–1929) produced a series of plays more concerned with "expressionistic" technique than with social problems. See John Dos Passos, "Did the New Playwrights' Theatre Fail?" *NM*, August 1929, p. 13.

3. Granville Hicks *et al.*, *Proletarian Literature in the United States* (New York, 1935), pp. 261, 264.

4. Crowther, p. 2.

5. "Change the World," *DW*, Nov. 5, 1940, p. 7. Gold was an editor of *New Masses*, 1926–1929, and a columnist for the *DW* during the thirties and forties. He has continued to write for the *Worker*. Gold revealed the Party's decisions on literary matters through his columns, but the decisions were made by V. J. Jerome, who was the Party's boss on cultural matters. See HCU-AA, *Hearings*, April 10, 1952, pp. 2407–2414.

NOTES TO CHAPTER 1

1. Ben Blake, *The Awakening of the American Theatre* (New York, 1935), p. 15.

2. Huntley Carter, *The New Spirit in the Russian Theatre, 1917–1928* (New York, 1929), pp. 260–261. Also see Pavel A. Markov, *The Soviet Theatre* (London, 1939), p. 139.

3. Tom Thomas, "World Congress of Workers' Theatre Groups," *NM*, November 1930, p. 21.

4. *Ibid.* Thomas reported that there were 7,000 troupes in Russia in 1927 and 200 in Germany and Czechoslovakia by 1930. Also see Harry Jaffe, "More on Soviet Blue Blouse," *NM*, December 1930, p. 20; and Carter, p. 261, who reported that there were 5,000 to 6,000 Soviet troupes in the late 1920's.

5. *Vote Communist*, WT, June–July 1932, pp. 15–17.

6. Hallie Flanagan, "Workers' Plays at Vassar College," *WT*, June–July 1932, p. 4.

7. Trans. B. Stern and George Lewis, *WT*, June–July 1932, pp. 11–14.

8. John Bonn, "Situations and Tasks of the Workers' Theatres in the U.S.A.," *WT*, June–July 1932, pp. 8–9.

9. Deutchman, "Proletarian Theatre," *NM*, June 1931, p. 21.

10. Blake, p. 20.

11. James Warren, "How Members of the W.L.T. Live and Work," *DW*, Dec. 28, 1934, p. 7. The sample performances are taken from advertisements in the *DW*.

12. Deutchman, p. 21.

13. Peter Martin, "A Day with the Shock Troupe," *DW*, May 23, 1934, p. 5.

14. Peter Martin, "The Theatre of Action," *DW*, Feb. 17, 1934, p. 7. For a full-length play on this case, see the discussion of *They Shall Not Die* in the chapter on the Theatre Guild.

15. Gregory Novikov, *Newsboy* (NYPL, Thea Coll, mimeographed, n.d.). This version is subtitled "An adaptation for the American League against War and Fascism by Gregory Novikov from the poem by V. J. Jerome, as co-ordinated by the Workers' Laboratory Theatre."

16. "Workers' Laboratory Theatre Reorganizes," *DW*, Feb. 27, 1935, p. 5.

17. *Ibid.* Others listed on the Advisory Board were Virgil Geddes, Robert Forsythe, Erskine Caldwell, Alfred Kreymborg, and William Browder. *NT*, March 1935, p. 3, does not include the above names. Others on the Executive Board were Charles Friedman, Stephen Karnot, Jack Remick, Leo Hurwitz, Sam Clark, and Peter Martin. The last three were not listed in *NT*.

18. "The Theatre of Action," *DW*, May 27, 1935, p. 5. Leon Alexander was the *DW*'s chief drama reviewer during the 1934–35 season.

19. Leon Alexander, "World of the Theatre," *DW*, Dec. 1, 1934, p. 7. Also see Stanley Burnshaw, "Other Current Shows," *NM*, Dec. 11, 1934, p. 29. Burnshaw was the principal drama critic for *NM*, 1934–1936.

20. Herbert Kline, *"The Young Go First,"* *NT*, July 1935, p. 30, joined the other leftist critics in attacking the political deviation. Kline was an editor of *NT*, 1934–1936. See also Nathaniel Buchwald, "The Real McCoy," *DW*, May 31, 1935, p. 5. Buchwald reviewed plays for Marxist magazines, 1932–1938.

21. Theodore Repard, "A Strike Put on the Stage," *DW*, March 5, 1936, p. 7. See also Edwin Seaver, "The New Play," *SW*, March 8, 1936, p. 6. *The Crime* was performed on a double bill with a scene from Bertolt Brecht's *Mother*.

22. Jack Shapiro, "Theatre Collective," *NT*, October 1934, p. 15.

23. "Theatre," *NM*, June 1933, pp. 29–30. For an account of the Group Theatre's production, see the chapter on the Group.

24. *DW*, May 26, 1934, p. 3.

25. *"Marion Models, Inc.,"* *NT*, July–August 1934, p. 11.

26. Shapiro, p. 15.

27. "The Theatre Collective," *NT*, October 1934, p. 15.

28. Mark Marvin, "World of the Theatre," *DW*, Sept. 25, 1935, p. 5. Marvin was an editor of *NT*, 1935–1936. For an account of the Odets play, see the chapter on the Group Theatre.

29. *DW*, Jan. 28, 1936, p. 4. Produced with Philip Stevenson's *You Can't Change Human Nature* and M. Jagendorf's *The Pastry Baker*. For an account of *Private Hicks*, see the chapter on the New Theatre League. Maltz wrote plays for Theatre Union.

30. "The Theatre Collective," *NT*, May 1936, p. 27. Gassner, later the author of such books as *Masters of the Drama*, wrote articles and reviews for *NT*, 1935–1937.

NOTES TO CHAPTER 2

1. John Bonn, "First National Workers' Theatre Conference," *WT*, May 1932, p. 6.

2. John Bonn, "Situations and Tasks," *WT*, August 1932, pp. 11–12.

3. John Bonn, "Dram Buro Report," *WT*, May 1932, p. 7.

4. *WT*, May 1932, pp. 2, 6.

5. John Bonn, "First National," pp. 5–6. Also see Bonn, "Situations and Tasks," *WT*, June–July 1932, pp. 8–9.

6. John Bonn, "Dram Buro," p. 7.

7. This performance was given at the Civic Repertory Theatre, May 20, 1934.

8. *Dimitroff*, in *NT*, July–August 1934, p. 24.

9. Blake, "The Theatre," *NM*, April 10, 1935, p. 26.

10. Anne Howe, "The Stage Was Not Set," *NT*, June 1934, pp. 14–15.

11. *NT*, June 1934, pp. 3–4. The change also displeased John Howard Lawson, who complained that *New Theatre* failed as both a philosophical and an artistic guide. See "Play on Dimitroff," *DW*, July 23, 1934, p. 5. Lawson attempted to fulfill the need for a book that related the theatre to Marxism when he wrote *Theory and Technique of Playwriting* (New York, 1936). Lawson maintained that dramatic conflict should always lead to social choice. The character, in brief, must be converted to Marxism. For an account of Lawson's conversion, see my chapter on the Group Theatre.

12. "Vital Articles," *DW*, Oct. 11, 1934, p. 5. Ettinger, a writer

for the *DW*, appeared on the editorial board of *NT* one month after this attack and remained an editor until June 1935.

13. *NT*, June 1934, pp. 3–4.

14. George Lewis, "We Need Anti-war Plays," *WT*, August 1932, p. 6.

15. "Building a Repertory," *WT*, June–July 1932, p. 7. Shapiro was active in the WLT and the Theatre Collective. *Hands Off!* was published in *WT*, June–July 1932, pp. 17–19.

16. *NT*, September 1934, p. 3.

17. "Send Us Scripts," *NT*, September 1934, p. 26.

18. "Appeal to Playwrights," *NT*, October 1934, p. 5.

19. Michael Gold, "*Stevedore*," *NM*, May 1, 1934, p. 28.

20. Conrad Seiler, "Workers' Theatre: A Criticism," *NT*, June 1934, p. 17.

21. "We Answer the Call," *WT*, June–July 1932, p. 3.

22. Seiler, p. 17.

23. "The World of the Theatre," *DW*, Nov. 10, 1933, p. 5. Edgar was the chief drama critic for *DW* during the 1933–34 season.

24. "Workers' Theatres," *NM*, August 1933, p. 27. Ben Blake and Harry Elion were also in the WLT.

NOTES TO CHAPTER 3

1. *NT*, February 1935, p. 3. The names of the old and new organizations were used interchangeably for the first few months of 1935.

2. Alice Evans, "New Theatre League," *DW*, June 1, 1935, p. 7.

3. Similarly, after the Second World War we discovered that we did not agree with the Soviet Russians on the meaning of "free and democratic elections" in Eastern Europe.

4. Granville Hicks, *Where We Came Out* (New York, 1954), pp. 41–45.

5. Ben Blake, "The Theatre," *NM*, April 16, 1935, p. 26.

6. "The Theatre," *NM*, Nov. 12, 1935, p. 27.

7. Evans, p. 7.

8. "Plays of the Month," *NT*, January 1935, p. 24.

9. "Middle-Ground Writers," *NM*, April 30, 1935, p. 19.

10. At the première, *Waiting for Lefty* was on a double bill with Philip Stevenson's *God's in His Heaven*. At subsequent performances such dramas as *Dimitroff* by Smith and Kazan were used.

11. This scene appeared in the version published in *NT*, February 1935, pp. 13–20, and also in *Three Plays* (New York, 1935). The scene is omitted from *Six Plays* (New York, 1939). As Odets drifted away from communism, he naturally omitted his most obviously Communistic scene.

For a fuller account of Odets' brief Party membership, see the chapter on the Group Theatre and also HCU-AA, *Hearings*, May 19 and 20, 1952, pp. 3453–3512.

12. *Waiting for Lefty* in *Three Plays*, p. 52.

13. *Ibid.*, pp. 53–54.

14. When Odets uses Biblical allusions to add a tone of supernatural prophecy to his revolutionary hopes, the dialogue becomes rhapsodic. See, for instance, *Three Plays*, p. 42.

15. *Ibid.*, p. 28.

16. *Waiting for Lefty* was Odets' only agitprop. His later plays and one earlier one (*Awake and Sing*) follow the patterns of conventional drama. Likewise the Marxist sentiments of his later plays (except *Till the Day I Die*) are extremely vague by comparison with *Waiting for Lefty*.

17. *DW*, June 17, 1935, p. 4.

18. Charles Hatchard, "The Theatre," *NM*, April 30, 1935, pp. 27–28. See also Anita Block, *The Changing World in Plays and Theatre* (Boston, 1939), pp. 284–285.

19. "Workers Stink," *New Leader*, March 16, 1935, Sec. 2, p. 1.

20. "*New Leader* Attack," *DW*, March 27, 1935, p. 7. There was no retraction, but a milder review appeared the following week: Joseph Shipley, "Driving Drama," *New Leader*, March 30, 1935, p. 8, found the play moving despite its exaggerations.

21. "Cheers Greet New Revolutionary Play," *DW*, Jan. 12, 1935, p. 7. Also see Stanley Burnshaw, "The Theatre," *NM*, Jan. 29, 1935, pp. 27–28.

22. The plays were Philip Barber's *The Klein-Ohrbach Strike*, Art Smith's *Tide Rises*, and Elizabeth England's *Take My Stand*.

23. *DW*, Jan. 9, 1936, p. 4. Also on the bill were *Unto Such Glory*, a short comedy by Paul Green, and "Angelo Herndon," a mass chant by Joseph North and Elizabeth England.

24. "The Theatre," *NM*, Jan. 21, 1936, p. 29.

25. Printed in *NT*, April 1936, pp. 15–30. The play was acted by the *Let Freedom Ring* Acting Company.

26. *NT*, April 1936, p. 3.

27. "Great Anti-War Play," *DW*, April 21, 1936, p. 7.

28. "New Strike Play," *DW*, Dec. 14, 1937, p. 7. Englander reviewed plays for *DW* in 1937.

29. Manngreen, "Left on Broadway," *DW*, May 3, 1938, p. 7. *Plant in the Sun* was paired successively with Theodore Kaghan's *Hello Franco*, Marc Blitzstein's *I've Got the Tune*, and Philip Stevenson's *Transit*.

30. "New Theatres," *DW*, Jan. 14, 1941, p. 7.

31. Ralph Warner, "Broadway Languid," *DW*, May 16, 1941, p. 7. Warner was chief drama critic for *DW*, 1940–1944.

32. "American Brand of Fascism," *SW*, May 25, 1941, p. 7.
33. "Prospects for the New Theatre," *NT*, September 1935, p. 24.
34. "Shifting Scenes," *NT*, September 1936, p. 24.
35. *Curtain Call*, October 1937, p. 3.
36. Alice Evans, "A Challenge," *NTN*, December 1939, pp. 6–7. As we have noted, the New Theatre of Manhattan did produce such a revised play in 1941.
37. "Footlights across America for Peace," *NTN*, November 1939, p. 3.
38. "Repertory Ramblings," *NTN*, August–September 1940, p. 5.
39. "Little Ladies of the Stage," *DW*, Oct. 29, 1936, p. 7. Dexter was chief drama critic for the *DW*, 1936–1937.
40. Alex Marden, "Social Playwrights," *DW*, Dec. 30, 1937, p. 7.
41. Mark Marvin, "An American People's Theatre," *NT*, December 1935, pp. 24–25.
42. Herbert Kline, "The New Theatres Meet," *NT*, May 1936, p. 3.
43. "National Membership Drive," *Curtain Call*, October 1937, p. 7.
44. "Statement of Profit and Loss," *NTN*, July 1940, p. 2.
45. For example, an advertisement in *NM*, March 19, 1935, p. 28, listed these Group members as teachers at the New Theatre School: Elia Kazan, "Technique of Directing"; J. Edward Bromberg, "Technique of Acting"; and Cheryl Crawford, "Theatre Management and Organization."
46. "Back Where We Came From," *NTN*, February 1940, p. 22.
47. *"Inside America,"* *DW*, Oct. 18, 1940, p. 7.
48. "Notice," *NTN*, November 1940, p. 3.
49. Ben Irwin, "Editorial," *NTN*, December 1940, p. 1.
50. Ben Irwin, "Editorial," *NTN*, January 1941, p. 1.

NOTES TO CHAPTER 4

1. George Sklar and Albert Maltz, "The Need for a Workers' Theatre," *DW*, Dec. 16, 1933, p. 7.
2. *DW*, Oct. 16, 1933, p. 5.
3. Anita Block, *The Changing World in Plays and Theatre* (Boston, 1939), p. 275.
4. "Towards a Workers' Theatre," *New Republic*, Dec. 27, 1933, p. 184.
5. "Timely Topics," *New Leader*, Dec. 2, 1933, p. 8.
6. Margaret Larkin, "Theatre Union—Its Tasks and Problems," *DW*, May 15, 1935, p. 5.
7. *DW*, Jan. 9, 1936, p. 7.
8. Larkin, p. 7.
9. Molly Day Thacher, "Revolutionary Staging for Revolutionary

Plays," *NT*, July–August 1934, p. 26. Miss Thacher, wife of Elia Kazan, was later a playreader for the Group Theatre.

10. Larkin, p. 7.

11. "On Writing and Selecting Plays for Workers," *DW*, Feb. 27, 1935, p. 5.

12. "The Theatre," *NM*, Jan. 16, 1934, p. 29.

13. See Jack Shapiro, *"Peace on Earth,"* *NT*, January 1934, p. 11; and Joseph Freeman, *"Peace on Earth,"* *DW*, Dec. 2, 1933, p. 7. Freeman was an editor of *NM*, 1926–1939. For an account of his Party activities see his *An American Testament* (New York, 1936). He later left the Party.

This advertisement appeared Feb. 14, 1934, p. 5.

14. Quoted by Paul Peters, *"Peace on Earth,"* *DW*, Dec. 5, 1933, p. 5.

15. Thacher, p. 26.

16. Dec. 30, 1933, p. 7. The statistics are in Burns Mantle, *The Best Plays of 1933–1934* (New York, 1934), pp. 265, 511. Unless otherwise noted, all subsequent statistics concerning the New York engagements of plays have been taken from the yearly volumes of this Burns Mantle series. Plays in the series are arranged chronologically for each season. Information regarding the casts, directors, and scene designers for all productions can also be found in these volumes.

17. Sender Garlin, "When Negro, White Unite," *DW*, May 16, 1934, p. 5.

18. A. Lunacharsky, "Problems of Style in Socialist Art," *The International Theatre*, Bulletin No. 5 (Moscow, 1933), pp. 3–7. Lunacharsky was a Soviet commissar and theorist.

19. "Straight from the Shoulder," *NT*, November 1934, pp. 11–12.

20. "Theatre Union Replies," *NT*, November 1934, p. 12. Oak admitted his own Communist affiliations in *DW*, March 21, 1935, p. 7.

21. See Harold Edgar, "Play of New Orleans," *DW*, April 20, 1934, p. 5; and Jack Shapiro, *"Stevedore,"* *NT*, May 1934, p. 13.

22. Philip Sterling, "Stirring Labor Play," *DW*, Oct. 4, 1934, p. 5.

23. *Professor Mamlock*, another drama by Wolf, was to be presented by Federal Theatre in 1937. This playwright was a German Communist who fled his native land when Hitler came to power.

24. "World of the Theatre," *DW*, Dec. 11, 1934, p. 5.

25. *"Sailors of Cattaro,"* *DW*, Feb. 5, 1935, p. 7.

26. "Change the World," *DW*, Dec. 26, 1934, p. 5.

27. "Actors Arrested in Store Picketing," *New York Times*, Feb. 10, 1935, Sec. 1, p. 17.

28. Friedman, "The Editor Comments," *New Leader*, March 2, 1935, p. 8. For Oak's reply, see "Theater Union," *DW*, March 21, 1935, p. 7.

29. For the definition of proletarian tragedy, see Philip Rahv, "The

Literary Class War," *NM*, August 1932, p. 7, and A. B. Magil, "Pity and Terror," *NM*, December 1932, p. 16. Magil was an editor of *NM*, 1932–1948.

30. Albert Maltz, *Black Pit* (New York, 1935), p. 108.

31. "The Theatre," *NM*, April 2, 1935, pp. 42–43. Joseph North was an editor of *NM*, 1934–1948.

32. "On the Theatre Union's Play," *DW*, April 29, 1935, p. 5. Stachel was listed as "a member of the Central Committee of the Communist Party," *SW*, Oct. 11, 1937, p. 6.

33. "Joseph North Answers," *DW*, April 30, 1935, p. 5.

34. "*Black Pit* Is the Real Stuff," *DW*, May 7, 1935, p. 5; "Splendidly Realistic Portrayal," *DW*, May 18, 1935, p. 7. Robert Forsythe, pen name of Kyle Crichton, was a columnist for *NM* in the mid-thirties.

35. "More about Black Pit," *DW*, May 30, 1935, p. 5.

36. Mordecai Gorelik, "Epic Realism: Brecht's Notes on the *Threepenny Opera*," *Theatre Workshop*, April–July 1937, pp. 29–40.

37. Bertolt Brecht, *Mother*, adapted by Paul Peters (NYPL, Thea Coll, mimeographed, 1935), p. 26.

38. This scene (Act I, Scene 3) was often produced by amateur theatres of the left under the title *The Little Green Bundle*.

39. Gorelik, p. 40.

40. "Brief an das Arbeitertheater Theatre Union in New York," in *Stücke für das Theateram Schiffbauerdamm*, III (Berlin, 1957), 156–163.

It is interesting to note that in 1938 Brecht, temporarily abandoning the theatrical devices of his "epic theatre," wrote *Señora Carrar's Rifles*, a realistic, highly emotional one-act drama about a Spanish mother who is converted from neutrality to Communist militancy when one of her innocent sons is killed by the nationalists. Brecht, who complained that Theatre Union had added too many realistic details—such as cabbage cooking on the stove—to *Mother*, directed Señora Carrar to bake bread in the later play. *Señora Carrar's Rifles*, translated by Keene Wallis and printed in *Theatre Workshop*, April–June 1938, pp. 30–50, was not performed in New York City.

41. This sketch was written by Emanuel Eisenberg, who was press representative for the Group Theatre in the last years of the decade. The typewritten script is at the Educational Department of the ILGWU in New York City.

42. "*Mother*," *DW*, Nov. 22, 1935, p. 5.

43. "Change the World," *DW*, Dec. 5, 1935, p. 7; "Change the World," *DW*, Dec. 6, 1935, p. 9.

44. Lunacharsky, pp. 3–7. Also see Louis Fischer, in *The God*

That Failed, ed. Richard Crossman (New York, 1950), pp. 205–206.

45. "Change the World," *DW*, Dec. 11, 1935, p. 5.

46. "Change the World," *DW*, Dec. 30 and 31, 1935, p. 7.

47. "A Play of Fascist Italy," *DW*, April 3, 1936, p. 7.

48. "A Worker Looks at Broadway," *NT*, May 1936, p. 26. *NT* identified Mullen as a novelist and a union organizer.

49. *DW*, Oct. 8, 1936, p. 7, and Nov. 24, 1936, p. 7. See also *New York Times*, Aug. 30, 1936, Sec. 9, p. 1.

50. "The Curtain Rises," *NT*, November 1936, p. 4.

51. *Marching Song* (NYPL, Thea Coll, typewritten, 1937), Act 2, p. 32.

52. "A Bourgeois Hamlet in Our Time," *NM*, April 10, 1934, pp. 28–29.

53. Charles E. Dexter, "In the Multitude," *DW*, March 1, 1937, p. 7. Also see Nathaniel Buchwald, "*Marching Song*," *DW*, March 2, 1937, p. 7; Dexter, "*Marching Song*," *DW*, Feb. 19, 1937, p. 7; and "Lawson's Play," *DW*, Feb. 20, 1937, p. 7.

54. Albert Maltz, "*Marching Song*," *NT and F*, March 1937, p. 13; Alexander Taylor, "Sights and Sounds," *NM*, March 2, 1937, p. 27. Taylor was the chief drama critic for *NM* during the 1936–37 season. Also see John Gassner, "Wings over Broadway," *NT and F*, April 1937, pp. 19–20.

55. *NM*, March 16, 1937, pp. 30–31.

56. The *New York Times*, Aug. 29, 1937, Sec. 10, p. 1, reported the official dissolution of the company. In dissolving, Theatre Union paid tribute to Charles R. Walker, its founder, Victor Wolfson, its business manager, and Margaret Larkin, its press representative and secretary.

57. "Thus the Union Figures," *New York Times*, Jan. 26, 1936, Sec. 9, p. 3. These figures were based on all Theatre Union productions through *Mother*. Theatre Union claimed an average attendance of 990 at each performance out of a possible 1,100. During this same period, it claimed a total audience of 523,000, of whom 23,000 had been admitted without charge.

58. "A Worker Looks at Broadway," *NT*, May 1936, p. 26.

59. "Change the World," *DW*, Dec. 31, 1935, p. 7.

60. "Change the World," *DW*, Oct. 9, 1937, p. 7.

61. *Ibid.*

NOTES TO CHAPTER 5

1. Fannia M. Cohn and Irwin Swerdlow, *In Union There Is Strength* (New York, 1933), p. 30.

2. New York *Herald Tribune*, Jan. 30, 1938, Sec. 6, p. 5.

3. *Playbill for Labor Stage*, Dec. 25, 1937.

4. *New York Times,* May 30, 1941, p. 13.

5. "The Veteran *Pins and Needles,*" *Playbill* (Windsor Theatre), July 31, 1939, p. 1.

6. Irwin Shapiro, *"Steel,"* NT and F, March 1937, p. 63.

7. Ben Burns, "The Labor Unions Go Broadway," *DW,* Sept. 28, 1937, p. 7.

8. Stanley Burnshaw, "The Theatre," *NM,* Oct. 22, 1935, p. 28.

9. "The A.F.L. Theatre," *DW,* June 17, 1936, p. 7.

10. *"Pins and Needles*—Labor Stage," *NT,* July 1936, p. 24.

11. "The Veteran *Pins and Needles,*" p. 1.

12. Labor Stage had a seating capacity of 299. The Windsor Theatre could seat 903 persons.

13. Henry W. L. Dana, "Five Years of Labor Theatre," *DW,* June 3, 1938, p. 7, read satire into the lyrics. This interpretation is possible but not probable in light of Schaeffer's aim, which did include a social message as well as satire.

The script of *Pins and Needles,* never published, is at the Education Department of the ILGWU in New York City. All quotations are taken from these manuscripts.

Many of the songs were published. Permission secured from the copyright owner, Mills Music, Inc.

14. See the chapter on the Mercury Theatre for details of Blitzstein's trouble with the WPA Theatre.

15. "Sparkling Revue," *DW,* Nov. 29, 1937, p. 7.

16. "The General Is Unveiled," "Little Red Schoolhouse," "Vassar Girl Finds Job," and "FTP Plowed Under" were dropped.

17. N.C., "Somebody Has Given the Revised *Pins* the Needles," *DW,* Nov. 30, 1939, p. 7.

18. "The Theatre and the A.F. of L.," *NM,* Nov. 5, 1935, p. 5.

19. Burns, p. 7.

20. *Ibid.*

21. New York State Committee, Communist Party, *No Career in No Man's Land* (New York, 1940), pp. 8–9, 12.

22. "Keen Social Satire," *DW,* Feb. 19, 1941, p. 7. Labor Stage still exists on paper, but it has been virtually inactive since the closing of *Pins and Needles.*

NOTES TO CHAPTER 6

1. Clarence J. Wittler, *Some Social Trends in WPA Drama* (Washington, D.C., 1939), pp. 8–9.

2. The government had operated a smaller theatrical program under the Civil Works Administration and then under the Federal Emergency Relief Administration for two years, starting in December 1933.

3. Hallie Flanagan, *Arena* (New York, 1940), p. 17.

4. *Ibid.,* pp. 45, 29.

5. *Ibid.,* pp. 45–46. On p. 361 she estimated that only 10 per cent of Federal Theatre productions were socially significant.

6. *Ibid.*

7. *Ibid.,* pp. 183–184. See also p. 204 for her sarcastic comments on Leninist drama.

8. *Ibid.,* p. 173. Thomas, later convicted for accepting "kick-backs" from his employees, served time in prison. See *New York Times,* Dec. 1, 1949, p. 1.

9. "Inciting to Riot," *Liberty,* May 23, 1936, p. 4.

10. *Congressional Record,* 80, Part 5 (April 20, 1936), 5696–5699.

11. Garet Garrett, "Federal Theatre for the Masses," June 20, 1936, p. 8, and Harrison Grey Fiske, "The Federal Theatre Doom-Boggle," Aug. 1, 1936, p. 8; the editorial was "Once Upon a Time," June 26, 1937, p. 22.

12. Quoted by Fiske, p. 72.

13. *Arena,* pp. 200–201.

14. *Congressional Record,* 80, Part 6 (April 27, 1936), 6165–6166.

15. *Arena,* pp. 57, 343.

16. *Ibid.,* p. 58.

17. *Ibid.,* p. 36.

18. "The Inside Story of a Murder," *DW,* Dec. 23, 1940, p. 7.

19. *Arena,* pp. 65–66.

20. *Ibid.*

21. Rice's statement to the press was reprinted in *NT,* February 1936, p. 2.

22. Arthur Arent, *Triple-A Plowed Under* in *Federal Theatre Plays,* ed. Pierre de Rohan (New York, 1938), pp. 34–35.

23. "The Theatre," *NM,* April 28, 1936, p. 27.

24. "Federal Theatre Play," *SW,* March 22, 1936, p. 6.

25. See "Text of Platform," *DW,* June 29, 1936, pp. 1–2. Also see "Browder in Radio Interview," *DW,* Oct. 8, 1936, p. 5. In this transcript of a radio interview, Earl Browder promised that the transition to a workers' state would be peaceful if the capitalists peacefully surrendered.

26. Hallie Flanagan, "Introduction," *Federal Theatre Plays,* p. x.

27. "A Worker Looks at Broadway," *NT,* May 1936, p. 27.

28. "1935," *SW,* May 17, 1936, p. 6.

29. Jay Gerlando, "Theatre," *DW,* March 26, 1936, p. 7, asserted that this play had been given a dull production. Gerlando reviewed plays for the *DW* during the 1935–36 season.

30. "Theatre," *DW,* May 25, 1936, p. 7.

31. "The Theatre," *NM,* June 2, 1936, pp. 29–30.

32. "Change the World," *DW,* Dec. 6, 1935, p. 9. Blankfort, deny-

ing actual collaboration with Gold, testified that the latter gave him the script for repairs and that he repaired it without consulting with Gold. See HCU-AA, *Hearings*, Jan. 28, 1952, p. 2343. Blankfort reviewed plays for the *DW* in 1935 and 1936, and for *NM* in 1934 and 1935. He told the House Committee that he was not a Communist, only a fellow traveler who wanted free theatre tickets.

33. See, for example, Michael Gold and Michael Blankfort, *Battle Hymn* (NYPL, Thea Coll, mimeographed by Federal Play Bureau, 1936), p. 2-3-3. Wage earners and slaves are equated throughout the play.

34. "Text of Platform," *DW*, June 29, 1936, p. 1.

35. *Ibid.*

36. Elizabeth Lawson, "A True Play," *DW*, May 26, 1936, p. 7; Howard Horstmann, "Then and Now," *SW*, June 7, 1936, p. 12; and James Robie, *"Battle Hymn," DW*, July 3, 1936, p. 7.

37. *Arena*, pp. 76–77.

38. "The Negro Theatre Triumphs," *DW*, June 29, 1936, p. 9.

39. *Arena*, pp. 72–73.

40. "Labor's Struggle Dramatized," *DW*, July 29, 1936, p. 7.

41. "The Theatre," *NM*, Aug. 4, 1936, p. 29.

42. "Second Play of Social Farceur," *DW*, Sept. 21, 1936, p. 7.

43. *Arena*, pp. 117–121.

44. *Ibid.*, p. 129.

45. *Ibid.*, p. 127.

46. Sinclair Lewis and John C. Moffitt, *It Can't Happen Here* (NYPL, Thea Coll, mimeographed by Federal Play Bureau, 1936), p. 2-4-8.

47. "Sinclair Lewis," *DW*, Oct. 29, 1936, p. 7. Also see A.W.T., "Sights and Sounds," *NM*, Nov. 10, 1936, p. 29.

48. "Living Newspaper's *Power*," *DW*, Feb. 25, 1937, p. 7. Also see Dexter, "Finding a Hero for *Power*," *DW*, March 3, 1937, p. 7, and Alexander Taylor, "Sights and Sounds," *NM*, March 9, 1937, p. 29.

49. "W.P.A.'s *The Sun and I*," *DW*, March 1, 1937, p. 7.

50. "Sights and Sounds," *NM*, March 9, 1937, p. 29.

51. The Nazis were often called the "instruments of German finance capital." For example, see "A United Front to Fight Fascism," *DW*, March 25, 1933, p. 1. See also Arthur Koestler, in *The God That Failed*, ed. R. Crossman (New York, 1950), pp. 15–75. Koestler blamed the Communist Party for fighting the Socialists more vehemently than it fought the Nazis.

52. Charles E. Dexter, *"Professor Mamlock," DW*, April 15, 1937, p. 7. Also see Alexander Taylor, "The Theatre," *NM*, April 27, 1937, p. 31.

53. Oscar Saul and Lou Lantz, *The Revolt of the Beavers* (NYPL, Thea Coll, typewritten, 1936), p. 1-2-18.

54. "*Revolt of the Beavers,*" *DW*, May 24, 1937, p. 9.

55. "Once Upon a Time," June 26, 1937, p. 22.

56. See *Processional* (NYPL, Thea Coll, typewritten, 1937).

57. "*Processional,*" *SW*, Oct. 17, 1937, p. 12. Also Judith Reed, "Lawson's Play Belongs to the Past," *DW*, Oct. 20, 1937, p. 7.

58. Dave Jones, "Living Newspaper Play," *DW*, Jan. 19, 1938, p. 7. Walter Ralston, "Sights and Sounds," *NM*, Feb. 1, 1938, pp. 28–29.

59. "Toller's Play," *DW*, Jan. 31, 1938, p. 9. Cambridge reviewed plays for the *DW* in 1938 and 1939.

60. John Cambridge, "Lincoln's Youth and Love," *DW*, March 21, 1938, p. 7. Eleanor Flexner, "Federal Theatre Interprets Lincoln," *NM*, March 29, 1938, pp. 27–29. Miss Flexner wrote reviews for *NM* in 1937 and 1938.

61. Bernard Shaw, *On the Rocks* (NYPL, Thea Coll, typewritten, 1938), Act 2, p. 54. See photo facing Act 1, p. 1. The American audience must have regarded Sir Arthur as the *raisonneur,* inasmuch as the actor portraying him was made up to resemble Shaw.

62. "The Stage," *SW*, June 26, 1938, p. 12. Also see Cambridge, "*On the Rocks,*" *DW*, June 18, 1938, p. 7.

63. "*Big Blow,*" *DW*, Oct. 3, 1938, p. 7.

64. "Negro W.P.A. Actors," *DW*, Dec. 19, 1938, p. 7.

65. Quoted in *NM*, Dec. 27, 1938, p. 29.

66. "Federal Theatre's *Androcles,*" *NM*, Dec. 27, 1938, p. 29.

67. George Sklar, *Life and Death of an American* (NYPL, Thea Coll, typewritten, 1939), Act 2, p. 38.

68. Milton Meltzer, "Sklar's New Play," *NM*, June 6, 1939, pp. 29–30. Also see John Cambridge, "The Stage," *SW*, May 22, 1938, p. 12.

69. Hallie Flanagán, *What Was Federal Theatre?* (American Council on Public Affairs, 1939), pp. 2–3, 61. Mrs. Flanagan estimated that half of this number represented performers, and half, other project personnel.

70. *Arena*, pp. 333–352.

71. John Cambridge, "The Stage," *SW*, June 18, 1939, p. 7. The *DW* offered advice to Federal Theatre on many occasions. The Party was chiefly worried about cuts in personnel.

72. Reprinted from the *Midwest Daily Record* in *DW*, Sept. 21, 1939, p. 7.

73. *Arena*, pp. 335–336.

74. See Eric Stone, "New Group Shows Promise," *DW*, Oct. 27, 1936, p. 7; Ben Compton, "Indications," *DW*, Dec. 11, 1936, p. 7;

"A Statement," *NT and F*, March 1937, p. 3; and Ralph Warner, "Growing Pains," *SW*, June 1, 1941, p. 7.
75. *NTN*, April 1940, p. 5.

NOTES TO CHAPTER 7

1. John Houseman, "Again—A People's Theatre," *DW*, Sept. 18, 1937, p. 7.
2. "Steel Strike Opera," *New York Times*, June 17, 1937, p. 1.
3. *Ibid.*
4. *SW*, Nov. 28, 1937, p. 11.
5. "Steel Strike Opera," p. 1.
6. *Ibid.*
7. Marc Blitzstein, *The Cradle Will Rock*, in *The Best Short Plays of the Social Theatre*, ed. William Kozlenko (New York, 1939), p. 167.
8. Marc Blitzstein, "Author of *The Cradle*," *DW*, Jan. 3, 1938, p. 7.
9. Edith Hale, "Author and Composer Blitzstein," *DW*, Dec. 7, 1938, p. 7.
10. Blitzstein, "Author of *The Cradle*," p. 7. Blitzstein treated the same themes once again in January 1941, when his opera *No for an Answer* was produced by W. E. Watts in a concert version at the Mecca Auditorium for three performances. See Blitzstein, *No for an Answer* (NYPL, Thea Coll, typewritten, 1941).
11. Hale, p. 7.
12. Charles E. Dexter, "Does Ban Mean W.P.A. Censorship?" *DW*, June 18, 1937, p. 7.
13. The production returned to the smaller Mercury Theatre on Feb. 28, 1938, for the remainder of the run.
14. "*Cradle* Rocks at Mercury," *DW*, Dec. 7, 1937, p. 7. Also see Englander, "The Stage," *SW*, Dec. 12, 1937, p. 10.
15. Houseman, p. 7.
16. "The Stage," *DW*, Nov. 13, 1937, p. 7. Also see Englander, "The Stage," *SW*, Nov. 21, 1937, p. 10.
17. "The Stage," *SW*, May 8, 1938, p. 12.
18. "Mercury Wins Wide Acclaim," *SW*, Feb. 6, 1938, p. 13.
19. "Shaw's *Heartbreak House*," *DW*, May 2, 1938, p. 7.
20. Prior to *Danton's Death*, Welles produced *Five Kings*, a compilation of scenes from various Shakespearean history plays for the Theatre Guild. This production failed out of town. See Lawrence Langner, *The Magic Curtain* (New York, 1951), pp. 269–273.
21. Oct. 20, 1938, p. 7.
22. Georg Büchner, *Danton's Death*, in *Plays of Georg Büchner*,

trans. Geoffrey Dunlop (New York, 1952), p. 142. For the Lenin quotation, see Michael Blankfort, "Foreword," in Friedrich Wolf, *The Sailors of Cattaro* (New York, 1935), p. vi.

23. *"Danton's Death,"* DW, Nov. 4, 1938, p. 7.

24. "Big Themes in the Theatre," *NM*, Nov. 15, 1938, p. 28. Miss McKenney, author of the "My Sister Eileen" stories, wrote reviews for *NM*, 1938–1939.

25. The notorious "War of the Worlds" was broadcast on Oct. 31, 1938.

26. "Stage Version of *Native Son,*" *DW*, March 27, 1941, p. 7. Also see Samuel Sillen, "Bigger Thomas on the Boards," *NM*, April 8, 1941, pp. 27–28.

27. Richard Wright, in *The God That Failed,* ed. R. Crossman (New York, 1950), pp. 115–162. Wright was expelled from the Party at the time when Federal Theatre was still operating, that is, before June 1939.

28. Ralph Warner, "Hearst Attempts to Sabotage," *SW*, March 30, 1941, p. 7.

NOTES TO CHAPTER 8

1. Philip Moeller, Teresa Helburn, Lee Simonson, Lawrence Langner, Maurice Wertheim, Helen Westley, and Alfred Lunt, "Introduction," *The Theatre Guild Anthology* (New York, 1936), p. ix. The above-named were the directors of the Guild. Langner and Miss Helburn were in charge of most of the productions.

2. *Ibid.*

3. "Change the World," *DW*, April 11, 1934, p. 5.

4. "The Theatre Guild Plays," *NM*, Jan. 5, 1937, p. 23.

5. "Theatre Guild and Its Record," *DW*, March 19, 1937, p. 7.

6. "Change the World," *DW*, Nov. 29, 1940, p. 7.

7. January 1934, pp. 6–7. Others replying to the questionnaire were Paul Green, George Sklar, John Howard Lawson, Alfred Harding, Paul and Claire Sifton, Emjo Basshe, John Wexley, and Liston M. Oak.

8. *"Red Rust,"* DW, Dec. 20, 1929, p. 2.

9. "Theatre," *NM*, February 1930, pp. 14–15.

10. "Notes of the Month," *NM*, April 1930, p. 5.

11. This translation has not been published. The synopsis is taken from an English adaptation by F. Polianovska and Barbara Nixon.

12. *"Roar China,"* DW, Nov. 15, 1930, p. 4.

13. "Theatre," *NM*, December 1930, p. 17.

14. *"The Good Earth,"* DW, Nov. 8, 1932, p. 2.

15. "The World of the Theatre," *DW*, Feb. 6, 1934, p. 7.

16. F. Raymond Daniell, "An Alabama Court in Forty-fifth Street," *New York Times*, March 4, 1934, Sec. 9, p. 1. This reporter, who had covered the case for the *Times*, found the play both realistic and accurate.

17. "*They Shall Not Die*," *DW*, Feb. 23, 1934, p. 7.

18. "Change the World," *DW*, April 11, 1934, p. 5.

19. *Ibid.*

20. Murray Kempton, *Part of Our Time* (New York, 1955), p. 253, estimated that the Party collected almost a million dollars for the boys even though the actual costs of the defense did not exceed $60,000.

The *New York Times* reported on Oct. 13, 1934, that Samuel Leibowitz and the newly formed non-Communist Scottsboro Committee had warned the public not to contribute money to Communist collectors. Leibowitz had broken with the ILD at this time because some of its members had attempted to bribe a witness.

21. "Change the World," *DW*, April 19, 1934, p. 5. See also Anita Block, *The Changing World in Plays and Theatre* (Boston, 1939), p. 262. Left-wing reviewers noticed the same lack of audience response.

22. "The Theatre," *NM*, Jan. 1, 1935, pp. 44–45.

23. "The Drama in Transition," *NT*, August 1935, pp. 28–29.

24. *Ibid.*, p. 14.

25. Paul Peters, George Sklar, *et al.*, *Parade* (NYPL, Thea Coll, typewritten, 1935), p. 22.

26. "World of the Theatre," *DW*, May 24, 1935, p. 7.

27. *NT*, June 1935, p. 9.

28. "Pacifist Pipe-Dream," *DW*, Sept. 27, 1935, p. 5.

29. *Idiot's Delight* (New York, 1938), pp. 189–190.

30. "The New Play," *SW*, March 29, 1936, p. 6.

31. "How Poverty Breeds Crime," *DW*, Jan. 15, 1937, p. 7. Sidney Harmon was associate producer.

32. Taylor, "Sights and Sounds," *NM*, Feb. 23, 1937, p. 27. Dexter, "Anderson Ends His Season," *DW*, Feb. 11, 1937, p. 7.

33. "Stage," *DW*, Oct. 16, 1937, p. 7.

34. Sayers, "Sights and Sounds," *NM*, Dec. 7, 1937, p. 26. Englander, "Ghosts of the Guild Stage," *DW*, Nov. 25, 1937, p. 7.

35. "Political Satire," *NM*, May 17, 1938, p. 29. Also see John Cambridge, "*Washington Jitters*," *DW*, May 4, 1938, p. 7.

36. "The Stage," *SW*, Feb. 12, 1939, p. 7.

37. Eugene Lyons, *The Red Decade* (New York, 1941), pp. 200–203. See also the following editorials: "Un-neutral Neutrality," *SW*, March 7, 1937, p. 10; and "Senator Borah—Victim of 'Isolationist' Fallacy," *DW*, July 8, 1939, p. 6.

38. *New York Times*, March 9, 1938, p. 21. Lawrence Langner,

The Magic Curtain (New York, 1951), p. 254, blamed the split on the playwrights' annoyance at the irritating criticism so often offered by members of the Guild's board.

39. "Abraham Lincoln Lives Again," *NM*, Nov. 1, 1938, p. 27. Also see John Cambridge, *"Abe Lincoln in Illinois,"* *DW*, Oct. 19, 1938, p. 7. The quotation comes from Robert E. Sherwood, *Abe Lincoln in Illinois* (New York, 1939), p. 137.

40. "A Preface to the Politics of *Knickerbocker Holiday*," *Knickerbocker Holiday* (Washington, D.C., 1938, pp. vii–viii.

41. Cambridge, "Reviewer in Doubt," *DW*, Oct. 24, 1938, p. 7; McKenney, "Sights and Sounds," *NM*, Nov. 1, 1938; pp. 27–28. Also see Miss McKenney's attack on Anderson's preface, "Notes on Maxwell Anderson," *NM*, Nov. 29, 1938, p. 27.

42. *American Landscape* (New York, 1939), p. 142.

43. "Elmer Rice on Americanism," *NM*, Dec. 20, 1938, pp. 27–28.

44. "Elmer Rice's New Play," *DW*, Dec. 9, 1938, p. 7. Also see Cambridge, "The Stage," *SW*, Dec. 11, 1938, p. 12.

45. "A Lively Theatre Week," *NM*, Dec. 12, 1939, p. 29. Bessie reviewed plays for *NM*, 1939–1944.

46. Ernest Hemingway, *The Fifth Column*, adapted by Benjamin Glazer (NYPL, Thea Coll, typewritten, 1940), Scene 8, p. 23. This speech and the interventionist tone were among Glazer's many additions. For comparison see *The Fifth Column* (New York, 1939). Hemingway wrote the play in 1937 originally.

47. "The Guild Version," *DW*, March 9, 1940, p. 7.

48. *"The Fifth Column,"* *NM*, March 19, 1940, pp. 28–31. This exoneration of Hemingway may have been an attempt to entice him into what remained of the united front. With the publication of *For Whom the Bell Tolls* in 1940, the Party gave up and attacked the famous novelist. See Bessie, "Hemingway's *For Whom the Bell Tolls,"* *NM*, Nov. 5, 1940, pp. 25–29, for the attack.

49. *"There Shall Be No Night,"* *DW*, May 2, 1940, p. 7. Also see Robert E. Sherwood, "Preface," *There Shall Be No Night* (New York, 1939), pp. xxvii–xxix. This playwright became disillusioned with the Soviet Union at the start of the Russo-Finnish War.

50. "Behind the Mannerheim Line," *NM*, May 14, 1940, p. 27.

51. "Change the World," *DW*, Nov. 29, 1940, p. 7.

52. *"Love's Old Sweet Song,"* *SW*, May 5, 1940, p. 7. Also see Alvah Bessie, "William Saroyan: Requiescat," *NM*, May 21, 1940, p. 29.

53. Alvah Bessie, *"Flight to the West,"* *NM*, Jan. 14, 1941, p. 29. Also see Ralph Warner, "Elmer Rice Drops War Tracts," *DW*, Jan. 3, 1941, p. 7; and Warner, "Public Rejects War Plays," *SW*, Feb. 23, 1941, p. 7.

54. *"Liberty Jones,"* *NM*, Feb. 25, 1941, pp. 28–29.

55. *"Liberty Jones,"* SW, Feb. 9, 1941, p. 7.

56. Maxwell Anderson, *Candle in the Wind* (Washington, D.C., 1941), p. 116.

57. "Helen Hayes Starred," DW, Oct. 25, 1941, p. 7. Also see Warner, "The Theatre," SW, Nov. 2, 1941, p. 7; and Alvah Bessie, "Anderson's New Play," NM, Nov. 4, 1941, pp. 28–30.

58. *"Hope for a Harvest,"* DW, Nov. 29, 1941, p. 7.

59. "Poor Harvest," NM, Dec. 9, 1941, pp. 26–27.

NOTES TO CHAPTER 9

1. The members are listed in Claire and Paul Sifton, *1931–* (New York, 1931), p. ix.

2. Harold Clurman, *The Fervent Years* (New York, 1945), pp. 36–38.

3. Harold Clurman, "The Group Theatre Speaks for Itself," *New York Times*, Dec. 13, 1931, Sec. 8, p. 2.

4. *Fervent Years*, p. 44. On p. 139 Clurman reported that Stella Adler, after weeks of study with Stanislavsky in Paris in 1934, decided that the Group had overemphasized the exercises involving the remembered emotions.

5. "What the Group Theatre Wants," *Playbill* (Mansfield Theatre), Dec. 10, 1931, pp. 4–5.

6. Cheryl Crawford, letter to John Mason Brown, "Two on the Aisle," New York *Post*, Jan. 27, 1933, p. 7.

7. See Clurman, *Fervent Years*, pp. 55–58, for an explanation of the Group's finances and salary arrangements. Although the Guild contributed half the production costs and the full services of its publicity department, the senior company had nothing to do with the artistic direction of the Group.

Although the Guild's presentation of *Red Rust* in 1929 had involved people who were later to become active in the Group, *The House of Connelly* was the Group's first presentation.

8. *1931–* (New York, 1931).

9. "A Proletarian Play on Broadway," NM, January 1932, pp. 27–28.

10. *Fervent Years*, pp. 71–72. Theatre Collective, having clarified the revolutionary sentiments of the play, revived it in 1933 for a run of four performances.

11. *Ibid.*, pp. 50, 91–93.

12. HCU-AA, *Hearings*, April 10, 1952, pp. 2407–2414. Kazan named eight other actors as members of the Group cell during 1934–1936: Lewis Leverett and J. E. Bromberg (the two leaders), Phoebe

Brand, Morris Carnovsky, Tony Kraber, Paula Miller (Mrs. Lee Strasberg), Clifford Odets, and Art Smith.

Odets, testifying on May 19 and 20, 1952, pp. 3453–3512, corroborated much of Kazan's testimony. Odets said that he remained a Party member for less than a year, and Kazan asserted that Paula Miller was not a member for a long period either. Testifying on April 24, 1951, pp. 389–393, Carnovsky invoked the Fifth Amendment, as did Bromberg, who testified on June 26, 1951, pp. 717–738.

Kazan asserted that Party orders were transmitted to the cell by V. J. Jerome, who was "some sort of 'cultural' commissar," and by Andrew Overgaard, who was a union leader. Jerome, who was a member of the National Agit-Prop (the Party's agitation and propaganda agency), was active in New York during the early thirties; in 1936 he became active in Hollywood, where he remained through the forties. Testifying on March 8, 1951, pp. 55–76, Jerome used the Fifth Amendment.

13. "*Success Story,*" *DW*, Oct. 3, 1932, p. 1.

14. "The World of the Theatre," *DW*, Oct. 3, 1933, p. 5.

15. D. A. Doran, Jr., was the associate producer.

16. "Lawson Makes His Reply," New York *Daily Mirror*, March 28, 1934, p. 20.

17. Melvin Levy, "The World of the Theatre," *DW*, March 28, 1934, p. 7. Levy wrote *Gold Eagle Guy*, which the Group produced the following season.

18. "A Bourgeois Hamlet in Our Time," *NM*, April 10, 1934, pp. 28–29.

19. " 'Inner Conflict' and Proletarian Art," *NM*, April 17, 1934, pp. 29–30.

20. "A Reply to Lawson," *NM*, April 24, 1934, pp. 28–29.

21. Pp. 6–7.

22. See *DW*, May 18, 1934, p. 1, for the story of Lawson's arrest.

23. "John Howard Lawson Appeals," *DW*, May 18, 1934, p. 2.

24. HCU AA, *Hearings*, Jan. 28, 1952, pp. 2300–2336. Although Levy quit the Party, he remained a fellow traveler. Late in the 1940's, believing that the Party was defunct, he joined the Communist Political Association in Hollywood. This organization, which he also left, did not attempt to influence his writing.

25. "World of the Theatre," *DW*, Dec. 4, 1934, p. 5. Also see Alexander, "Plays of the Month," *NT*, January 1935, pp. 24–25.

26. "The Theatre," *NM*, Dec. 11, 1934, p. 29.

27. Clifford Odets, *Awake and Sing*, in *Three Plays* (New York, 1935), p. 108.

28. *Ibid.*, p. 70.

29. "World of the Theatre," *DW*, Feb. 20, 1935, p. 5.

30. "The Theatre," *NM*, March 5, 1935, p. 28.

31. "The Theatre," *NM*, March 26, 1935, p. 27.
32. *Ibid.*, pp. 27–28.
33. "*Till the Day I Die*," *NT*, May 1935, p. 16.
34. "The Theatre," *NM*, April 9, 1935, p. 27.
35. February 1935, p. 4.
36. "World of the Theatre," *DW*, April 1, 1935, p. 5.
37. "Theatre," *DW*, Dec. 4, 1935, p. 5.
38. "Change the World," *DW*, Dec. 5, 1935, p. 7.
39. The improbability of Leo Gordon's final speech about the bright future was ridiculed by Joseph Schrank in his sketch "Paradise Mislaid," which was part of *Pins and Needles*. To the embezzlement, the dispossession, and the death, Schrank added the revelation that the daughter had three illegitimate children—a theme suggested by *Awake and Sing*.
40. "Interpretation and Characterization," *NT*, January 1936, p. 21.
41. Clurman, "Introduction," in Clifford Odets, *Paradise Lost* (New York, 1936), p. x.
42. "Clifford Odets Writes a Tragedy," *DW*, Dec. 13, 1935, p. 7. Blankfort testified that the *DW* dropped him as a play reviewer because the editors did not like his praise of *Paradise Lost*. See HCU-AA, *Hearings*, Jan. 28, 1952, pp. 2323–2366.
43. "Odets and the Middle Class," *DW*, Feb. 7, 1936, p. 7. Also see Stanley Burnshaw, "The Theatre," *NM*, Feb. 11, 1936, p. 28; and Clara Bagley, "The New Play," *SW*, Feb. 16, 1936, p. 6.
44. HCU-AA, *Hearings*, May 19–20, 1952, pp. 3453–3512.
45. Piscator, a German revolutionary producer, directed radical theatres in Berlin in the 1920's and early 1930's. After escaping from Hitler, he settled in New York.
Milton Shubert was the associate producer. The play was translated by Louise Campbell.
46. *Fervent Years*, p. 174.
47. "Drama vs. Melodrama," *NT*, April 1936, pp. 8–10. Theodore Repard, "Theatre," *DW*, March 17, 1936, p. 7, liked the spectacle of the production, as did Stanley Burnshaw, "The Theatre," *NM*, March 31, 1936, p. 28.
48. "A Worker Looks at Broadway," *NT*, May 1936, p. 25. Mullen disliked the production.
49. Harold Clurman, letter to Howard Barnes, "The Playbill," New York *Herald Tribune*, Feb. 16, 1936, Sec. 5, p. 1. Also see Miss Crawford's letter to John Mason Brown, "Two on the Aisle," New York *Post*, April 17, 1936, p. 16.
50. "Case of the Group Theatre," *NT*, July 1936, p. 5.
51. "Group Theatre Scores Some Hits," *DW*, Nov. 21, 1936, p. 7. In 1941 a more strongly anti-war version of the play (music omitted)

was offered without success by the Popular Theatre, a minor and unsuccessful theatre group.

52. "The Diluted Theatre," *NT and F*, March 1937, p. 30.

53. Lee Strasberg, "Showing the Movie Screen," *DW*, Jan. 5, 1937, p. 7.

54. Ben Compton, "Facts and the Group Theatre," *SW*, Jan. 10, 1937, p. 12.

55. *Fervent Years*, p. 206. Clurman, while promising to try to employ all Group actors, said he would not pay anyone not actually appearing in a production. During the preceding years all members were paid whether they acted or not, as long as the Group had a play on the boards. •

The Actors' Committee—Luther Adler, Roman Bohnen, and Elia Kazan—continued to act only as an advisory council. Clifford Odets and Morris Carnovsky were later added to the committee.

56. "Group Back on Broadway," *DW*, Nov. 12, 1937, p. 7.

57. "Farewell to Silk, Hello Lisle," *DW*, Dec. 3, 1937, p. 7.

58. "Odets' *Rocket to the Moon*," *DW*, Nov. 28, 1938, p. 7. For a milder review, see Ruth McKenney, "The New Odets Play," *NM*, Nov. 6, 1938, p. 28.

59. "*Gentle People*," *DW*, Jan. 7, 1939, p. 7.

60. "Gentle People in Trouble," *NM*, Jan. 17, 1939, pp. 29–30.

61. N.C., "*Thunder Rock*," *DW*, Nov. 16, 1939, p. 7. Also see Alvah Bessie, "*Thunder Rock*," *NM*, Nov. 28, 1939, pp. 28–31.

62. This bit of isolationism, reported by the two critics, does not appear in the revised edition of the play. See Robert Ardrey, *Thunder Rock* (New York, 1941), for the revised version.

63. "The Dilemma of Clifford Odets," *NM*, March 5, 1940, pp. 28–29. Also see Abel Gorham, "Hollywood and Broadway," *DW*, Feb. 27, 1940, p. 7. Abel Gorham reviewed plays for the *DW* during 1939 and 1940.

64. "Mr. Shaw Retreats," *NM*, Dec. 31, 1940, pp. 29–30.

65. "*Retreat to Pleasure*," *DW*, Dec. 19, 1940, p. 7.

66. For a full account of the demise, see *Fervent Years*, pp. 271–280.

67. "Machines before the Footlights," *NM*, Aug. 26, 1941, pp. 26–31.

NOTES TO CHAPTER 10

1. "Aristophanes' Sportive Satire," *DW*, June 11, 1930, p. 2.

2. The evidence was slight, but Mooney was sentenced to life in prison. He was pardoned in 1939.

3. Burns Mantle, *Best Plays of 1931–1932* (New York, 1932),

pp. 435–436. A revised version of the play was produced by Labor Stage in 1936.

4. Nov. 21, 1931, p. 2.

5. "A Play with Propaganda," *WT*, August 1932, pp. 7–8.

6. Mantle, *Best Plays of 1931–1932*, p. 508.

7. "A Play with Propaganda," pp. 7–8.

8. Shumlin was connected with several Party fronts, including the Theatre Arts Committee (TAC) and the Joint Anti-Fascist Refugee Committee. He quit the latter group in 1947 when he and the other board members were convicted on contempt of Congress because they had refused to submit the records of the organization. Shumlin, desiring to purge himself of contempt, said that he had no control over the records. As a result, his sentence was suspended. See *New York Times*, July 17, 1947, p. 1.

9. "*Clear All Wires*," *DW*, Sept. 20, 1932, p. 2.

10. "Stage and Screen," *DW*, Feb. 7, 1933, p. 2.

11. "Change the World," *DW*, Sept. 18, 1934, p. 5.

12. Notes to *The Threepenny Opera*, in *From the Modern Repertoire*, ed. Eric Bentley, Series One (Denver, 1949), p. 396.

13. *The Threepenny Opera*, trans. Desmond Vesey and Eric Bentley, in *The Modern Theatre*, ed. Eric Bentley, Vol. 1 (Garden City, 1955), p. 193. The Cochran-Krimsky version was not published. Marc Blitzstein's version of *The Threepenny Opera*, which opened at the Theatre de Lys on Sept. 23, 1955, ran 2,611 performances.

14. "Stage and Screen," *DW*, April 24, 1933, p. 4.

15. Burns Mantle, *Best Plays of 1933–1934* (New York, 1934), p. 436.

16. "The World of the Theatre," *DW*, Oct. 6, 1933, p. 5.

17. Mantle, *Best Plays of 1933–1934*, p. 460.

18. Kaufman *et al.*, *Let 'Em Eat Cake* (New York, 1933), p. 55.

19. "The World of the Theatre," *DW*, Nov. 2, 1933, p. 5. Also see Ben Blake, "*Let 'Em Eat Cake*," *NT*, January 1934, pp. 11–12.

20. "The World of the Theatre," *DW*, Jan. 15, 1934, p. 5.

21. "The Theatre," *NM*, Jan. 30, 1934, pp. 28–29.

22. Mantle, *Best Plays of 1933–1934*, p. 8.

23. "Elmer Rice," *NT*, September 1934, p. 7. Also see Albert Maltz's review of this article, "Current *New Theatre*," *DW*, Sept. 17, 1934, p. 5.

24. Sender Garlin, "Change the World," *DW*, Sept. 18, 1934, p. 5. Also see George Willson, "The Theatre," *NM*, Sept. 25, 1934, p. 28; and Ben Blake, "*Judgment Day*," *NT*, October 1934, p. 17.

25. "World of the Theatre," *DW*, Oct. 30, 1934, p. 5.

26. "Two Authors between Two Worlds," *NT*, December 1934, pp. 19–20.

27. "Elmer Rice Says Farewell to Broadway," *New York Times,* Nov. 11, 1934, Sec. 9, p. 1.

28. Leon Alexander, "World of the Theatre," *DW,* Nov. 12, 1934, p. 7; Joshua Kunitz, "The Theatre," *NM,* Nov. 20, 1934, p. 26; and Stanley Burnshaw, "The Theatre," *NM,* Nov. 27, 1934, p. 27.

29. Edwin Rolfe, "An Interview with Archibald MacLeish," *DW,* March 15, 1935, p. 5. Also see Al Saxe, "World of the Theatre," *DW,* March 18, 1935, p. 7.

30. Jerome's speech was printed in *NM,* April 2, 1935, pp. 43–44.

31. "Change the World," *DW,* Oct. 23, 1935, p. 7.

32. "The Theatre," *NM,* Oct. 29, 1935, pp. 27–28.

33. "World of the Theatre," *DW,* Nov. 5, 1935, p. 5.

34. "The Theatre," *NM,* Nov. 26, 1935, pp. 28–29.

35. "Change the World," *DW,* Dec. 5, 1935, p. 7.

36. "Change the World," *DW,* Dec. 10, 1935, p. 7.

37. Burns Mantle, *Best Plays of 1935–1936* (New York, 1936), p. 457.

38. "Theatre," *DW,* Jan. 14, 1936, p. 7. Also see Stanley Burnshaw, "The Theatre," *NM,* Jan. 21, 1936, p. 28, for further details.

39. *"Ten Million Ghosts,"* *DW,* Oct. 26, 1936, p. 7. Also see Dexter, "Recommending Some Reading," *SW,* Nov. 15, 1936, p. 12; and A.W.T., "Sights and Sounds," *NM,* Nov. 3, 1936, p. 29.

40. Lillian Hellman offered to testify about her own activities but refused to talk about others. Since the congressmen refused to accept any conditions, she invoked the Fifth Amendment on most of the questions. See HCU-AA, *Hearings,* May 21, 1952, pp. 3541–3549.

Stalin's views on the relation of capitalism and fascism were quoted by Fritz Heckert, "What Is Happening in Germany," *DW,* May 17, 1933, p. 4.

41. Charles E. Dexter, "Strikes and Strike Breakers," *DW,* Dec. 18, 1936, p. 7. Also see Alexander Taylor, "Sights and Sounds," *NM,* Dec. 20, 1936, p. 27.

42. "A Comparative Study," *NT and F,* March 1937, pp. 15–16.

43. "The Theatre," *NM,* Feb. 9, 1937, pp. 30–31.

44. *"Tide Rising,"* *DW,* Jan. 29, 1937, p. 7.

45. "A Note from the Author," *Tide Rising* (New York, 1937), pp. 7–10.

46. "It's All Aboard for Utopia," *DW,* April 13, 1937, p. 7. Also see Dexter, "Comedy, Pathos, and Day-Dreams," *DW,* April 14, 1937, p. 7.

47. "Sights and Sounds," *NM,* April 20, 1937, p. 35.

48. Burns Mantle, *Best Plays of 1937–1938* (New York, 1938), p. 401. The other professional plays about the Spanish War were Maxwell Anderson's *Key Largo* (produced by the Playwrights' Com-

pany) and the Theatre Guild production of *The Fifth Column* by Ernest Hemingway and Benjamin Glazer.

49. "Sights and Sounds," *NM*, Dec. 21, 1937, p. 28. Burrows reviewed some plays for *NM* during the 1937–38 season.

50. "*Siege* Fails," *DW*, Dec. 10, 1937, p. 7.

51. John Cambridge, "Caldwell's *Journeyman*," *DW*, Feb. 14, 1938, p. 7. Also see Nathaniel Buchwald, "Sights and Sounds," *NM*, Feb. 15, 1938, pp. 25–26.

52. "A Comedy for the 'Ruling Clawss,'" *DW*, Nov. 5, 1937, p. 7.

53. "Sights and Sounds," *NM*, Nov. 23, 1937, p. 28.

54. "The Stage," *SW*, May 22, 1938, p. 12.

55. *Ibid.*

56. Eugene Lyons, *The Red Decade* (New York, 1941), pp. 296–297.

57. June 26, 1938, p. 12.

58. "The Stage," *SW*, May 22, 1938, p. 12.

59. *DW*, April 24, 1940, p. 7.

60. *NTN*, February 1940, p. 17.

61. "The Stage," *SW*, Nov. 6, 1938, p. 16.

62. "Democracy Boosted," *DW*, Nov. 14, 1938, p. 7.

63. "Anti-Fascist Comedy," *NM*, Nov. 22, 1938, p. 30.

64. "*The American Way*," *DW*, Jan. 27, 1939, p. 7. Also see Cambridge, "The Stage," *SW*, Jan. 29, 1939, p. 7; and Ruth McKenney, "Written in Anger," *NM*, Feb. 7, 1939, pp. 29–30.

65. Ruth McKenney, "*The Little Foxes*," *NM*, Feb. 28, 1939, pp. 29–30. Also see John Cambridge, "The Stage," *SW*, Feb. 19, 1939, p. 7.

66. "17 Battery Place," *NM*, Nov. 21, 1939, p. 30.

67. Abel Gorham, "Thurber-Nugent Comedy," *DW*, Jan. 12, 1940, p. 7. Also see Alvah Bessie, "War of the Sexes," *NM*, Jan. 23, 1940, p. 31.

68. "*Medicine Show*," *DW*, April 16, 1940, p. 7. Also see Alvah Bessie, "Medicine for the People," *NM*, April 23, 1940, p. 31.

69. April 17, 1940, p. 7.

70. "Miners' Life Depicted," *DW*, Nov. 29, 1940, p. 7.

71. "*The Corn Is Green*," *SW*, Dec. 15, 1940, p. 7.

72. Burns Mantle, *Best Plays of 1940–1941* (New York, 1941), p. 94.

73. "*Watch on the Rhine*," *DW*, April 4, 1941, p. 7.

74. "*Watch on the Rhine*," *NM*, April 15, 1941, pp. 26–28.

75. "Audiences Want Plays," *SW*, April 20, 1941, p. 7.

76. The figure of 1,500 is approximate, a round compromise between the totals listed by *Variety*, May 29, 1957, p. 70, and those

derived from the listings of Burns Mantle. The figure excludes Broadway productions by Federal Theatre, the Group Theatre, the Theatre Guild, the Playwrights' Company, and the Mercury Theatre.

NOTES TO CHAPTER 11

1. For the Communist position on war, see J. P., "Be Prepared against Imperialist War," *DW*, July 30, 1930, p. 4; and Alex Bittleman, "Organize for the Struggle against War," *DW*, July 11, 1931, p. 6.

2. See, for example, "Unite Your Ranks against War," *DW*, Oct. 3, 1935, p. 1, for the Party's position on the Ethiopian War. See also Earl Browder, "The Democratic Front in the 1940 Elections," *DW*, Dec. 14, 1938, p. 6, for the Communist view on Spain and China. Browder's plea for a united front against fascism was to be conveniently forgotten more than a year before the 1940 elections.

3. National Committee, Communist Party, U.S.A., "Keep America out of the Imperialist War," *DW*, Sept. 19, 1939, p. 1.

4. See "Wall Street Uses Finland for War," *DW*, Dec. 1, 1939, p. 1. Russia's territorial expansions during this period were usually labeled "liberations" or "peaceful" settlements of old disputes.

5. "A Season on the Boards," *NM*, May 7, 1940, p. 29.

6. National Committee, Communist Party, U.S.A., "The People's Program of Struggle," *DW*, June 30, 1941, p. 1.

7. "C.P. National Committee Vows Support in Crisis," *DW*, Dec. 8, 1941, p. 1.

8. See the Party platforms in *DW*, July 27, 1932, p. 3, and July 26, 1934, p. 3.

9. See the Party platform in *DW*, June 29, 1936, pp. 1–2.

10. See the Party platform in *DW*, July 26, 1934, p. 3, for the orthodox position. See the Party platform in *DW*, June 29, 1936, pp. 1–2, for the united front view.

11. Nathaniel Buchwald's Yiddish adaptation of this play, retitled *Trickenish* and presented in 1931 by the Artef, a Yiddish workers' theatre, had a more clearly pro-Communist ending.

12. *Hearings*, May 19, 1952, p. 3481.

13. See V. I. Lenin, "Party Organization and Party Literature," trans. Ralph B. Winn, *Dialectics*, No. 5, 1938, pp. 2–5. Also see "Lenin on Working Class Literature," trans. Anna Rochester, *NM*, October 1929, p. 7.

14. January 1934, p. 2.

15. "The Crisis in the Theatre," *NM*, Dec. 15, 1936, pp. 35–36.

BIBLIOGRAPHY

I. PLAYS

ABBOTT, GEORGE. *Sweet River.* NYPL, Thea Coll, typewritten, 1936.
AIKEN, G. L. *Uncle Tom's Cabin,* revised by A. E. Thomas. New York, 1934.
ANDERSON, MAXWELL. *Both Your Houses.* New York, 1937.
——. *Candle in the Wind.* Washington, D.C., 1941.
——. *Key Largo.* Washington, D.C., 1939.
——. *Knickerbocker Holiday.* Washington, D.C., 1938.
——. *The Masque of Kings.* Washington, D.C., 1937.
——. *Night over Taos.* New York, 1935.
——. *Valley Forge.* Washington, D.C., 1934.
——. *The Wingless Victory.* Washington, D.C., 1936.
——. *Winterset.* Washington, D.C., 1936.
ARDREY, ROBERT. *Thunder Rock.* New York, 1941.
ARENT, ARTHUR, and the Editorial Staff of the Living Newspaper. *Injunction Granted.* NYPL, Thea Coll, mimeographed by National Service Bureau, 1938.
——. *1935.* NYPL, Thea Coll, mimeographed by Federal Play Bureau, 1938.
——. *One-Third of a Nation,* in *Federal Theatre Plays,* ed. Pierre de Rohan. New York, 1938.
——. *Power,* in *Federal Theatre Plays,* ed. Pierre de Rohan. New York, 1938.
——. *Triple-A Plowed Under,* in *Federal Theatre Plays,* ed. Pierre de Rohan. New York, 1938.
ARISTOPHANES. *Lysistrata,* adapted by Gilbert Seldes. New York, 1930.
AUDEN, W. H. *The Dance of Death.* London, 1933.
BARRY, PHILIP. *Liberty Jones.* New York, 1941.
BEHRMAN, S. N. *Biography.* New York, 1933.
——. *No Time for Comedy.* New York, 1939.
——. *Rain from Heaven.* New York, 1935.
BEIN, ALBERT. *Let Freedom Ring.* New York, 1936.
BENGAL, BEN. *Plant in the Sun,* in *The Best Short Plays of the Social Theatre,* ed. William Kozlenko. New York, 1939.
BLANKFORT, MICHAEL. *The Brave and the Blind.* New York, 1937.
——. *The Crime.* New York, 1936.

263

BLANKFORT, MICHAEL, and MICHAEL GOLD. *Battle Hymn,* NYPL, Thea Coll, mimeographed by Federal Play Bureau, 1936.

BLITZSTEIN, MARC. *The Cradle Will Rock.* New York, 1938.

——. *No for an Answer.* NYPL, Thea Coll, typewritten, 1941.

BOLITHO, WILLIAM. *Overture—1920.* New York, 1931.

BONN, JOHN E. *15 Minute Red Revue,* trans. B. Stern and George Lewis, *WT,* June–July 1932, pp. 11–14.

BOOTHE, CLARE. *Margin for Error.* New York, 1940.

BORUFF, JOHN, and WALTER HART. *Washington Jitters.* New York, 1938.

BOUCICAULT, DION. *The Poor of New York.* New York, 1857.

BRECHT, BERTOLT. *The Informer,* trans. Ruth Norden, in *Six Anti-Nazi One Act Plays,* ed. Stephen Moore. New York, 1939. (A scene from *The Private Life of the Master Race.*)

——. *Justice,* anon. trans., in *V for Victory.* NYPL, Thea Coll, mimeographed by the IWO, 1941. (A scene from *The Private Life of the Master Race.*)

——. *Die Mutter,* in *Stücke für das Theater am Schiffenbauerdamm,* Vol. 3. Berlin, 1957. (Contains one scene of the Peters adaptation, and also the projection titles of the Theatre Union production.)

——. *Mother,* adapted by Paul Peters. NYPL, Thea Coll, mimeographed, 1935.

——. *Señora Carrar's Rifles, Theatre Workshop,* April–June, 1938, pp. 30–50.

——. *The Sixth Column,* adapted from *The Informer* by Ruth Holder. NYPL, Thea Coll, typewritten, 1940.

——. *The Threepenny Opera,* revised trans. Eric Bentley and Desmond Vesey, in *The Modern Theatre,* ed. Eric Bentley, Vol. 1. Garden City, 1955.

——. *The Threepenny Opera,* trans. Eric Bentley and Desmond Vesey in *From the Modern Repertoire,* ed. Eric Bentley, Series One. Denver, 1949.

BRENNAN, FREDERICK H. *The Wookey.* New York, 1941.

BREWER, GEORGE. *Tide Rising.* New York, 1937.

BÜCHNER, GEORG. *Danton's Death,* trans. Geoffrey Dunlop, in *Plays of Georg Büchner.* New York, 1952.

BUCHWALD, NATHANIEL. *Hands Off!* in *WT,* June–July 1932, pp. 17–19.

CAPEK, KAREL. *The Mother,* trans. Paul Selver. London, 1939.

CHLUMBERG, HANS. *Miracle at Verdun,* trans. Julian Leigh. New York, 1931.

CLARKE, HAROLD, and MAXWELL NURNBERG. *Chalk Dust.* NYPL, Thea Coll, mimeographed by Federal Play Bureau, 1936.

COHN, FANNIA, and IRWIN SWERDLOW. *All for One.* NYPL, Thea Coll, mimeographed by the ILGWU, 1933.

——. *In Union There Is Strength*. NYPL, Thea Coll, mimeographed by the ILGWU, 1933.

COLES, STEDMAN, and JEROME BROOKMAN. *Press Time*, NYPL, Thea Coll, typewritten, 1938.

CONKLE, ELLSWORTH P. *Prologue to Glory*, in *Federal Theatre Plays*, ed. Pierre de Rohan. New York, 1938.

——. *200 Were Chosen*. New York, 1937.

DAVIS, PHILIP H. *Trojan Incident*. NYPL, Thea Coll, typewritten, 1938.

DEKKER, THOMAS. *The Shoemakers' Holiday*, in *Elizabethan Plays*, ed. Hazleton Spencer. Boston, 1933.

DEVAL, JACQUES. *Lorelei*. NYPL, Thea Coll, typewritten, 1938.

DIX, BEULAH M., and BERTRAM MILLHAUSER. *Ragged Army*. NYPL, Thea Coll, typewritten, 1934.

ENGLAND, ELIZABETH. *Take My Stand*. New York, 1935.

ENGLAND, ELIZABETH, and JOSEPH NORTH. "Angelo Herndon." NYPL, Thea Coll, mimeographed by the New Theatre League, 1935.

EPSTEIN, JULIUS J., and PHILIP. *And Stars Remain*. New York, 1937.

EURIPIDES. *The Trojan Women*, trans. Gilbert Murray. New York, 1915.

FARAGOH, FRANCIS E. *Sunup to Sundown*. NYPL, Thea Coll, typewritten, 1937.

FLANAGAN, HALLIE, and MARGARET ELLEN CLIFFORD. *Can You Hear Their Voices?* Poughkeepsie, N.Y., 1931. (Based on a story by Whittaker Chambers.)

GARRETT, OLIVER H. P. *Waltz in Goose Step*. NYPL, Thea Coll, typewritten, 1938.

GOLDEN, I. J. *Precedent*. New York, 1931.

GORKI, MAXIM. *A Night's Lodging*, trans. Edwin Hopkins. Boston, 1920.

GREEN, PAUL. *The House of Connelly*. New York, 1931.

——. *Hymn to the Rising Sun*, in *The Best Short Plays of the Social Theatre*, ed. William Kozlenko. New York, 1939.

——. *Johnny Johnson*. New York, 1937.

——. *Roll Sweet Chariot*. New York, 1935.

——. *Unto Such Glory*, in *In the Valley*. New York, 1928.

HARE, WALTER B. *Over Here*. Boston, 1919.

HAYES, ALFRED, and LEON ALEXANDER. *Journeyman*. NYPL, Thea Coll, typewritten, n.d.

HECHT, BEN. *To Quito and Back*. New York, 1937.

HELLMAN, LILLIAN. *Days to Come*, in *Four Plays*. New York, 1942.

——. *The Little Foxes*. New York, 1939.

——. *Watch on the Rhine*. New York, 1941.

HEMINGWAY, ERNEST. *The Fifth Column*. New York, 1939.

——. *The Fifth Column*, adapted by Benjamin Glazer. NYPL, Thea Coll, typewritten, 1940.

HEYWARD, DUBOSE. *Brass Ankle.* New York, 1931.

HOLMES, JOHN HAYNES, and REGINALD LAWRENCE. *If This Be Treason.* New York, 1935.

HOWARD, SIDNEY. *The Ghost of Yankee Doodle.* New York, 1938.

——. *Paths of Glory.* New York, 1936.

HUGHES, LANGSTON. *Don't You Want to Be Free,* in *One Act Play Magazine,* II (October 1938), 359–393.

——. *Scottsboro Limited.* New York, 1932.

KAGHAN, THEODORE. *Hello Franco.* NYPL, Thea Coll, typewritten, n.d.

KATAYEV, VALENTIN. *The Path of Flowers,* adapted by Irving Talmadge. NYPL, Thea Coll, typewritten, 1936.

——. *Squaring the Circle,* trans. Charles Malamuth and Eugene Lyons, in *Six Soviet Plays,* ed. Eugene Lyons. Boston, 1934.

KAUFMAN, GEORGE S., and EDNA FERBER. *The Land Is Bright.* Garden City, 1941.

KAUFMAN, GEORGE S., and MOSS HART. *The American Way,* in *Six Plays.* New York, 1942.

——. *I'd Rather Be Right.* New York, 1937.

KAUFMAN, GEORGE S., and MORRIE RYSKIND. *Let 'Em Eat Cake.* New York, 1933.

——. *Of Thee I Sing.* New York, 1932.

KAZAN, ELIA, and ART SMITH. *Dimitroff,* NT, July–August 1934, pp. 20–24.

KENNELL, RUTH, and JOHN WASHBURNE. *They All Come to Moscow.* NYPL, Thea Coll, typewritten, 1933.

KINGSLEY, SIDNEY. *Dead End.* New York, 1936.

——. *Men in White.* New York, 1933.

——. *Ten Million Ghosts.* NYPL, Thea Coll, typewritten, 1936.

KIRKLAND, JACK. *Tobacco Road.* New York, 1952.

KIRSCHON, V., and A. OUSPENSKY. *Red Rust,* adapted by Frank and Virginia Vernon. New York, 1930.

KOZLENKO, WILLIAM. *This Earth Is Ours,* in *The Best Short Plays of the Social Theatre,* ed. William Kozlenko. New York, 1939.

KRAFT, H. S. *The Bishop of Munster,* in *Six Anti-Nazi Plays,* ed. Stephen Moore. New York, 1939.

KRASNA, NORMAN. *The Man with Blond Hair.* NYPL, Thea Coll, typewritten, 1941.

KREYMBORG, ALFRED. "America, America!" in *Proletarian Literature in the United States,* ed. Granville Hicks, *et al.* New York, 1935.

LASHIN, ORRIE, and MILO HASTINGS. *Class of '29.* NYPL, Thea Coll, typewritten, 1936.

LAWRENCE, REGINALD, and S. K. LAUREN. *Men Must Fight.* NYPL, Thea Coll, typewritten, 1933.

LAWSON, JOHN HOWARD. *Gentlewoman,* in *With a Reckless Preface.* New York, 1934.

——. *Marching Song.* New York, 1937.

——. *Marching Song.* NYPL, Thea Coll, typewritten, 1937.

——. *Processional* (original version). New York, 1925.

——. *Processional* (Federal Theatre version). NYPL, Thea Coll, typwritten, 1937.

——. *The Pure In Heart,* in *With a Reckless Preface.* New York, 1934.

——. *Success Story.* New York, 1932.

LEVY, MELVIN. *Gold Eagle Guy.* New York, 1935.

LEWIS, SINCLAIR, and JOHN C. MOFFITT. *It Can't Happen Here.* NYPL, Thea Coll, mimeographed by Federal Play Bureau, 1936.

MACLEISH, ARCHIBALD. *Panic.* Boston, 1935.

MACOWAN, NORMAN. *Glorious Morning.* New York, 1939.

MALTZ, ALBERT. *Black Pit.* New York, 1935.

——. *Private Hicks,* in *The Best Short Plays of the Social Theatre,* ed. William Kozlenko. New York, 1939.

——. *Rehearsal,* in *One Act Play Magazine,* I (March 1938), 994–1020.

MARTIN, PETER. *Daughter.* NYPL, Thea Coll, mimeographed by the New Theatre League, n.d.

NOVIKOV, GREGORY. *Newsboy.* NYPL, Thea Coll, mimeographed, n.d.

ODETS, CLIFFORD. *Awake and Sing,* in *Three Plays.* New York, 1935.

——. *Golden Boy,* in *Six Plays.* New York, 1939.

——. *Night Music.* New York, 1940.

——. *Paradise Lost.* New York, 1936.

——. *Rocket to the Moon,* in *Six Plays.* New York, 1939.

——. *Till the Day I Die,* in *Three Plays.* New York, 1935.

——. *Waiting for Lefty* (original version), in *Three Plays.* New York, 1935.

——. *Waiting for Lefty* (revised version), in *Six Plays.* New York, 1939.

O'NEIL, GEORGE. *American Dream.* New York, 1933.

PETERS, PAUL, and GEORGE SKLAR. *Stevedore.* New York, 1934.

PETERS, PAUL, GEORGE SKLAR, FRANK GABRIELSON, DAVID LESAN, KYLE CRICHTON, and JEROME MOROSS. *Parade,* NYPL, Thea Coll, typewritten, 1935.

PISCATOR, ERWIN, and LENA GOLDSCHMIDT. *The Case of Clyde Griffiths,* trans. Louise Campbell. NYPL, Thea Coll, typewritten, 1936.

PRATT, THEODORE. *Big Blow.* NYPL, Thea Coll, typewritten, 1938.

RAND, AYN. *The Unconquered.* NYPL, Thea Coll, typewritten, 1940.

RAPHAELSON, SAMSON. *White Man.* NYPL, Thea Coll, typewritten, 1929.

READE, LESLIE. *The Shatter'd Lamp.* NYPL, Thea Coll, typewritten, 1934.

RICE, ELMER. *The Adding Machine.* Garden City, 1923.

RICE, ELMER. *American Landscape*. New York, 1939.
——. *Between Two Worlds*, in *Two Plays*. New York, 1935.
——. *Flight to the West*. New York, 1941.
——. *Judgment Day*. New York, 1934.
——. *We the People*. New York, 1933.
ROBERTS, WALTER C. *Red Harvest*. New York, 1937.
ROLLAND, ROMAIN. *The Game of Love and Death*, trans. Eleanor S. Brooks. New York, 1926.
——. *Wolves*, trans. Barrett H. Clark. New York, 1937.
ROME, HAROLD, ARTHUR ARENT, MARC BLITZSTEIN, EMANUEL EISENBERG, CHARLES FRIEDMAN, DAVID GREGORY, and JOSEPH SCHRANK. *Pins and Needles*. Typewritten script at the Educational Department of the ILGWU.
SAROYAN, WILLIAM. *Love's Old Sweet Song*, in *Three Plays*. New York, 1940.
——. *My Heart's in the Highlands*. New York, 1939.
SAUL, OSCAR, and H. R. HAYS. *Medicine Show*. NYPL, Thea Coll, typewritten, 1940.
SAUL, OSCAR, and LOU LANTZ. *The Revolt of the Beavers*. NYPL, Thea Coll, typewritten, 1936.
SHAKESPEARE, WILLIAM. *Julius Caesar*, in *The Living Shakespeare*, ed. Oscar J. Campbell. New York, 1949.
SHAW, GEORGE BERNARD. *Androcles and the Lion*. New York, 1916.
——. *Androcles and the Lion* (Negro version). NYPL, Thea Coll, typewritten, 1938.
——. *The Apple Cart*. London, 1930.
——. *Geneva*. London, 1939.
——. *Heartbreak House*. New York, 1944.
——. *On the Rocks*, in *Too True to Be Good*. New York, 1934.
——. *On the Rocks* (Federal Theatre version). NYPL, Thea Coll, typewritten, 1938.
——. *The Simpleton of the Unexpected Isles*, in *The Six of Calais* . . . New York, 1936.
SHAW, IRWIN. *Bury the Dead*, in *The Best Short Plays of the Social Theatre*, ed. William Kozlenko. New York, 1939.
——. *The Gentle People*. New York, 1939.
SHDANOFF, GEORGE. *The Possessed*. NYPL, Thea Coll, typewritten, 1939.
SHEEAN, VINCENT. *An International Incident*. NYPL, Thea Coll, typewritten, 1940.
SHERWOOD, ROBERT E. *Abe Lincoln in Illinois*. New York, 1939.
——. *Idiot's Delight*. New York, 1938.
——. *There Shall Be No Night*. New York, 1940.
SIFTON, PAUL and CLAIRE. *1931–*. New York, 1931.
Skits and Sketches (New Theatre League Collection with a TAC section). New York, 1939.

SKLAR, GEORGE. *Life and Death of an American.* NYPL, Thea Coll, typewritten, 1939.

SKLAR, GEORGE, and ALBERT MALTZ. *Peace on Earth.* New York, 1936.

SPEWACK, SAM and BELLA. *Clear All Wires.* New York, 1932.

——. *Leave It to Me.* NYPL, Thea Coll, typewritten, 1938.

STAVIS, BARRIE and LEONA. *The Sun and I.* NYPL, Thea Coll, typewritten, 1937.

STEVENSON, PHILIP. *Back Where We Came From* (originally, *You Can't Change Human Nature*). NYPL, Thea Coll, typewritten, 1935.

——. *God's in His Heaven.* New York, 1934.

——. *Transit,* in *Contemporary One Act Plays,* ed. William Kozlenko. New York, 1938.

SUNDGAARD, ARNOLD. *Everywhere I Roam.* NYPL, Thea Coll, typewritten, 1938.

THURBER, JAMES, and ELLIOTT NUGENT. *The Male Animal.* New York, 1940.

TOLLER, ERNST. *Man and the Masses,* trans. Louis Untermeyer. Garden City, 1924.

——. *No More Peace,* trans. Edward Crankshaw and W. H. Auden. New York, 1937.

TREADWAY, SOPHIE. *Hope for a Harvest.* New York, 1942.

TRETYAKOV, S. *Roar China,* trans. F. Polianovska and Barbara Nixon. London, 1931.

VIERTEL, JOSEPH M. *So Proudly We Hail.* NYPL, Thea Coll, typewritten, 1936.

Vote Communist, WT, June–July 1932, pp. 15–17.

WARE, ALICE H. *Mighty Wind A Blowin'.* New York, 1936.

WEXLEY, JOHN. *Running Dogs,* in *The Best Short Plays of the Social Theatre,* ed. William Kozlenko. New York, 1939.

——. *They Shall Not Die.* New York, 1934.

WILLIAMS, EMLYN. *The Corn Is Green.* New York, 1941.

WOLF, FRIEDRICH. *Professor Mamlock,* trans. Anne Bromberger. New York, 1935.

——. *The Sailors of Cattaro.* New York, 1935.

WOLFSON, VICTOR. *Excursion.* NYPL, Thea Coll, typewritten, 1937.

WRIGHT, RICHARD, and PAUL GREEN. *Native Son.* New York, 1941.

ZWEIG, STEFAN. *Jeremiah,* trans. Eden and Cedar Paul. New York, 1929.

II. BOOKS AND PUBLIC DOCUMENTS

AARON, DANIEL. *Writers on the Left.* New York, 1962.

BENTLEY, ERIC. *The Playwright as Thinker.* New York, 1946.

BLAKE, BEN. *The Awakening of the American Theatre*. New York, 1935.

BLOCK, ANITA. *The Changing World in Plays and Theatre*. Boston, 1939.

BROWDER, EARL. *Communism and Culture*. New York, 1941.

———. *Communism in the United States*. New York, 1935.

———. *The Communist Party of the U.S.A.* New York, 1941.

BROWN, B. W. *Theatre at the Left*. Providence, 1938.

BROWN, E. J. *The Proletarian Episode in Russian Literature, 1928–1932*. New York, 1953.

CARTER, HUNTLEY. *The New Spirit in the European Theatre, 1914–1924*. New York, 1926.

———. *The New Spirit in the Russian Theatre, 1917–1928*. New York, 1929.

CLURMAN, HAROLD. *The Fervent Years*. New York, 1945.

———. *The Fervent Years*. New York, 1957. (Contains a chapter on the theatre from 1945 to 1955.)

Communist Party, U.S.A., New York State Committee. *No Career in No Man's Land*. New York, 1940.

CONGDON, DON, ed. *The Thirties: A Time to Remember*. New York, 1962.

CROSSMAN, RICHARD, ed. *The God That Failed*. New York, 1950. (Essays by Arthur Koestler, Ignazio Silone, Richard Wright, André Gide, Louis Fischer, and Stephen Spender.)

DRAPER, THEODORE. *The Roots of American Communism*. New York, 1957.

EATON, WALTER P. *The Theatre Guild, the First Ten Years*. New York, 1929.

FLANAGAN, HALLIE. *Arena*. New York, 1940.

———. *Shifting Scenes of the Modern European Theatre*. New York, 1928.

———. *What Was Federal Theatre?* American Council on Public Affairs, 1939.

FLEXNER, ELEANOR. *American Playwrights: 1918–1938*. New York, 1938.

FOX, RALPH. *The Novel and the People*. New York, 1937.

FREEMAN, JOSEPH. *An American Testament*. New York, 1936.

GAGEY, EDMOND M. *Revolution in American Drama*. New York, 1947.

GASSNER, JOHN. *Masters of the Drama*. First ed. New York, 1940.

———. *Masters of the Drama*. Third ed. New York, 1954.

GOLD, MICHAEL. *The Hollow Men*. New York, 1941.

———. *Jews without Money*. New York, 1935.

GORELIK, MORDECAI. *New Theatres for Old*. New York, 1940.

HICKS, GRANVILLE. *The Great Tradition*. New York, 1935.

———. *Where We Came Out*. New York, 1954.

HICKS, GRANVILLE, MICHAEL GOLD, ISIDOR SCHNEIDER, JOSEPH NORTH, PAUL PETERS, ALAN CALMER, and JOSEPH FREEMAN, eds. *Proletarian Literature in the United States.* New York, 1935.

HOFFMAN, 1 ED J. *The Twenties.* New York, 1955.

HOOK, SIDNEr. *Marx and the Marxists.* New York, 1955.

HOUGHTON, NORRIS. *Moscow Rehearsals.* New York, 1936.

KAZIN, ALFRED. *On Native Grounds.* New York, 1942.

KEMPTON, MURRAY. *Part of Our Time.* New York, 1955.

KRUTCH, JOSEPH WOOD. *The American Drama since 1918.* New York, 1939.

——. *The American Drama since 1918.* Revised ed. New York, 1957.

LANGNER, LAWRENCE. *The Magic Curtain.* New York, 1951.

LANIA, LEO. *Today We Are Brothers,* trans. Ralph Marlowe. Boston, 1942.

LAWSON, JOHN HOWARD. *Theory and Technique of Playwriting.* New York, 1936.

LENIN, V. I. *Collected Works of V. I. Lenin,* authorized trans. V. I. Lenin Institute. 23 vols. Moscow and New York, 1927–1945.

——. *Marx. Engels. Marxism,* ed. J. Fineberg, trans. Marx-Engels-Lenin Institute. Moscow and London, 1934.

——. *Selected Works,* ed. J. Fineberg, trans. Marx-Engels-Lenin Institute. 12 vols. Moscow and New York, 1935–1938.

LIFSHITS, M. *The Philosophy of Art of Karl Marx,* trans. Ralph B. Winn, Critics Group Series No. 7. New York, 1938.

LUKACS, GYÖRGY. *Karl Marx und Friedrich Engels als Literaturhistoriker.* Berlin, 1948.

——. *Studies in European Realism,* trans. Edith Bone. London, 1950.

LYONS, EUGENE. *The Red Decade.* New York, 1941.

MANTLE, BURNS. *The Best Plays of 1929–1930* through *The Best Plays of 1941–1942.* 13 vols. New York, 1930 through 1942.

MARKOV, PAVEL A. *The Soviet Theatre.* London, 1939.

MARX, KARL, and FRIEDRICH ENGELS. *Capital, the Communist Manifesto and Other Writings,* ed. Max Eastman. New York, 1932.

——. *Correspondence 1846–1895,* ed. V. Adoratsky, trans. Dona Torr. London, 1934.

——. *Karl Marx, Friedrich Engels, Historisch-kritische Gesamtausgabe,* ed. V. Adoratsky of Marx-Engels Institute. Moscow, 1927–1935.

——. *Literature and Art.* New York, 1947.

——. *Selected Works,* ed. V. Adoratsky, trans. Marx-Engels-Lenin Institute. 2 vols. Moscow and New York, 1936.

——. *Über Kunst und Literatur.* Berlin, 1948.

MERSAND, JOSEPH. *The Drama of Social Significance, 1930–1940.* New York, 1940.

PISCATOR, ERWIN. *Das Politische Theater.* Berlin, 1929.

PLEKHANOV, GEORGII. *Art and Society*, trans. Paul Leitner, Alfred Goldstein, and C. H. Crout, Critics Group Series No. 3. New York, 1936.

SHERWOOD, ROBERT E. *Roosevelt and Hopkins*. 2 vols. New York, 1950.

SPENDER, STEPHEN. *Forward from Liberalism*. London, 1937.

SPRIGG, C. ST. JOHN (Christopher Caudwell, pseud.). *Studies in a Dying Culture*. London, 1938.

STALIN, IOSIF. *Works*, trans. Marx-Engels-Lenin Institute. 13 vols. Moscow, 1952–1955.

STRACHEY, JOHN. *Literature and Dialectical Materialism*. New York, 1934.

——. *The Theory and Practice of Socialism*. New York, 1936.

United States Congress. *Congressional Record*, 80, Part 5 (April 20, 1936), 5696–5699; Part 6 (April 24, 1936), 6074–6075; Part 6 (April 27, 1936), 6165–6166; Part 6 (May 7, 1936), 6792.

United States Congress. House. Committee on Un-American Activities. *Cumulative Index to Publications*. Washington, D.C., 1955.

——. *Hearings* (Testimony of V. J. Jerome), March 8, 1951, pp. 55–76.

——. *Hearings* (Testimony of Morris Carnovsky), April 24, 1951, pp. 389–393.

——. *Hearings* (Testimony of J. Edward Bromberg), June 26, 1951, pp. 717–738.

——. *Hearings* (Testimony of Melvin Levy), Jan. 28, 1952, pp. 2309–2326.

——. *Hearings* (Testimony of Michael Blankfort), Jan. 28, 1952, pp. 2327–2366.

——. *Hearings* (Testimony of Elia Kazan), April 10, 1952, pp. 2407–2414.

——. *Hearings* (Testimony of Clifford Odets), May 19 and 20, 1952, pp. 3453–3512.

——. *Hearings* (Testimony of Lillian Hellman), May 21, 1952, pp. 3541–3549.

WHITMAN, WILLSON. *Bread and Circuses*. New York, 1937.

WITTLER, CLARENCE J. *Some Social Trends in WPA Drama*. Washington, D.C., 1939.

III. ARTICLES AND REVIEWS

"Actors Arrested in Store Picketing," *New York Times*, Feb. 10, 1935, Sec. 1, p. 17.

ALEXANDER, LEON. "Plays of the Month," *NT*, January 1935, pp. 24–25.

——. "The Theatre of Action," *DW*, May 27, 1935, p. 5.

——. "World of the Theatre," *DW*, Oct. 30, 1934, p. 5; Nov. 12, 1934, p. 7; Dec. 1, 1934, p. 7; Dec. 4, 1934, p. 5; Dec. 11, 1934, p. 5; April 1, 1935, p. 5.

ARENT, ARTHUR. "Technique of the Living Newspaper," *Theatre Arts Monthly*, XXII (November 1938), 820–825.

"Aristophanes' Sportive Satire," *DW*, June 11, 1930, p. 2.

"Back Where We Came From," *NTN*, February 1940, p. 22.

BAGLEY, CLARA. "The New Play," *SW*, Feb. 16, 1936, p. 6.

BEIN, ALBERT. "Change the World," *DW*, Dec. 10, 1935, p. 7.

BESSIE, ALVAH. "Anderson's New Play," *NM*, Nov. 4, 1941, pp. 28–30.

——. "Behind the Mannerheim Line," *NM*, May 14, 1940, p. 27.

——. "The Dilemma of Clifford Odets," *NM*, March 5, 1940, pp. 28–29.

——. "*The Fifth Column,*" *NM*, March 19, 1940, pp. 28–31.

——. "*Flight to the West,*" *NM*, Jan. 14, 1941, p. 29.

——. "Hemingway's *For Whom the Bell Tolls,*" *NM*, Nov. 5, 1940, pp. 25–29.

——. "*Liberty Jones,*" *NM*, Feb. 25, 1941, pp. 28–29.

——. "A Lively Theatre Week," *NM*, Dec. 12, 1939, p. 29.

——. "Medicine for the People," *NM*, April 23, 1940, p. 31.

——. "Mr. Shaw Retreats," *NM*, Dec. 31, 1940, pp. 28–30.

——. "Poor Harvest," *NM*, Dec. 9, 1941, pp. 26–27.

——. "A Season on the Boards," *NM*, May 7, 1940, p. 29.

——. "*Thunder Rock,*" *NM*, Nov. 28, 1939, pp. 28–31.

——. "War of the Sexes," *NM*, Jan. 23, 1940, p. 31.

——. "*Watch on the Rhine,*" *NM*, April 15, 1941, pp. 26–28.

——. "William Saroyan: Requiescat," *NM*, May 21, 1940, p. 29.

BIBERMAN, ABNER. "The Theatre," *NM*, March 26, 1935, p. 27.

BITTLEMAN, ALEX. "Organize for the Struggle against War," *DW*, July 11, 1931, p. 6.

BLAKE, BEN. "*Judgment Day,*" *NT*, October 1934, p. 17.

——. "*Let 'Em Eat Cake,*" *NT*, January 1934, pp. 11–12.

——. "The Theatre," *NM*, April 16, 1935, p. 26.

——. "Two Authors between Two Worlds," *NT*, December 1934, pp. 19–20.

BLANKFORT, MICHAEL. "Clifford Odets Writes a Tragedy," *DW*, Dec. 13, 1935, p. 7.

——. "Pacifist Pipe-Dream," *DW*, Sept. 27, 1935, p. 5.

——. "Theatre," *DW*, Dec. 4, 1935, p. 5; Jan. 14, 1936, p. 7; Jan. 22, 1936, p. 7.

——. "The Theatre," *NM*, Jan. 1, 1935, pp. 44–45; March 5, 1935, p. 28; March 26, 1935, pp. 27–28.

——. "World of the Theatre," *DW*, Nov. 5, 1935, p. 5.

BLITZSTEIN, MARC. "Author of *The Cradle,*" *DW*, Jan. 3, 1938, p. 7.

Bonn, John E. "Dram Buro Report," *WT*, May 1932, p. 7.
———. "First National Workers' Theatre Conference," *WT*, May 1932, pp. 5–6.
———. "Situations and Tasks of the Workers' Theatres in the U.S.A.," *WT*, June–July 1932, pp. 8–9.
———. "Situations and Tasks," *WT*, August 1932, pp. 11–12.
Browder, Earl. "The Democratic Front in the 1940 Elections," *DW*, Dec. 14, 1938, p. 6.
———. "The Roosevelt 'New Deal' and Fascism," *DW*, July 8, 1933, p. 5.
"Browder in Radio Interview," *DW*, Oct. 8, 1936, p. 5.
Buchwald, Nathaniel. "Cheers Greet New Revolutionary Play," *DW*, Jan. 12, 1935, p. 7.
———. "*Marching Song*," *DW*, March 2, 1937, p. 7.
———. "*Marion Models, Inc.*," *NT*, July–August 1934, p. 11.
———. "The Real McCoy," *DW*, May 31, 1935, p. 5.
———. "*Sailors of Cattaro*," *DW*, Feb. 5, 1935, p. 7.
———. "Sights and Sounds," *NM*, Feb. 15, 1938, pp. 25–26.
———. "World of the Theatre," *DW*, Feb. 20, 1935, p. 5; May 24, 1935, p. 7.
Burns, Ben. "The Labor Unions Go Broadway," *DW*, Sept. 28, 1937, p. 7.
Burnshaw, Stanley. "Middle-Ground Writers," *NM*, April 30, 1935, p. 19.
———. "Other Current Shows," *NM*, Dec. 11, 1934, p. 29.
———. "The Theatre," *NM*, Nov. 27, 1934, p. 27; Dec. 11, 1934, pp. 28–29; Jan. 29, 1935, pp. 27–28; April 9, 1935, p. 27; Oct. 22, 1935, p. 28; Oct. 29, 1935, pp. 27–28; Nov. 26, 1935, pp. 28–29; Jan. 21, 1936, pp. 28–29; Feb. 11, 1936, p. 28; March 31, 1936, p. 28; April 28, 1936, p. 27; June 2, 1936, pp. 29–30.
Burrows, Jack. "Sights and Sounds," *NM*, Nov. 23, 1937, p. 28; Dec. 21, 1937, p. 28.
C., N. "*Thunder Rock*," *DW*, Nov. 16, 1939, p. 7.
———. "Somebody Has Given the Revised *Pins* the Needles," *DW*, Nov. 30, 1939, p. 7.
"C.P. National Committee Vows Support in Crisis," *DW*, Dec. 8, 1941, p. 1.
Cambridge, John. "*Abe Lincoln in Illinois*," *DW*, Oct. 19, 1938, p. 7.
———. "*The American Way*," *DW*, Jan. 27, 1939, p. 7.
———. "*Big Blow*," *DW*, Oct. 3, 1938, p. 7.
———. "Caldwell's *Journeyman*," *DW*, Feb. 14, 1938, p. 7.
———. "*Danton's Death*," *DW*, Nov. 4, 1938, p. 7.
———. "Democracy Boosted," *DW*, Nov. 14, 1938, p. 7.
———. "Elmer Rice's New Play," *DW*, Dec. 9, 1938, p. 7.
———. "*Gentle People*," *DW*, Jan. 7, 1939, p. 7.

——. "Shaw's *Heartbreak House*," *DW*, May 2, 1938, p. 7.

——. "Lincoln's Youth and Love," *DW*, March 21, 1938, p. 7.

——. "Mercury Wins Wide Acclaim," *SW*, Feb. 6, 1938, p. 13.

——. "Negro W.P.A. Actors," *DW*, Dec. 19, 1938, p. 7.

——. "Odets' *Rocket to the Moon*," *DW*, Nov. 28, 1938, p. 7.

——. "*On the Rocks*," *DW*, June 18, 1938, p. 7.

——. "Reviewer in Doubt," *DW*, Oct. 24, 1938, p. 7.

——. "The Stage," *SW*, May 8, 1938, p. 12; May 22, 1938, p. 12; June 26, 1938, p. 12; Nov. 6, 1938, p. 16; Dec. 11, 1938, p. 12; Jan. 29, 1939, p. 7; Feb. 12, 1939, p. 7; Feb. 19, 1939, p. 7; June 18, 1939, p. 7.

——. "Toller's Play," *DW*, Jan. 31, 1938, p. 9.

——. "*Washington Jitters*," *DW*, May 4, 1938, p. 7.

CLURMAN, HAROLD. "The Group Theatre Speaks for Itself," *New York Times*, Dec. 13, 1931, Sec. 8, p. 2.

——. "Interpretation and Characterization," *NT*, January 1936, p. 21.

——. "The Playbill," New York *Herald Tribune*, Feb. 16, 1936, Sec. 5, p. 1.

Communist Party, U.S.A., National Committee. "Keep America out of the Imperialist War," *DW*, Sept. 19, 1939, p. 1.

——. "The People's Program of Struggle," *DW*, June 30, 1941, p. 1.

——. Platform, *DW*, July 27, 1932, p. 3.

——. Platform, *DW*, July 26, 1934, p. 3.

——. Platform, *DW*, June 29, 1936, pp. 1–2.

——. Platform, *DW*, June 2, 1940, pp. 1 and 4.

COMPTON, BEN. "Facts and the Group Theatre," *SW*, Jan. 10, 1937, p. 12.

——. "Indications," *DW*, Dec. 11, 1936, p. 7.

——. "Labor's Struggle Dramatized," *DW*, July 29, 1936, p. 7.

CRAWFORD, CHERYL. "Two on the Aisle," New York *Post*, Jan. 27, 1933, p. 7.

——. "Two on the Aisle," New York *Post*, April 17, 1936, p. 16.

CROWTHER, BOSLEY. "Theatre of the Loft," *New York Times*, April 14, 1935, Sec. 9, p. 2.

"The Curtain Rises," *NT*, November 1936, p. 4.

DANA, HENRY W. L. "Five Years of Labor Theatre," *DW*, June 1, 1938, p. 7; June 2, 1938, p. 7; June 3, 1938, p. 7.

DANIELL, F. RAYMOND. "An Alabama Court in Forty-fifth Street," *New York Times*, March 4, 1934, Sec. 9, p. 1.

DAVIS, BEN, JR. "Richard Wright's *Native Son*," *DW*, April 14, 1940, p. 4.

DAY, AGNES. "17 Battery Place," *NM*, Nov. 21, 1939, p. 30.

DENNEN, LEON. "Theatre," *NM*, December 1930, p. 17.

DEUTCHMAN. "Proletarian Theatre," *NM*, June 1931, p. 21.

DEXTER, CHARLES E. "Anderson Ends His Season," *DW*, Feb. 11, 1937, p. 7

DEXTER, CHARLES E. "Comedy, Pathos, and Day-Dreams," *DW*, April 14, 1937, p. 7.

——. "Does Ban Mean W.P.A. Censorship?" *DW*, June 18, 1937, p. 7.

——. "Finding a Hero for *Power*," *DW*, March 3, 1937, p. 7.

——. "Group Back on Broadway," *DW*, Nov. 12, 1937, p. 7.

——. "Group Theatre Scores Some Hits," *DW*, Nov. 21, 1936, p. 7.

——. "How Poverty Breeds Crime," *DW*, Jan. 15, 1937, p. 7.

——. "In the Multitude," *DW*, March 1, 1937, p. 7.

——. "It's All Aboard for Utopia," *DW*, April 13, 1937, p. 7.

——. "Lawson's Play," *DW*, Feb. 20, 1937, p. 7.

——. "Little Ladies of the Stage," *DW*, Oct. 29, 1936, p. 7.

——. "Living Newspaper's *Power*," *DW*, Feb. 25, 1937, p. 7.

——. "*Marching Song*," *DW*, Feb. 19, 1937, p. 7.

——. "Political Satire," *NM*, May 17, 1938, p. 29.

——. "*Professor Mamlock*," *DW*, April 15, 1937, p. 7.

——. "Recommending Some Reading," *SW*, Nov. 15, 1936, p. 12.

——. "Second Play of Social Farceur," *DW*, Sept. 21, 1936, p. 7.

——. "Sinclair Lewis," *DW*, Oct. 29, 1936, p. 7.

——. "Strikes and Strike Breakers," *DW*, Dec. 18, 1936, p. 7.

——. "*Ten Million Ghosts*," *DW*, Oct. 26, 1936, p. 7.

——. "Theatre Guild and Its Record," *DW*, March 19, 1937, p. 7.

——. "*Tide Rising*," *DW*, Jan. 29, 1937, p. 7.

——. "WPA's *The Sun and I*," *DW*, March 1, 1937, p. 7.

DOS PASSOS, JOHN. "Did the New Playwrights' Theatre Fail?" *NM*, August 1929, p. 13.

DREIBLATT, MARTHA. "Author of Theatre Union's New Play," *DW*, Oct. 31, 1935, p. 7.

EDGAR, HAROLD. "Play of New Orleans," *DW*, April 20, 1934, p. 5.

——. "*They Shall Not Die*," *DW*, Feb. 23, 1934, p. 7.

——. "The World of the Theatre," *DW*, Oct. 3, 1933, p. 5; Oct. 6, 1933, p. 5; Nov. 2, 1933, p. 5; Nov. 10, 1933, p. 5; Jan. 15, 1934, p. 5; Feb. 6, 1934, p. 7.

ENGLANDER, ERIC. "A Comedy for the 'Ruling Clawss,'" *DW*, Nov. 5, 1937, p. 7.

——. "*Cradle* Rocks at Mercury," *DW*, Dec. 7, 1937, p. 7.

——. "Ghosts of the Guild Stage," *DW*, Nov. 25, 1937, p. 7.

——. "New Strike Play," *DW*, Dec. 14, 1937, p. 7.

——. "*Processional*," *SW*, Oct. 17, 1937, p. 12.

——. "*Siege* Fails," *DW*, Dec. 10, 1937, p. 7.

——. "Sparkling Revue," *DW*, Nov. 29, 1937, p. 7.

——. "The Stage," *DW*, Nov. 13, 1937, p. 7; *SW*, Nov. 21, 1937, p. 10; Dec. 12, 1937, p. 10.

ETTINGER, MANFRED. "Vital Articles," *DW*, Oct. 11, 1934, p. 5.

EVANS, ALICE. "A Challenge," *NTN*, December 1939, pp. 6–7.

——. "New Theatre League," *DW*, June 1, 1935, p. 7.

"Every Measure to Support the Soviet Union!" *SW*, June 29, 1941, p. 5.

"Farewell to Silk, Hello Lisle," *DW*, Dec. 3, 1937, p. 7.

FISKE, HARRISON G. "The Federal Theatre Doom-Boggle," *Saturday Evening Post*, Aug. 1, 1936, p. 8.

FLANAGAN, HALLIE. "Introduction," *Federal Theatre Plays*, ed. Pierre de Rohan. New York, 1938.

———. "A Theatre Is Born," *Theatre Arts Monthly*, XV (November 1931), 908–915.

———. "Workers' Plays at Vassar College," *WT*, June–July 1932, p. 4.

FLEXNER, ELEANOR. "Federal Theatre Interprets Lincoln," *NM*, March 29, 1938, pp. 27–29.

"Footlights across America for Peace," *NTN*, November 1939, p. 3.

FORSYTHE, ROBERT. "*Black Pit* Is the Real Stuff," *DW*, May 7, 1935, p. 5.

FRANKFIELD, PHIL. "Splendidly Realistic Portrayal," *DW*, May 18, 1935, p. 7.

FREEMAN, JOSEPH. "Elmer Rice," *NT*, September 1934, p. 7.

———. "*Peace on Earth*," *DW*, Dec. 2, 1933, p. 7.

FRIEDMAN, SAMUEL H. "The Editor Comments," *New Leader*, March 2, 1934, p. 8.

GARDENER, WILLIAM. "The Theatre," *NM*, Jan. 16, 1934, p. 29; Jan. 30, 1934, pp. 28–30.

GARLIN, SENDER. "Change the World," *DW*, Sept. 18, 1934, p. 5.

———. "When Negro, White Unite," *DW*, May 16, 1934, p. 5.

GARRETT, GARET. "Federal Theatre for the Masses," *Saturday Evening Post*, June 20, 1936, p. 8.

GASSNER, JOHN. "The Diluted Theatre," *NT and F*, March 1937, pp. 30–32.

———. "The Drama in Transition," *NT*, August 1935, pp. 13–14, 28–29.

———. "Drama vs. Melodrama," *NT*, April 1936, pp. 8–10.

———. "The Theatre Collective," *NT*, May 1936, p. 27.

———. "Wings over Broadway," *NT and F*, April 1937, pp. 19–20.

GEDDES, VIRGIL. "Appeal to Playwrights," *NT*, October 1934, p. 5.

GERLANDO, JAY. "Odets and the Middle Class," *DW*, Feb. 7, 1936, p. 7.

———. "Theatre," *DW*, March 26, 1936, p. 7.

GERSON, S. W. "Great Anti-War Play," *DW*, April 21, 1936, p. 7.

GOLD, MICHAEL. "A Bourgeois Hamlet in Our Time," *NM*, April 10, 1934, pp. 28–29.

———. "Change the World," *DW*, April 11, 1934, p. 5; Oct. 23, 1935, p. 7; Dec. 5, 1935, p. 7; Dec. 6, 1935, p. 7; Dec. 11, 1935, p. 5; Oct. 9, 1937, p. 7; Nov. 5, 1940, p. 7; Nov. 29, 1940, p. 7.

———. "Notes of the Month," *NM*, April 1930, p. 5.

———. "A Reply to Lawson," *NM*, April 24, 1934, pp. 28–29.

GOMEZ, MANUEL. "A Proletarian Play on Broadway," *NM*, January 1932, pp. 27–28.

GORELIK, MORDECAI. "Epic Realism: Brecht's Notes on the *Three-Penny Opera*," *Theatre Workshop*, April–July 1937, pp. 29–40.

GORHAM, ABEL. "Hollywood and Broadway," *DW*, Feb. 27, 1940, p. 7.

——. "Thurber-Nugent Comedy," *DW*, Jan. 12, 1940, p. 7.

HALE, EDITH. "Author and Composer Blitzstein," *DW*, Dec. 7, 1938, p. 7.

HALL, MACDONALD. "Federal Theatre Play," *SW*, March 22, 1936, p. 6.

HATCHARD, CHARLES. "The Theatre," *NM*, April 30, 1935, pp. 27–28.

HAYES, ALFRED. "Change the World," *DW*, Dec. 26, 1934, p. 5.

HECKERT, FRITZ. "What Is Happening in Germany," *DW*, May 17, 1933, p. 4.

HICKERSON, HAROLD. "Theatre," *NM*, Feb. 1930, pp. 14–15.

HORSTMAN, HOWARD. "Then and Now," *SW*, June 7, 1936, p. 12.

HOUSEMAN, JOHN. "Again—A People's Theatre," *DW*, Sept. 18, 1937, p. 7.

HOWE, ANNE. "The Stage Was Not Set," *NT*, June 1934, pp. 14–15.

INGRAHAM, INIGO. "Theatre," *DW*, May 25, 1936, p. 7.

"*Inside America*," *DW*, Oct. 18, 1940, p. 7.

IRWIN, BEN. "The A.F.L. Theatre," *DW*, June 17, 1936, p. 7.

——. "Editorial," *NTN*, December 1940, p. 1; January 1941, p. 1.

——. "*Pins and Needles*—Labor Stage," *NT*, July 1936, p. 24.

J., A. "Stage and Screen," *DW*, Feb. 7, 1933, p. 2.

JAFFE, HARRY. "More on Soviet Blue Blouse," *NM*, December 1930, p. 20.

JONES, DAVE. "Living Newspaper Play," *DW*, Jan. 19, 1938, p. 7.

KARNOT, ETIENNE. "Theatre," *NM*, June 1933, pp. 29–30.

KLEIN, GERTRUDE W. "Workers Stink," *New Leader*, March 16, 1935, Sec. 2, p. 1.

KLINE, HERBERT. "The New Theatres Meet," *NT*, May 1936, p. 3.

——. "*The Young Go First*," *NT*, July 1935, p. 30.

KUNITZ, JOSHUA. "The Theatre," *NM*, Nov. 20, 1934, p. 26.

L., V. "The Guild Version," *DW*, March 9, 1940, p. 7.

LARKIN, MARGARET. "Theatre Union—Its Tasks and Problems," *DW*, May 15, 1935, p. 5.

LAWSON, ELIZABETH. "A True Play," *DW*, May 26, 1936, p. 7.

LAWSON, JOHN HOWARD. "A Comparative Study," *NT and F*, March 1937, pp. 15–16.

——. "The Crisis in the Theatre," *NM*, Dec. 15, 1936, pp. 35–36.

——. "'Inner Conflict' and Proletarian Art," *NM*, April 17, 1934, pp. 29–30.

——. "John Howard Lawson Appeals," *DW*, June 22, 1934, p. 2.

——. "Lawson Makes His Reply," New York *Daily Mirror*, March 28, 1934, p. 20.

——. "Machines before the Footlights," *NM*, Aug. 26, 1941, pp. 26–31.

——. "Play on Dimitroff," *DW*, July 23, 1934, p. 5.

——. "Straight from the Shoulder," *NT*, November 1934, pp. 11–12.

——. "The Theatre Guild Plays," *NM*, Jan. 5, 1937, p. 23.

——. "Towards a Revolutionary Theatre," *NT*, June 1934, pp. 6–7.

LENIN, V. I. "Lenin on Working Class Literature," trans. Anna Rochester, *NM*, October 1929, p. 7.

——. "Party Organization and Party Literature," trans. Ralph B. Winn, *Dialectics*, No. 5 (1938), pp. 2–5.

LEVY, MELVIN. "The World of the Theatre," *DW*, March 28, 1934, p. 7.

LEWIS, GEORGE. "We Need Anti-War Plays," *WT*, August 1932, p. 6.

LORIN, WILLIAM. "*1935*," *SW*, May 17, 1936, p. 6.

LUNACHARSKY, A. "Problems of Style in Socialist Art," *The International Theatre*, Bulletin No. 5 (1933), pp. 3–7.

M., H. "Federal Theatre's *Androcles*," *NM*, Dec. 27, 1938, pp. 28–29.

——. "Gentle People in Trouble," *NM*, Jan. 17, 1939, pp. 29–30.

MACFADDEN, BERNARR. "Inciting to Riot," *Liberty*, May 23, 1936, p. 4.

MAGIL, A. B. "Pity and Terror," *NM*, December 1932, p. 16.

MALTZ, ALBERT. "Change the World," *DW*, Dec. 30, 1935, p. 7; Dec. 31, 1935, p. 7.

——. "Current *New Theatre*," *DW*, Sept. 17, 1934, p. 5.

——. "*Marching Song*," *NT and F*, March 1937, p. 13.

MANNGREEN. "Left on Broadway," *DW*, May 3, 1938, p. 7; Oct. 20, 1938, p. 7.

MARDEN, ALEX. "Social Playwrights," *DW*, Dec. 30, 1937, p. 7.

MARTIN, PETER. "A Day with the Shock Troupe," *DW*, May 23, 1934, p. 5.

——. "The Theatre of Action," *DW*, Feb. 17, 1934, p. 7.

MARVIN, MARK. "An American People's Theatre," *NT*, December 1935, pp. 24–25.

——. "Prospects for the New Theatre," *NT*, September 1935, p. 24.

——. "Shifting Scenes," *NT*, September 1936, p. 24.

——. "The Theatre," *NM*, Nov. 12, 1935, p. 27.

——. "World of the Theatre," *DW*, Sept. 25, 1935, p. 5.

McKENNEY, RUTH. "Abraham Lincoln Lives Again," *NM*, Nov. 1, 1938, p. 27.

——. "Anti-Fascist Comedy," *NM*, Nov. 22, 1938, p. 30.

——. "Big Themes in the Theatre," *NM*, Nov. 15, 1938, pp. 28–29.

——. "Elmer Rice on Americanism," *NM*, Dec. 20, 1938, pp. 27–28.

——. "*The Little Foxes*," *NM*, Feb. 28, 1939, pp. 29–30.

——. "The New Odets Play," *NM*, Dec. 6, 1938, p. 28.

——. "Notes on Maxwell Anderson," *NM*, Nov. 29, 1938, p. 27.

McKenney, Ruth. "Sights and Sounds," NM, Nov. 1, 1939, pp. 27–28.

——. "Written in Anger," NM, Feb. 7, 1939, pp. 29–30.

Meltzer, Milton. "Sklar's New Play," NM, June 6, 1939, pp. 29–30.

Meredith, Burgess. "Confessions of a Fellow Traveler," Common Sense, October 1939, pp. 3–6.

Moeller, Philip, Theresa Helburn, Lee Simonson, Lawrence Langner, Maurice Wertheim, Helen Westley, Alfred Lunt. "Introduction," The Theatre Guild Anthology. New York, 1936.

Morrow, Mary. "Revolt of the Beavers," DW, May 24, 1937, p. 9.

Mullen, John. "A Worker Looks at Broadway," NT, May 1936, pp. 25–27.

"National Membership Drive," Curtain Call, October 1937, p. 7.

"New Theatres," DW, Jan. 14, 1941, p. 7.

North, Joseph. "Joseph North Answers," DW, April 30, 1935, p. 5.

——. "Red Rust," DW, Dec. 20, 1929, p. 2.

——. "The Theatre," NM, April 2, 1935, pp. 42–43.

"Notice," NTN, November 1940, p. 3.

Oak, Liston M. "Theatre Union," DW, March 21, 1935, p. 7.

——. "Theatre Union Replies," NT, November 1934, p. 12.

Olgin, M. J. "Mother," DW, Nov. 22, 1935, p. 5.

"Once Upon a Time," Saturday Evening Post, June 26, 1937, p. 22.

P., J. "Be Prepared against Imperialist War," DW, July 30, 1930, p. 4.

Page, Myra. "Roar China," DW, Nov. 15, 1930, p. 4.

Peters, Paul. "On Writing and Selecting Plays for Workers," DW, Feb. 27, 1935, p. 5.

——. "Peace on Earth," DW, Dec. 5, 1933, p. 5.

Rahv, Philip. "The Literary Class War," NM, August 1932, p. 7.

Ralston, Walter. "Sights and Sounds," NM, Feb. 1, 1938, pp. 28–29.

Reed, Judith. "Lawson's Play Belongs to the Past," DW, Oct. 20, 1937, p. 7.

——. "Stage," DW, Oct. 16, 1937, p. 7.

Repard, Theodore. "The Negro Theatre Triumphs," DW, June 29, 1936, p. 9.

——. "A Play of Fascist Italy," DW, April 3, 1936, p. 7.

——. "A Strike Put on the Stage," DW, March 6, 1936, p. 7.

——. "Theatre," DW, March 17, 1936, p. 7.

"Repertory Ramblings," NTN, August–September 1940, p. 5.

Rice, Elmer. "Elmer Rice Says Farewell to Broadway," New York Times, Nov. 11, 1934, Sec. 9, p. 1.

Robie, James. "Battle Hymn," DW, July 3, 1936, p. 7.

Rolfe, Edwin. "An Interview with Archibald MacLeish," DW, March 15, 1935, p. 5.

S., V. "Clear All Wires," DW, Sept. 20, 1932, p. 2.

——. "The Good Earth," DW, Nov. 8, 1932, p. 2.

SAXE, ALFRED. "A Play with Propaganda," *WT*, August 1932, pp. 7–8.
——. "World of the Theatre," *DW*, March 18, 1935, p. 7.
SAYERS, MICHAEL. "Sights and Sounds," *NM*, Dec. 7, 1937, p. 26.
SEAVER, EDWIN. "The New Play," *SW*, March 8, 1936, p. 6; March 29, 1936, p. 6.
SEILER, CONRAD. "Workers' Theatre: a Criticism," *NT*, June 1934, p. 17.
"Senator Borah—Victim of 'Isolationist' Fallacy," *DW*, July 8, 1939, p. 6.
"Send Us Scripts," *NT*, September 1934, p. 26.
SHAPIRO, IRWIN. *"Steel,"* *NT and F*, March 1937, p. 63.
SHAPIRO, JACK. *"Peace on Earth,"* *NT*, January 1934, p. 11.
——. *"Stevedore,"* *NT*, May 1934, p. 13.
——. "Theatre Collective," *NT*, October 1934, p. 15.
SHERIDAN, HELEN. *"New Leader Attack,"* *DW*, March 27, 1935, p. 7.
SHIPLEY, JOSEPH. "Driving Drama," *New Leader*, March 30, 1935, p. 8.
SILLEN, SAMUEL. "Bigger Thomas on the Boards," *NM*, April 8, 1941, pp. 27–28.
SIMONSON, LEE. "Prospects for the American Theatre," *NT*, January 1934, p. 7.
SKLAR, GEORGE. "Workers' Theatre Advances," *NT*, September 1934, p. 8.
SKLAR, GEORGE, and ALBERT MALTZ. "The Need for a Workers' Theatre," *DW*, Dec. 16, 1933, p. 7.
STACHEL, JACK. "On the Theatre Union's Play," *DW*, April 29, 1935, p. 5.
"Stage and Screen," *DW*, April 24, 1933, p. 4; Jan. 9, 1936, p. 4.
"A Statement," *NT and F*, March 1937, p. 3.
"Statement of Profit and Loss," *NTN*, July 1940, p. 2.
"Steel Strike Opera," *New York Times*, June 17, 1937, p. 1.
STERLING, PHILIP. "Stirring Labor Play," *DW*, Oct. 4, 1934, p. 5.
STEVENS, NORMAN. "Case of the Group Theatre," *NT*, July 1936, p. 5.
STONE, ERIC. "New Group Shows Promise," *DW*, Oct. 27, 1936, p. 7.
STRASBERG, LEE. "Showing the Movie Screen," *DW*, Jan. 5, 1937, p. 7.
"Success Story," *DW*, Oct. 3, 1932, p. 1.
TAYLOR, ALEXANDER. "Sights and Sounds," *NM*, Nov. 3, 1936, p. 29; Nov. 10, 1936, p. 29; Dec. 29, 1936, p. 27; Feb. 23, 1937, p. 27; March 2, 1937, p. 27; March 9, 1937, p. 29; April 20, 1937, p. 35.
——. "The Theatre," *NM*, Aug. 4, 1936, p. 29; Feb. 9, 1937, pp. 30–31; April 27, 1937, p. 31.
THACHER, MOLLY DAY. "Revolutionary Staging for Revolutionary Plays," *NT*, July–August 1934, p. 26.
"The Theatre and the A.F. of L.," *NM*, Nov. 5, 1935, p. 5.

"The Theatre Collective," *NT*, October 1934, p. 15.

THOMAS, NORMAN. "Timely Topics," *New Leader*, Dec. 2, 1933, p. 8.

THOMAS, TOM. "World Congress of Workers' Theatre Groups," *NM*, November 1930, p. 31; December 1930, p. 20.

"Thus the Union Figures," *New York Times*, Jan. 26, 1936, Sec. 9, p. 3.

TOOEY, PAT. "More about *Black Pit*," *DW*, May 30, 1935, p. 5.

"Towards a Workers' Theatre," *New Republic*, Dec. 27, 1933, p. 184.

"Unite Your Ranks against War," *DW*, Oct. 3, 1935, p. 1.

"A United Front to Fight Fascism," *DW*, March 25, 1933, p. 1.

"Un-neutral Neutrality," *SW*, March 7, 1937, p. 10.

"Up from Union Square," *New York Times*, Aug. 30, 1936, Sec. 9, p. 1.

"The Veteran *Pins and Needles*," *Playbill* (Windsor Theatre), July 31, 1939, p. 1.

"Wall Street Uses Finland for War," *DW*, Dec. 1, 1939, p. 1.

WARNER, RALPH. "American Brand of Fascism," *SW*, May 25, 1941, p. 7.

——. "Audiences Want Plays," *SW*, April 20, 1941, p. 7.

——. "Broadway Languid," *DW*, May 16, 1941, p. 7.

——. "*The Corn Is Green*," *SW*, Dec. 15, 1940, p. 7.

——. "Elmer Rice Drops War Tracts," *DW*, Jan. 3, 1941, p. 7.

——. "Growing Pains," *SW*, June 1, 1941, p. 7.

——. "Hearst Attempts to Sabotage," *SW*, March 30, 1941, p. 7.

——. "Helen Hayes Starred," *DW*, Oct. 25, 1941, p. 7.

——. "*Hope for a Harvest*," *DW*, Nov. 29, 1941, p. 7.

——. "The Inside Story of a Murder," *DW*, Dec. 23, 1940, p. 7.

——. "Keen Social Satire," *DW*, Feb. 19, 1941, p. 7.

——. "*Liberty Jones*," *SW*, Feb. 9, 1941, p. 7.

——. "*Love's Old Sweet Song*," *SW*, May 5, 1940, p. 7.

——. "*Medicine Show*," *DW*, April 16, 1940, p. 7.

——. "Miners' Life Depicted," *DW*, Nov. 29, 1940, p. 7.

——. "Public Rejects War Plays," *SW*, Feb. 23, 1941, p. 7.

——. "*Retreat to Pleasure*," *DW*, Dec. 19, 1940, p. 7.

——. "Stage Version of *Native Son*," *DW*, March 27, 1941, p. 7.

——. "The Theatre," *SW*, Nov. 2, 1941, p. 7.

——. "*There Shall Be No Night*," *DW*, May 2, 1940, p. 7.

——. "*Watch on the Rhine*," *DW*, April 4, 1941, p. 7.

WARREN, JAMES. "How Members of the W.L.T. Live and Work," *DW*, Dec. 28, 1934, p. 7.

WATSON, MORRIS. "The Living Newspaper," *NT*, June 1936, p. 8.

"We Answer the Call," *WT*, June–July 1932, pp. 3–4.

"What the Group Theatre Wants," *Playbill* (Mansfield Theatre), Dec. 10, 1931, pp. 4–5.

"What Is Americanism," *DW*, July 4, 1934, p. 6.

WILLSON, GEORGE. "The Theatre," *NM*, Sept. 25, 1934, p. 28.
WITTENBERG, RALPH. *"Till the Day I Die,"* NT, May 1935, p. 16.
"Workers' Laboratory Theatre Reorganizes," *DW*, Feb. 27, 1935, p. 5.
"Workers' Theatres," *NM*, August 1933, p. 27.
WRIGHT, RICHARD. "Negro Tradition in the Theatre," *DW*, Oct. 15, 1937, p. 9.

Index